JUST WAR IN COMPARATIVE PERSPECTIVE

The contributors to this book analyse how the different cultures, religions, and nations of the world justify war, and the limits which these groups place on the conduct of wars. Chapters in the book cover religious and secular perspectives, modern and pre-modern perspectives, and case studies. Together they form a unique and wide-ranging comparative contribution to what is one of the most important ethical debates facing humankind. The book should interest anyone concerned with issues of international affairs and international law, war, philosophy, or religion.

Just War in Comparative Perspective

Edited by
PAUL ROBINSON

ASHGATE

Published by
Ashgate Publishing Limited
Gower House
Croft Road
Aldershot
Hampshire GU11 3HR
England

Ashgate Publishing Company
Suite 420
101 Cherry Street
Burlington, VT 05401-4405
USA

Ashgate website: http://www.ashgate.com

British Library Cataloguing in Publication Data
Just war in comparative perspective
    1.Just war doctrine
    I.Robinson, Paul
    172.4'2

Library of Congress Cataloging-in-Publication Data
Just war in comparative perspective / edited by Paul Robinson.
      p. cm.
    Includes bibliographical references and index.
    ISBN 0-7546-3587-2 (alk. paper)
    1. Just war doctrine. I. Robinson, Paul (Paul F.)

    U21.2.J85 2003
    172'42--dc21

    2003043033

ISBN 0 7546 3587 2

Printed and bound in Great Britain by Antony Rowe Ltd, Chippenham, Wiltshire

Contents

List of Contributors

Francis X. Clooney, S.J. is a Professor of Theology at Boston College where he has taught since 1984. Author of seven books and currently writing a book on Hindu Goddesses and Christian theology, he has lived and taught in India and Nepal. He is a specialist in the classic religious traditions of Hindu India, and a comparative theologian interested in how the study of Hinduism challenges and transforms Christian identity. He is the Coordinator for Interreligious Dialogue for the Society of Jesus in the United States and, during 2002-2004, the Visiting Academic Director of the Centre for Hindu Studies at the University of Oxford.

Paul Dearey is Lecturer in Ethics and Christian Theology at the University of Hull. He has published a number of articles on matters of Catholic interest, and is a member of the editorial board of *Catholic Horizons*.

Elizabeth J. Harris is Secretary for Inter-Faith Relations in the Methodist Church in London, and is also Honorary Lecturer at the Postgraduate Institute of Theology and Religions, University of Birmingham.

Brendan Howe is an Assistant Professor of Security and Diplomacy at Ewha University in Seoul, Korea. Related previous publications include a chapter 'On The Justifiability of Military Intervention' in Richard Norman and Alexander Moseley (eds.), *Human Rights and Military Intervention* (Aldershot: Ashgate, 2002); 'Southeast Asian Counter-Insurgency Techniques: The Malayan Experience', *Journal of Postgraduate Research,* January 2002; 'Can NATO Intervention in Yugoslavia be Justified by Existing International Legal Norms?', *Irish Studies in International Affairs*, vol.11, November 2000; and 'An Analysis of Walzer's Contributions to Debates on Domestic and International Social Organisation', *Alumnus,* October 2000. His research currently focuses on international societal constraints upon crisis decision-making.

Thomas M. Kane teaches Strategic Studies at the University of Hull. His books *Military Logistics and Strategic Performance* and *Chinese Grand Strategy and Maritime Power* are in print with Frank Cass.

John Kelsay is Richard L. Rubenstein Professor and Chair in the Department of Religion, Florida State University, Tallahassee, Florida, USA. His publications include *Islam and War: A Study in Comparative Ethics* (Louisville, Ky: Westminster/John Knox Press, 1993), and two co-edited volumes: *Cross, Crescent and Sword* (Westport, Ct.: Greenwood Press, 1990), and *Just War and Jihad* (Westport, Ct., Greenwood Press, 1991).

Alexander Moseley is the author of *A Philosophy of War* (Algora, 2002), and is currently working on two follow-up volumes. He is Political Theory Editor for the Internet Encyclopedia, and co-editor (with Richard Norman) of *Human Rights and Military Intervention* (Aldershot: Ashgate, 2002).

Paul Robinson is Lecturer in Security Studies at the University of Hull, and the author of various works on military history and contemporary security, including *The White Russian Army in Exile* (Oxford: Clarendon Press, 2002). He has served as an officer in both the British and Canadian armies.

Gurharpal Singh is Nadir Dinshaw Chair in Inter-Religious Relations in the Department of Theology at the University of Birmingham. He is the author of numerous works, including *Ethnic Conflict in India: A Case-Study of Punjab* (Basingstoke: Palgrave, 2000).

Rob van den Toorn studied international and European law at the University of Nijmegen, and philosophy at the Erasmus University at Rotterdam. From 1981 to 1986 he was a member of the Dutch Parliament. He now works part-time as a refugee lawyer, and is also working part-time on a PhD thesis on just war and the ethics of care.

Frank R. Trombley is Reader in Religious Studies at the University of Wales, Cardiff. He has a PhD in Byzantine history from UCLA (1981), and is the author of a number of works on early Christianity.

Jenel Virden is Senior Lecturer and Head of American Studies at the University of Hull. She received her PhD from the University of Washington (Seattle), and is the author of *Goodbye Piccadilly: British War Brides in America* (Urbana: University of Illinois Press, 1996). She is also the British Association for American Studies representative to the European Association of American Studies.

Rev. Fr. Alexander F.C. Webster is Assistant Professorial Lecturer in the University Honors Program, the George Washington University (USA); Parish Priest of St. Mary Orthodox Church in Falls Church, Virginia; Chaplain (Lieutenant Colonel), Virginia Army National Guard; and author of numerous scholarly and op-ed articles and books, including *The Pacifist Option: The Moral Argument Against War in Eastern Orthodox Theology* (Lanham, MD: Rowman & Littlefield Publishers, 1998), *The Price of Prophecy: Orthodox Churches on Peace, Freedom, and Security* (2nd rev. ed.; Grand Rapids, MI: Wm. B. Eerdmans Pub. Co., 1995), and *The Romanian Legionary Movement: An Orthodox Christian Assessment of Anti-Semitism* (Carl Beck Papers, no.503; Pittsburgh, 1986).

George Wilkes is a Historian of Contemporary International and Interreligious Relations who lectures at the Centre for Jewish-Christian Relations and the University of Cambridge Divinity School/Theological Federation.

Acknowledgments

I would like to thank those people and institutions who helped me to bring together the wide variety of experience assembled in this book. These include the Department of Politics and the Centre for Security Studies at the University of Hull, and notably Professor Gurharpal Singh and Dr. Eric Grove, who provided financial support for my endeavours. I would also like to thank Matthew Mowthorpe from the Centre of Security Studies, and my wife Chione for her advice in editing this book and for her comments on various drafts of my own contribution.

Introduction

Paul Robinson

As this book goes to press, early in 2003, a fierce debate is taking place in the Western world as to whether an American-led attack on Iraq would constitute a just war.[1] Not merely dozens, but hundreds, of newspaper and magazine articles have appeared arguing the moral cases for and against.[2] The arguments on both sides have run the gamut from arcane legal views to practical assessments of the consequences of a second war against Iraq. It is very clear from this debate that there is no intellectual consensus on what rules apply to such moral considerations, and yet there is near-universal acceptance that some sort of threshold must be met prior to war. Across the Western world, theorists are breathing new life into an old tradition of thought, and for the first time are also seriously considering the alternate perspectives of other cultures in establishing the rules of just war.

This revival of interest is remarkable, since as little as fifteen years ago the just war doctrine, which has existed in various forms for many hundreds of years, was considered to have been rendered 'obsolete'[3] by modern warfare and weapons. First codified by St Augustine and elaborated by Thomas Aquinas and other foremost Western Christian philosophers, the theory reached essentially its modern form after the revisions of thinkers such as the Dutch international lawyer Hugo Grotius. Since his time, there has been little change to the accepted set of criteria which have to be met if a war is to be considered 'just'. These criteria cover two aspects of war: initiating it (*jus ad bellum*) and the actions one may undertake during it (*jus in bello*). Different authorities provide slightly different lists of criteria (compare for instance those in Chapters 13 and 14 of this book), but roughly speaking, they all equate to the following: one may righteously wage war if one has: a just cause; legitimate authority; a right intention; a reasonable chance of success; and all other reasonable alternatives to war have been exhausted (the principle of 'last resort'). One's actions during war can be considered just if one exercises discrimination in terms of who one targets; and if the amount of violence one uses is proportionate to the ends that one seeks. Not everybody accepts all of these principles, but in general most discussions of just war theory focus more on how to interpret them than on their essential validity.

The criteria of just war theory had fallen somewhat into disuse by the waning years of the twentieth century. After two world wars, and the invention of nuclear

---

1   For my own views on this issue, see my article 'A War for Fools and Cowards', *The Spectator*, 14/21 December 2002, pp.20-22

2   As an example, one anti-war website contains links to over 80 articles published in major newspapers and magazines: http://www.antiwar.com

3   I.D. de Lupis, *The Law of War* (Cambridge: Cambridge University Press, 1987).

weapons, theorists, as well as much of the general public, felt that war was becoming too dangerous to be contemplated except in the most extreme circumstances. Efforts to circumscribe the horrors of war by means of rules of behaviour (i.e. *jus in bello*) were clearly no longer enough. Twentieth-century Western leaders decided that the only solution was entirely to outlaw the initiation of war by states. The Kellogg-Briand Pact of 1928, for instance, defined armed aggression as 'an international crime', a view subsequently reinforced by the Charter of the United Nations, the judgments of the Nuremburg Trials condemning German officers for 'waging aggressive war', and various resolutions of the United Nations General Assembly. The International Court of Justice twice ruled that states had no right to intervene in the affairs of others. As the century entered its final decade, with two missile-armed superpowers standing ready to destroy each other, and possibly all human civilization as well, at the push of a button, it seemed that, in future, Western nations could only conceivably fight either when attacked or in support of a call by the United Nations. Just war theory was no longer needed.

The situation in the early twenty-first century is very different. The Cold War standoff had barely ended when the 50-year old NATO alliance launched its very first military action, in Bosnia, in 1995. This was promptly followed by an air campaign against Yugoslavia in 1999, and a war against Iraq is likely to join those two soon. With each successive operation, the Western powers are straying closer and closer to what used to be deemed aggressive war. This has not passed unnoticed. Public debate has differed sharply from that during such events as the British Falklands War and the 1991 Gulf War to free occupied Kuwait, which were portrayed as straightforward efforts to reverse aggression by others. The age-old questions of war are being discussed with a new sense of importance: When and under what circumstances is one entitled to undertake a military action? What constitutes a just cause? What authority is required for war (the United Nations, one's own state, etc)? What are the limits of force?

The debate has taken on an added complexity in our time. The 1999 war launched by NATO against Yugoslavia brought to the fore the question of whether humanitarian intervention constitutes a just cause for war. The 2001 terrorist attacks on the U.S. sparked heated debate about who has the right to wage war and what targets are legitimate. May only states wage war, or do oppressed groups and individuals have that right? If they do, are they bound by the same rules of non-combatant immunity as limit the behaviour of armies? Counter-terrorist strategy poses similar problems. Where, for instance, is the line drawn between assassination and overseas special forces operations? All these questions and more have now acquired a new urgency as policy-makers scramble to adapt to the rapidly changing international environment. For example, the 2002 American National Security Strategy promulgated a doctrine of pre-emptive action, provoking detailed discussions among international lawyers as to the rights and wrongs of pre-emptive strikes.[4] This policy may very soon see actual application in Iraq.

It appears that the trend is for the powerful military states of the West – in particular the United States and the United Kingdom – to claim both a right and a moral duty to enforce their standards of human rights throughout the world, and, in the interests of greater stability and security, to overthrow regimes in other countries which they believe threaten their interests. This new-found community spirit is not merely the product of modern idealism. With the risk of triggering global nuclear war removed, and with the development of 'smart' weapons which allow war to be waged more discriminately, thereby limiting the damage caused, the apparent costs of war have dropped dramatically. The temptation to resort to force as a solution, rather than to diplomacy or economics, has therefore increased.[5]

This places Western demands and Western self-justifications squarely at the centre of the world. In such circumstances, Western thinkers need to examine the views of other cultures. Around the world, all the major religious traditions and ethnic cultures have studied many of the same issues of war – matters such as the constitution of legitimate authority, the determination of what constitutes a legitimate target, and the degree to which the criteria of just war may be overruled in times of emergency, for instance – and they have often come to very similar conclusions. Apart from the case of Islamic thought, these traditions tend to be less developed than the very formal, codified just war theory developed in the West, but they are no less worthy of consideration.

Such consideration is all the more necessary because this century is likely to see many clashes between groups of people whose views of 'just war' differ. In an influential book written in 1996, Samuel Huntington argued that the world was about to witness the 'Clash of Civilizations'.[6] Huntington states that the wars of the future will be fought along the fault lines separating the main civilizations of the world. His ideas contain many flaws. Not least of these is the fact that the civilizations he lists (the West, Orthodoxy, Islam, Africa, etc.) are not homogeneous. There are, for instance, great divisions within the Islamic world. Nevertheless, there is some truth to his views, in that we can see that many recent conflicts have taken place, and continue to take place, between peoples of different cultures and religions. The wars in Yugoslavia, for instance, took place along the dividing line between Catholicism (Croatia), Eastern Orthodoxy (Serbia), and

---

4   For a discussion of the moral issues concerning humanitarian intervention, see Alexander Moseley and Richard Norman (eds.), *Human Rights and Military Intervention* (Aldershot: Ashgate, 2002).

5   Although it should be noted that despite the much smaller number of casualties in 'smart' war, the proportion of civilians killed has shifted from ten percent a hundred years ago to 90 percent today. A detailed tally of deaths in current conflicts can be found in the annual *SIPRI Yearbook*. The latest is *SIPRI Yearbook 2002: Armaments, Disarmament and International Security* (Oxford: Oxford University Press, 2002).

6   S. Huntington, *The Clash of Civilizations and the Remaking of World Order* (New York: Simon and Schuster, 1996).

Islam (Bosnia and Kosovo). The war in Kashmir is being fought along the line dividing the Muslim world (in the form of Pakistan) and the Hindu world (in the form of India). The September 2001 attacks on American targets revealed an intense hatred of Western culture and power among some disaffected elements of the Muslim Arab world. Many other examples could be listed.

Historically speaking, when different rules of war meet, they tend after a period of time to converge – a fact pointed out by several of the contributors to this volume. However, before the convergence takes place, there is often a rise in particularly atrocious violence. Traditionally, states and soldiers have tended to consider that the rules of war apply only to opponents who come from a similar background. Outsiders are outside the code and can be treated almost as one likes. One can see this throughout history. The ancient Greeks, for instance, permitted acts against the Persians which they did not permit against Greek enemies. Mediaeval Europeans distinguished between *bellum hostile*, in which Christians fought against other Christians and in which one was expected to obey the rules of war, and *bellum romanum*, in which one could treat enemies entirely as one pleased because they were heathens and barbarians. Similarly in more recent times, the German Army of World War Two mostly abided by the laws of war when fighting the Western Allies (despite occasional atrocities), but paid very little attention to these laws when combating what they considered the '*untermensch*' in Soviet Russia.

Given this, it is a matter of some urgency, and of more than simply academic concern, to develop a greater mutual understanding of the world's just war traditions. Research on the subject can lead to a direct impact on attitudes to the issues of war and peace in the current era. As an introduction to the subject, this book aims to provide as wide a set of perspectives as possible, examining the theories of the main world religions (Judaism, Roman Catholicism, Eastern Orthodoxy, Islam, Buddhism, Hinduism, and Sikhism), as well as views prevalent in specific countries and regions (Africa, China, and Russia), and various case studies, both historical and modern.

An interesting point to emerge from several of the chapters in the book is that, although the just war tradition is even now undergoing a revival, it is also under challenge from many quarters and principally from the very Christian churches that founded it. In Chapter 2, for instance, Paul Dearey notes that 'it would be mistaken to assume that the Roman Catholic social teaching is conclusively in favour of the ethics of just war'. He points to the growing emphasis placed on the ethics of peacemaking. Similarly, in Chapter 3, Fr. Alexander Webster also notes that within the Eastern Orthodox Churches many clergymen are questioning the idea that war can ever be just. In Chapter 14, Rob van den Toorn then points to an alternative system of ethics – that of the Ethics of Care. Elsewhere, we also see that the very notion of 'just war' is not universally accepted, even by those who consider war necessary, even obligatory. Necessity is an idea that raises its head almost as often as justice. This can be seen in what I term, in Chapter 4, 'the necessary war trajectory' in Russian thinking, and in the ideas of some Islamic thinking, as discussed by John Kelsay in Chapter 5, that in emergency circumstances people have an obligation to fight – that 'necessity makes the forbidden things permitted'. The Chinese Legalists took this idea to its logical conclusion, and adopted the view, as laid out by Thomas Kane in Chapter 9, that war lies outside the bounds of moral law. This position, however, was and remains the exception in human history. Nearly every society at every time has developed some code of conduct limiting and guiding the practice of war. It is a universal moral question.

We should also note that the theories that different cultures develop about war do have a definite impact upon the behaviour of people during war. Of course, one can take a somewhat cynical viewpoint, and suggest that in times of war moral considerations do not rate highly in the minds of those taking important decisions. Matters of personal and national interest, of power and possibilities, may rank more highly. Followers of the Realist School of International Relations theory would tend to support such a conclusion. Furthermore, in Chapter 12 of this book, Jenel Virden points out that, in World War II, even US Army Chaplains seemed to be very unconcerned about the justification of war and killing. Yet, despite this, it is clear that as an activity war is constrained by cultural expectations and norms, and has been throughout history. Western armed forces nowadays have to consult lawyers over almost every target that they strike, and their actions are exposed to the closest public scrutiny to determine whether they are keeping to the accepted moral standard. Peoples from all backgrounds determine their behaviour in the light of societal, cultural and religious influences, as much in the realm of war as in any other.

The justification or non-justification of war is one of the most important moral issues that face us, especially at a time when issues of war and peace occupy so high a place in the public consciousness. It is to be hoped that the variety of perspectives included in this book will go some way towards promoting greater understanding of the various views on this issue which exist around the world, and will thereby enable us to manage the difficult moral judgments that lie before us rather better than we may have done in the past.

PART I
JEWISH, CHRISTIAN AND ISLAMIC PERSPECTIVES

Chapter 1

Judaism and Justice in War

George Wilkes

The sword comes into the world for the delay of justice, and for the perversion of justice, and on account of the offence of those who interpret the Torah not according to its true sense. (Mishnah, *Chapters of the Fathers*, 5:11)

One who has mercy on the cruel will in the end be cruel to the merciful. (*Tanchuma*, Metzorah 1/*Koheleth Rabbah* 7)

Introduction

The present chapter sets out to sketch the historical development of Jewish equivalents of 'just war theory'.[1] Bearing in mind the comparative framework of the book, the chapter focuses in particular on the consistency with which Jewish traditions have been influenced by other civilizations across the millennia, a phenomenon which has yet to receive the academic attention it deserves. To be sure, the distinctive elements of Jewish legal traditions governing the conduct of war are so central that straightforward comparisons can be as misleading as they are inevitable. There is thus no tradition in rabbinic Judaism according to which a war may be 'holy', nor arguably can war be sanctified, biblical precedents notwithstanding. Nor have rabbinic Jewish commentators been impelled to examine whether a war, or participation in a war, is in itself 'just'. There is a literature which focuses on the justifications for war, but rabbinic law and theology focuses more consistently on the bases on which military conduct may be commanded or sanctioned than on the idea that a war can or need be 'justified' in religious terms. Equally, there is no Jewish tradition according to which battle is an extension of religious or spiritual 'struggle' by other means. The development of 'just war' and 'jihad' theory nevertheless finds close parallels in the key texts which traditionalist Jews raise in discussion of military conduct, presenting historian and military ethicist alike with grounds for a serious examination of the comparative context in which Jewish texts were conceived and written.

This chapter sketches a comparative context beginning with Semitic and Classical traditions before examining the relationship between Jewish, Christian

---

1   The author wishes to thank Professors Reuven Firestone, Moshe Herr, and Mark Saperstein for their welcome guidance on critical points – they bear no responsibility for any imperfections in the text, of course.

and Muslim traditions. We are attempting to construct a foundation on which scholars focused on different periods may build a clearer picture of the nature of cross-cultural influences – aware that the lack of explicit reference to comparative sources of the laws of war in traditional rabbinic commentaries has encouraged modern scholars, too, with few exceptions, to view the Jewish sources in isolation. The persistent relationship between Jewish and non-Jewish traditions need not, for our purposes, have been the product of direct encounter between Jewish legal authorities and their non-Jewish counterparts, nor even of direct knowledge of non-Jewish legal texts. Two further avenues of influence feed into the unacknowledged openness of Jewish commentators to the military practices of their neighbours. First, changes in the laws of war brought about by the social or cultural context in which armies were organized and supplied have been no less important in shaping Jewish military ethics than was the case for other peoples. Secondly, a central dimension to military ethics lies in the assessment of the value attached by other cultures to life, to change, to peace, and thence of the likely responses of other armies and peoples to military engagement or negotiations for peace. Without comparative judgements about Jewish and Arab religious and secular cultures, the exponent cannot relate the Mishnah's 'sword' to today's context, nor can he or she hope to suggest, with the Midrashic text above, the twisted relationship of cruelty and mercy in today's armed conflicts. The comparative context is thus of enduring importance for those to whom Jewish approaches to war constitute a matter of life and death.

The Development of Jewish Laws of War: Biblical Bases

The biblical laws of war form a cornerstone for rabbinic Jewish discussion of war. Expounding on the centrality of peace in Judaism, the sermon is as likely to resort to the first five books of the Bible as to the later prophetic books and to the Talmud. The biblical bases of this tradition is not exactly the 'ban' or 'Holy War' which Old Testament scholars since Wellhausen have often portrayed as central to Israelite religion,[2] but nor have rabbis traditionally accepted the current scholarship according to which the thinkers of the Hebrew Monarchy invented the slaughter of

---

2   For the history of Old Testament 'Holy War' scholarship, see G. von Rad, *Holy War in the Old Testament*, trans M.J. Dawn (Grand Rapids: Eerdmans, 1991). Those scholars who follow von Rad (e.g. S. Niditch, *War in the Hebrew Bible: A Study in the Ethics of Violence* (New York/London: OUP, 1993) have continued to refine his view that the 'ban' did not apply to the vast majority of biblical wars, and survived only in later biblical texts thanks to a prophetic critique of the pragmatic motivations for military campaigns under the Hebrew monarchy. On the conquest as myth and history, see G. Lüdemann, *The Unholy in Holy Scripture: The Dark Side of the Bible* (London: SCM Press, 1997), p.42, and C.S. Ehrlich, 'Joshua, Judaism and Genocide', in J.T. Borras and A. Saenz-Badillos (eds.), *Jewish Studies at the Turn of the Twentieth Century: Proceedings of the Sixth European Association of Jewish Studies Congress, Toledo, July 1998*, vol.I (Leiden: Brill, 1999), p.117 ff.

Canaanites in support of the idea that their ancestors had all followed Moses out of Egypt, standing at Sinai before purifying the land of idolatry. The result is a wealth of commentary tackling the details of Biblical engagements, conceived with an eye to reconciling Israelite conduct with the dictates of peace and justice.

A key method by which rabbinic tradition identified laws relating to war was through classifying each biblical war according to whether it was 'commanded' and 'obligatory' (a *milchemet mitzvah*), 'permitted' (a *milchemet reshut*) or contrary to divine law. According to the Mishnah,[3] the battles for self-defence recorded in the first five books of the Bible were 'obligatory', while the wars fought by King David to expand his territory were merely 'permitted' – a historical distinction used to imply progressive limits to religious sanctions for subsequent military engagement rather than to expose a broad Biblical mandate for further wars. The terms might be read simply in relation to the conditions under which combatants take up arms, the *milchemet mitzvah* obliging males of conscriptable age to fight, while a *milchemet reshut* permits conscientious objection. The bulk of the literature also treats the distinction as a basis for linking the discussion of justifiable cause for war and justifiable military conduct: a defensive war justifies some of the severity described in the earlier books of the Bible, while a war not fought against an immediate threat demands additional limitations on combat. In two cases, the Bible commands war without quarter: against the Amalekites, who have drawn this situation on themselves through their uncompromising hatred for the Israelites and by dint of their cruelty in attacking the vulnerable, non-combatant stragglers crossing the desert,[4] and against those Canaanites who refused to make peace with the conquering Israelites.[5] Here, rabbinic tradition recognizes something much like the Semitic 'herem' or 'ban', an ordained slaughter of men, women and children without mercy. From the Mishnah (second century) onwards, rabbinic literature dealt with these as exceptions, no longer relevant, it was noted, because the peoples concerned had intermarried to the point that they were no longer distinguishable.[6] Even the 'ban' on the Canaanites, according to rabbinic interpretation, was preceded by peace negotiations, a practice identified with all of the wars of the biblical patriarchs.[7] Biblical resources used to justify war today are thus hedged with rabbinic conditions, and if Israeli extremists have sought to compare Arabs with Amalek, Israel's enemies are also regularly compared, less damningly, to Jacob's brother and rival Esau, and, more sympathetically still, to Ishmael. In one sense, this is a simplifying typology, explaining the enmity of their non-Jewish neighbours through events dating to the origins of the Jewish people. In its everyday use, however, the biblical types are also a basis for examinations of the purported cultural dimensions to contemporary conflict.

---

3   *Sotah*, ch.8.
4   *Exodus* 17:8-16: *Deuteronomy* 25:17-19.
5   *Deuteronomy* 20:16.
6   *Mishnah, Yadayim* IV, 4; *Babylonian Talmud (BT), Kiddushin* V, 9; Maimonides, *Mishneh Torah, Hilkhot Melakhim*, V.
7   *Deuteronomy* 20, and commentary of *Sifre* on *Deuteronomy* 20:19.

Comparative perspectives make this a tool for critique of misunderstanding on all sides of the Middle Eastern cultural conflict.

In another sense, Jewish biblical exegesis ties approaches to war to comparisons between cultures. The first reference to war in the Bible has Abraham drawn into a conflict between Canaanite kings after Lot is taken captive (Genesis 14). According to one of the leading nineteenth century founders of 'Modern Orthodox' Judaism, Samson Raphael Hirsch, this underscores Abraham's mission to bring the values associated with ethical monotheism into a gentile world where war and conflict are the norm.[8] The association of gentiles, war and injustice, Jews, peace and the search for justice, runs through much rabbinic commentary, a suggestive parallel to the Islamic doctrine of the 'land of war'. The rabbis, following the prophets, started from the presupposition that 'the wars of the gentiles' would only end with the coming of the messiah. Genesis 14 is a key text for the discussion of the consequences this had for Jewish approaches to military affairs. The biblical account of Abraham giving chase and defeating Lot's captors established a broad precedent for going to war in defence of a third party which has been unjustly attacked.[9] The thrust of most of the early rabbinic literature on the subject was, however, to urge the dissociation of Jews from any aspect of war-making. A minority position which persisted into mediaeval times extended the precedent of Abraham giving chase into a mandate for serving in gentile armies, even as mercenaries. In the twentieth century, Israeli rabbis turned to these earliest sources for discussion of the ethics of arms manufacture and trade, which they concluded they were only able to sanction on the basis of the extremity of the military threat to the State of Israel.[10] Even then, the military conduct of states to which arms were sold would have to be scrutinized. The comparative study of military ethics is of direct relevance to this task.

The utility of comparative analysis can be clearly tested with respect to the basic conditions faced by the soldier of biblical and rabbinic text. In Genesis 14, after this first biblical battle, Abraham commands his retainers to divide their booty equally. Both the conduct of the military encounter and Abraham's instructions for the division of booty have exact parallels in the second millenium international treaties of Boghazkoi and Ugarit, concluded at the time Abraham is believed to have lived and long before the text of Genesis was finally edited.[11] Abraham's conduct made sense in an age of warring kings surrounded by small bands of retainers. A thousand years later, however, when the remainder of the biblical text was edited, warfare had transformed dramatically. The role of logistics in supporting an army had grown, and I Samuel (30:24) therefore records the

8   S.R. Hirsch, *Terumath Zvi: The Pentateuch*, ed. E. Oratz (New York: Judaica Press, 1986), p.68 f.

9   G. Horowitz, *The Spirit of Jewish Law* (New York: Central Book Co., 1953), p.146 ff.

10 J. Polak, 'Arms Transfers, the State of Israel, and Halakha', *Tradition*, vol.24, no.3, Spring 1989, pp.67-82.

11 J. Muffs, 'Abraham the Noble Warrior: Patriarchal Politics and Laws of War in Ancient Israel', *Journal of Jewish Studies*, vol.33, nos 1-2 (1982: Yadin Festschrift), pp.81-107.

enactment of King David according to which booty was to be shared equally between all soldiers, whether or not they had fought on the battlefield.[12]

For the authors of Deuterononomy and the Prophets, living in an age when popular militia fought hand-to-hand engagements behind a row of shields, a key feature of the success of an army was its morale. The promotion of courage in battle is thus a persistent theme in the prophetic literature – indeed, this is more true of the Jewish canon than it is of the Old Testament, since the canonical category 'The Prophets' includes most of the texts classed as history books in the Christian canon. As with the warring Spartans and Athenians, the key role played by shield formations meant that once one soldier ran from the battlefield, his immediate neighbours were left undefended, and the flight of a few soldiers could end in speedy defeat. A stark contrast separates the Spartan law, in which cowards faced shaming or death, and the key passages treating the biblical laws of war in Deuteronomy 20, providing for four categories of exemption for men of conscriptable age afraid of dying in combat – points still raised in Israeli court judgments of the rights of conscientious objectors.[13] Narrowly conceived, these exemptions relate to fear caused by the commission of grave sins[14] – unlike its better-known Christian and Muslim counterparts, Jewish just war theory did not provide for the absolution of sin or the attainment of paradise through battle.

In Deuteronomy 20, even in the context of the so-called 'ban' on the Canaanite peoples, the Children of Israel are commanded to lay siege to cities with consideration for their civilian populations, taking particular care at the onset of a siege to give its inhabitants the opportunity to remain non-combatant – the terms on which they may do so, and the consequences if they do not, bear comparison with Islamic law. The section ends with the injunction not to destroy fruit trees in the pursuit of a military campaign, a passage which the Talmud already extended to cover food stores, reading the purpose in relation to the impact of war on civilian populations,[15] and which Josephus records was also applied to burning the land and killing domestic animals.[16] Here again, the developing Jewish law on the subject bears comparison with Roman legal polemics against the poisoning of wells and with the Quranic injunction against destroying animals in the course of a military campaign. If the purpose of comparative study was to construct a single, overarching intercultural framework underpinning understandings of the laws of war, the differences of detail would probably appear overwhelming. But if the implications of the different focal points in each tradition cast light on the principles on which each are based, then this comparison can be of immediate utility. In the rabbinic tradition, these military injunctions have become an integral part of wider debate over ethical priorities and moral refinement. Subsequent literature has drawn from the prohibition against destroying trees a series of more

---

12 M. Elon, *Jewish Law*, vol.II, p.554. Compare *Numbers* 31:27.
13 D.B. Sinclair, 'Jewish Law in the State of Israel', *Jewish Law Annual*, no.9, p.262.
14 E.g. Rabbi Elchanan Samet, 'The Laws of War and the Torah's Attitude Towards War', Yeshivat Har Etzion, Parshat Ki Tetze, online at www.vbm-torah.org.
15 *Sifre* on *Deuteronomy* 20:19.
16 *Contra Apion*, II, 29.

general implications for humanity's stewardship of the environment. A leitmotif in rabbinic tradition is the assertion that ethical behaviour under wartime conditions underpins the whole ethical edifice of a religious tradition.   For this reason, according to one of the leading moderate 'settlers', Rabbi Aharon Lichtenstein, the Bible places a specific prohibition on stealing from gentiles (also covered by the general prohibition on theft) in the midst of a text treating the proper bases for Israel's behaviour in a national crisis.[17] On this count, too, the 'beautiful captive' passage in Deuteronomy 21 is considered by some the most important ethical reminder in the whole Torah.[18] There, the commandment to respect the feelings of the wives of their slain enemies – and to refrain from exercising the normal prerogatives of the powerful – is viewed as one of the most important biblical tests of moral fibre. There have been, as we shall see, commentators who argue war to be essentially lawless. The overwhelming thrust of rabbinic tradition, however, has held the contrary – justifiable conduct in war is a key to the establishment of international law in peacetime society as well.

Post-Biblical Developments in Comparative Perspective

The interaction of Jewish law with the military culture and ethics of the successive invaders of the Land of Israel can be seen again from the time of the restoration of independent Jewish rule under the Maccabees in the second century BCE. The repeated defeat and occupation of the Jewish kingdoms brought far-reaching changes in attitudes to the conduct of war, and this has shaped rabbinic 'just war' theory.

The revolt of the Maccabees signalled a theological shift in the understanding of God's role in war, popular initiative rather than divine leadership becoming the most important element in the decision to wage war.   Thus, military activity conducted on the Sabbath against an immediate threat became permissible. A pragmatic change, the decision to fight on the Sabbath nevertheless touches on the fundamentals of Jewish eschatology, for the Sabbath is treated as a taste of the messianic redemption, when war will be no more, and in the modern State of Israel the problems this raises have again proven a constant source of debate.[19] The recognition that divine protection could not be relied on during the Sabbath accompanied a theological revolution, with a popular revolt signalling the willingness of the Maccabees and their supporters to take steps to throw off tyrannical rule without waiting for signs of divine sanction.[20] The extent to which this development was influenced by the Greek thought of the time is also the subject of continuing debate in the Jewish world. A nationalist literature drawing strength from the Maccabee model grew from the nineteenth century, together with

---

17 'Protecting the Stranger', *Parshat Naso*, 5755, www.vbm-torah.org.
18 Rabbi Edward Feinstein, 'God's Four Questions', sermon for Yom Kippur 1993, www.vbs.org/rabbi/rabfeins/divre/fourqust.htm.
19 M. Elon, *Jewish Law*, vol.3, p.1036.
20 See discussion in M. Elon, *Jewish Law*, vol.3, pp.1035-6.

the modern Zionist movement, though there has also been a significant Liberal Jewish critique of this muscular Judaism on the grounds that it draws too much on fundamentally unethical Greek sources.[21] To the period of Greek influence before and after the Maccabees, too, Jewish tradition owes its first martyrological literature, encouraging later waves of suicidal acts under the Romans which the rabbis first struggled against, and then tried to assimilate.[22] Early rabbinic leaders opposed the zealot who deliberately sought martyrdom, in much the same way that the Church Fathers did. Not so all sections of the rabbinic community in subsequent generations. The persistent taboo on suicide in rabbinic Judaism meant that, in the 1930s, the declaration sanctioning suicidal missions of Abraham Isaac Kook, the first Ashkenazi Chief Rabbi of Mandate Palestine, became the subject of a fierce dispute amongst religious Zionists,[23] which in many respects parallels that amongst religious anti-Zionists in the Arab Islamic world today.

The attempt of the rabbinic authorities to interpret the law so as to limit war as much as possible should also be understood in the context of Roman occupation, with which the rabbis developed a very different relationship. Under the Romans, the rabbis faced periods of persecution, against which one strand of the rabbinic community, one emblematic leader of which was Rabbi Shimeon bar Yochai, encouraged firm and, if necessary, violent resistance. To Shimeon bar Yochai we owe the notorious statement, quoted in many anti-Jewish tracts but cited as a command with legal force by only a fringe within the rabbinic community, 'The best of the Gentiles you shall kill'.[24] His teacher, Rabbi Akiva, one of the greatest figures whose teachings feature in the rabbinic literature, concluded that the revolt of Bar Kochba was a mandated war, and that Bar Kochba was the Messiah. Yet Roman rule also witnessed periods of flourishing religious culture and relatively peaceful relations with the new rulers, without which Shimeon bar Yochai would have had far less reason to speak positively of 'the best' of the Gentiles. Rabbi Yohanan ben Zakkai, after escaping from the captured Jerusalem, was able to establish the greatest centres of Jewish learning seen to that date, providing a model whereby obedience to tyrants could be turned into a kind of passive resistance.

We know that rabbinic scholars entered into dialogues with Roman lawyers,[25] though scholars have yet to show that many rabbis knew much of the Roman laws of war then being reforged by dissident legal and philosophical voices. Those Latin words which the rabbinic texts in this period took in often related to military

---

21 See, notably, D. Marmur, *Beyond Survival: Reflections on the Future of Judaism* (London: Darton, Longman & Todd, 1982).

22 See D. Boyarin, *Dying for God: Martyrdom and the Making of Christianity and Judaism* (Stanford: Stanford University Press, 1999).

23 W.S. Wurzburger, *Ethics of Responsibility: Pluralistic Approaches to Covenantal Ethics* (Philadelphia: JPSA, 1994), p.92.

24 BT *Soferim* 15:10; *Mechilta* 14:7.

25 See, e.g., D. Novak, *The Image of the Non-Jew in Judaism: An Historical and Constructive Study of the Noahide Laws* (Lewiston, NY: Edwin Mellen, 1983).

vocabulary,[26] but the rabbis' turn against war-making may equally have been a direct reaction against the severity of Roman rule. When the Mishnah was compiled at the end of the second century, its authors concluded: 'One may not sell to idolators bears or lions nor anything that may be harmful to the public'.[27] It is difficult to imagine a situation of persecution in which the rabbis might have hoped to regulate the market in bears and lions. Here, the opposition of 'idolators' and 'the public' reflects an increasing tendency in the rabbinic literature to identify 'idolators' with the perpetrators of ethical outrage rather than with polytheism or the use of idols, and to reflect on a public morality embracing all parts of the societies in which Jews lived, not simply the rabbinic community itself.[28] The opportunities for the transfer of ideas from Roman law were correspondingly great, and those ideas which did not survive in the Talmud can at least be viewed through the discussions of the laws of war in Josephus and Philo.[29]

Later rabbis further restricted the conduct of military campaigns on the basis of an imaginative reading of the biblical passage commanding the Israelites to make war against Midian (Numbers 31:7), where 'as the Lord commanded Moses' was read as enjoining that, in besieging a city, 'it was permitted to surround the enemy only on three sides so that they might flee from the beleaguered city'.[30] By this later period, the rabbis were not only living under yet another set of rulers, the Persians, they had enjoyed a period of economic prosperity based on an increasingly commercial society for which war was a huge risk. In its discussion of capital punishment, the Mishnah makes clear that the rabbis were themselves clear that their discussion of the imposition of an ideal justice could only survive while Jews did not exercise the ultimate sanctions against murder.[31]

In the light of these conflicting tendencies in the early rabbinic community, the biblical passages relating to *jus ad bellum* received further refinement. The rabbis agreed that a king should only be able to embark upon a 'permitted war' upon the agreement of the Sanhedrin, which some commentators have portrayed as a political, and even a democratic, check, and which others have seen as a gathering of legal experts ensuring adherence to the law.[32] In the wake of the invasion of Lebanon in 1982, rabbinic discussion turned once again to the role of the Sanhedrin and of the priestly augury supposed to accompany the decision to make

---

26 S. Krauss, *Griechische und Lateinische Lohnwörter im Talmud, Midrasch und Targum*, (Olms: Georg Publishers, 1987).

27 *Avodah Zarah* I, 7; BT 15b-16a.

28 See Novak, op cit., passim.

29 See, e.g., Josephus, *Antiquities*, e.g. XII, 1:1, 6:2; *Contra Apion* I, 22; II, 29. For useful commentary on both figures, see Reuven Kimelman, 'War', in S. Katz (ed.), *Frontiers of Jewish Thought* (Washington DC: Bnai Brith, 1992), pp.301-32.

30 *Sifri*, Matot 157; *Yalkut Shimoni*.

31 Mishnah, *Makkot* 1:10.

32 See discussion in N. Zohar, 'Morality and War: A Critique of Bleich's Oracular Halakha', in D.H. Frank (ed.), *Commandment and Community: New Essays in Jewish Legal and Political Philosophy* (Albany, NY: SUNY, 1995), p.251 ff.

war – comparable to the auguries of ancient Greek and Roman war-making, and equally supposed by some to provide a check on war-making.[33]

A new category of war also appeared in the Talmud, of 'wars fought to reduce the number of idolators that they should not rise up against them'.[34] This was, according to the majority, a situation threatening the defence of the people in which Jews were obligated to fight, while Rabbi Yehudah argued that this was a situation which fell short of the conditions for a *milchemet mitzvah*, thus falling into the category of wars that were simply 'permitted'. This subsequently became the basis for discussing the permissibility of a pre-emptive strike. The rabbis still concluded that a declaration of war must precede the onset of initial hostilities by at least three days. Nevertheless, the discussion between Rabbi Yehudah and his colleagues suggested grounds for a debate over the permissibility of an attack where the hostile intentions of an enemy made an invasion appear likely. In addition, the reference to the *milchemet mitzvah* provides further grounds for debate over the conditions in which a pre-emptive strike is necessary on defensive grounds. In 1967, this debate over the pre-emptive strike in Judaism was rekindled by the Six Day War, and subsequently again by Israel's campaigns in Lebanon and in the territories.[35]

The scholarly literature on mediaeval and modern Jewish views of the laws of war is at present patchy. One key to this situation is the influence of Moses Maimonides. The discussion of the laws of war in Maimonides' *The Laws of Kings* has since become quasi-canonical in all sections of the Orthodox community, though Maimonides clearly took an extreme position on the rationale for a 'just war'. Motivated by his extreme position on the spread of 'idolatry' in his own day, particularly in the light of his experience of the cruelty of the invasion of Spain by the zealous Almohad dynasty, Maimonides blurred the distinction between the *herem* of Deuteronomy, the defensive *milchemet mitzvah*, and the 'voluntary' war, which many commentators have argued could only lawfully be pursued against the aggressive 'idolators' condemned in the Mishnah.[36] The practical implications of the extreme interpretations of Maimonides were at the time minimal, particularly since *The Laws of Kings* also gives due attention to the restrictions on warfare outlined in the rabbinic literature, the duty to seek peace before making war, and especially the duty of compassionate treatment of both combatant enemies and civilians.[37] With the birth of the State of Israel, however, the association between restraint and the 'idolatry' of Israel's enemies has again become a matter of political importance.[38]

---

33 Ibid.
34 Mishnah, *Sotah*, 44b.
35 J.D. Bleich, 'Preemptive War in Jewish Law', *Tradition*, vol.21, no.1, Spring 1983, pp.3-41.
36 G.J. Blidstein, 'Holy War in Maimonidean Law', in J. Kraemer (ed.), *Perspectives on Maimonides: Philosophical and Historical Studies* (Oxford: Littman, 1996), pp.209-220.
37 *Mishneh Torah, Hilchot Melakhim*, V.
38 See, e.g., sermons of Rabbi Shlomo Riskin on, for instance, *Leviticus*: 25:1-27:34, 19 May 2001, www.ohrtorahstone.org.il/parsha/5762/achareimot_kedoshim62.htm

In the modern Religious Zionist community, increasing attention has been given to the positions of the thirteenth-century Spanish rabbi Nachmanides, who took in key respects a more extreme position. While Nachmanides, too, stressed the duty of compassion and the imperative to seek peace, he also argued that restrictions on combat following from the prohibition of the destruction of fruit trees only applied if their sole purpose was to inflict needless suffering.[39] With the benefit of 700 years of hindsight, we might wish to see this as an early polemic against 'terrorism'. However, if the destruction of trees (or comparable actions) served a defensive purpose, or even if it was simply a matter of military advantage, Nachmanides concluded that it was permitted.

The significance of Nachmanides for the Religious Zionist community is perhaps better understood in the light of his biography. Soon after participating, under duress, in the Barcelona Disputation of 1263, Nachmanides fled and in 1267 led a large party of French rabbis to settle in the Crusader capital, Acre, before moving to Jerusalem. For Nachmanides, unlike Maimonides, the duty of regaining the Land of Israel was a biblical commandment incumbent on every Jew in all times, and, in including it in his definitive listing of the 613 biblical commandments, he criticised Maimonides for the omission.[40] Living during the embattled final years of the Crusader Kingdom, the conditions in which settlements in the Land were defended was a question of great importance, to Christians and to Jews alike. The Religious Zionist community turns to Nachmanides for a discussion of principles for the defence of outlying settlements in the West Bank/Judea and Samaria.[41] A comparison of the military ethics of Nachmanides and that of Christians and Muslims in the region at the time would therefore be of more than historical interest.

Jewish commentators writing over the last two millenia have naturally enough evidenced a persistent awareness of their military impotence. From the turn of the first millenium, rabbinic texts began to treat 'the wars of the lord' as an entirely spiritual phenomenon with no military implications. Commonly, books on 'The Wars of the Lord' deal with the ethical fight against temptation.[42] Bahya ibn Paquda's seminal *Hobot HaLebabot* (*Duties of the Heart*), a work which remains a cornerstone of Jewish ethical teaching, takes up the Islamic description of the greater *jihad* as an internal battle for spiritual purification.[43] In this version, a 'pious man' (sometimes assumed to be a Jew) tells soldiers returning from a fierce war to prepare for the 'greater *milchamah*', the battle against the 'evil inclination', many times more formidable than any other human foe, and always seeking to turn

39 Rabbi Michael Broyde, 'Fighting the War and the Peace', p.3, at
    www.jlaw.com/Articles/war3.html.
40 See further in C.B. Chauvel, *Rabenu Moshe ben-Nachman: toldot hayyav zemano vehiborav*, and Haim Rivlin, *Maalat Haaretz: Eretz Yisrael be peirush haRamban leTorah* (Jerusalem: HaMador HaDati, 1969).
41 See, e.g., I. Lustick, *For the Land and the Lord: Jewish Fundamentalism in Israel* (CFR, 1988), ch.5, passim.
42 E.g. Nehemiah Calomiti, *Sefer Milhemet ha-Emet* (Hoboken, NJ: Ktav, 1975).
43 *Sha'ar Yichud HaMa'aseh*, ch.5. See also M. Saperstein, *Jewish Preaching, 1200-1800: an Anthology* (New Haven: Yale University Press, 1985), p.355.

external contests into opportunities for a spiritual defeat. The parable was retold in abbreviated form in the ethical treatise *Orchot Tzaddikim* (*The Ways of the Righteous*), possibly written in fifteenth century Crete and widely used to this day in a Yiddish translation.[44] The Muslim precedent for the parable is unknown to most of the books' readers.

From the eleventh century, too, Hebrew works entitled 'The Wars of the Lord' are also often fashioned as polemics against 'heretics' or those whose opposition to the true faith has made them fit targets for a defensive *milchemet mitzvah*.[45] Military affairs were not classed among the problems covered by the comprehensive fifteenth century legal code, the *Shulchan Aruch*, and the literature which treated armed conflict as a Jewish concern was far more likely to cast Jews as civilian victims than as potential combatants.[46] The degree to which military might was alien to Jewish spirituality can be exaggerated, though the '*Haredi*' community does make much of the non-military tradition of rabbinic Judaism, both in their polemics against the State and in justifying refusal to perform military service.[47] In resurrecting the idea of a Jewish state in the nineteenth and early twentieth centuries, the Zionist movement created a problem for religious Jews. Jewish law had been focused on life in the Diaspora for so long that discussion of the military ethics of a Jewish polity was almost entirely hypothetical. Meanwhile, the nature of modern states, of modern warfare and of the international laws of war had moved a long way from the 'bears and lions' of talmudic discussion. Applying talmudic principles in the contemporary State of Israel would prove one of the most tendentious aspects of Israeli religious politics.

Israeli Divisions over the Use of Jewish Sources on the Laws of War

In contemporary rabbinic debate, 'Religious Zionists' have followed in some respects the same shift which has governed secular Israeli military ethics. Before 1967, the dominant tendency within the Israeli Defence Forces coupled the doctrine of the 'purity of arms' with a universalist, socialist credo according to which high standards in the conduct of war would impress upon the Arab world

---

44 *Orchot Tzaddikim: The Ways of the Righteous*, trans. S.J. Cohen (Hoboken NJ: Ktav, 1982), ch.1, 'On Pride', pp.36-7.
45 E.g. Jacob ben Reuven, *Milhamot ha-Shem*, 12th century; Abraham Maimonides, *Milhemet ha-Schem*, ed. R. Margolit (Jerusalem: Mossad HaRav Kook, 1997); Meir of Narbonne, *Milhemet haMitzvah*, 13th century; Judah b. Iaac ibn Shabbetai, *Milhemet ha-hokhmah veha-osher* (*The War of Wisdom and Happiness*), 13th century, ed. A.M. Haberman, (Jerusalem: Defus Merkaz, 1953); Moshe ben Nachman, *Milchamot HaShem*, 13th century.
46 This dominated Eastern European literature from the Chmielnicki massacres to the pogroms of the late 19th and early 20th centuries. The exceptions to this trend were mostly Biblical commentaries written in the Mediterranean, notably those of Sforno and Abrabanel.
47 E.g Rabbi Nosson Zeev Grossman, 'The Danger of Secular Control of Eretz Yisroel', *Dei'ah ve-Dibur*, 31 May 2000.

Israel's desire to live in peace.[48] Since that time, this force for moderation has increasingly faced competition from those who believe that force is the only language understood in the region, that retaliation is the most effective means to combat instability, and that Jews need not fear the 'becoming the enemy' syndrome. The more public interventions of religious leaders in military affairs have swung between these poles, following the fortunes of the peace process, from Left to Right and back again, marked both by an attempt to underscore a distinctive Jewish ethic, and by a constant comparison with the cultural values believed to motivate Arab attacks on Israel.

The dominant political tendencies amongst religious Israeli Jews interpret the contemporary significance of the classical Jewish sources on the laws of war through the lenses of three distinctive religious responses to the Zionist State. The 'Religious Zionist', or 'National Religious', community is overwhelmingly 'Modern Orthodox', with liberals joining the tiny 'Masorti' ('Conservative') and Reform communities. A smaller proportion of the population – 2% – are 'Haredi', either rejecting modernity, secularism and Zionism without quarter (the 'anti-Zionists') or prepared to strike some degree of compromise with the State (the 'non-Zionists'). A sizeable proportion of the ostensibly-secular Israeli population, particularly within the Sephardi community, has also been willing to support the political representatives of these religious factions. The core of the conflict between their respective interpretations of the laws of war thus primarily reflects an internal Israeli debate over the ideal relationship between a Jewish state and Israeli society. The competing approaches have largely been cast in terms of legal differences over the authority of various institutions of the state, the role and authority of the rabbinate, and the nature of rabbinic jurisprudence in relation to secular knowledge and military expertise. In this context, restrictions on 'just' warfare, the rights of non-combatants and the plight of the Palestinians have drawn the active support of only a minority within the religious section of Israeli society. Most of the rabbinic leadership has concluded, with Maimonides, that the defensive mandate for war applies in a wide sense because of the apparently implacable hostility of Israel's enemies.

In 1948, the balance between religious moderates and hardliners in many respects favoured the former. At the birth of the State, the National Religious Party's leader, Dr Zorah Wahrhaftig, played an important role in debate over the constitutional position of the Israeli Defence Forces, adding weight to the side of the debate in the Knesset (the parliament) which insisted the military ought to be firmly under the control of the legislature.[49] A more nationalistic wing also developed within the Religious Zionist camp, inspired by the mystic and Ashkenazi Chief Rabbi of Mandate Palestine, Abraham Isaac Kook. Kook's forceful support for Jewish efforts at self-defence, and his fulsome acceptance of the role of the executive in military affairs (the king as against the Sanhedrin, or

---

48 See, e.g., M. Pa'il, 'The Dynamics of Power: Morality in Armed Conflict After the Six Day War', in M. Fox (ed.), *Modern Jewish Ethics, Theory and Practice* (Columbus: Ohio State University Press, 1975), pp.191-200.

49 E. Rackman, *Modern Halakhah for Our Time* (Hoboken, NJ: Ktav, 1995) p.150.

the Israeli government rather than the rabbinate or the Knesset),[50] also gave his students and followers a lasting and influential association with the religious chaplaincy of the IDF. The Chief Rabbis of the IDF, the rabbis who broke the ground in ruling on the *halakhic* status of Israel's wars and the consequences of this for military conduct, have largely been followers of Kook. Frequently permissive in their rulings on army conduct, they have over the decades of Israel's existence taken a hard line in opposing arguments for restraint in pursuit of reconciliation with the Arab states. In the wake of the massacre of Arab civilians in the village of Kibiyeh in 1953, maverick Orthodox intellectual Yeshayahu Leibowitz published an influential article arguing that the attack, retribution for a series of killings of Jewish civilians nearby, smacked of the unrestrained conception of 'strict justice' for which Jacob cursed those of his sons who attacked the sons of Shechem after the rape of Dinah.[51] In response, one of the most influential figures within the National Religious movement, Rabbi Shaul Yisraeli,[52] published a qualified defence of both the actions of Jacob's sons and those of the soldiers responsible for Kibiyeh. In the 1990s, this hardline tendency threatened to create a split between the National Religious movement and the army itself: in 1995, the agreements with the Palestinians made by the State were countered by even those rabbis most closely associated with the IDF, who ruled that religious Jews should refuse to obey orders to withdraw from settlements in pursuit of the Oslo Accords. The executive had the power to wage a defensive war, but not the power to initiate a dangerous peace.[53]

The religious meaning of the State for the National Religious bloc has, however, encouraged a wide margin of tolerance for those actions of the government and army justified on defensive grounds. The victories of Israel have been marked with annual ceremonies given a special religious status by all sections of the Religious Zionist community, although the celebration of military victories has been a very controversial feature of Jewish history.[54] Since the surprise victory in the Six Day War of June 1967, the more extreme manifestations of hardline temperament have commonly been associated with a 'messianic' faith that the capture of the Temple Mount in Jerusalem, the biblical heartland of Judea and Samaria, as well as Gaza and the Golan Heights, signalled the onset of the 'Messianic Days'. A movement for a 'Greater Israel' – Gush Emunim ('The Bloc

---

50 R. Kimelman, 'Abravanel and the Jewish Republican Ethos', in Frank, op cit, pp.201-11.
51 'After Kibiyeh', *Beterem*, 1953, translated in E. Goldman (ed.), *Yeshayahu Leibowitz: Judaism, Human Values, and the Jewish State* (Cambridge, Mass.: Harvard University Press, 1992), pp.185-90.
52 'The Kibiyeh Incident in the Light of Halakha', *Ha'Torah Ve'Hamedinah*, nos 5-6, 1954. Commentary in Z. Yaron, 'Religion and Morality in Israel and in the Dispersion', in Fox, op cit., p.242.
53 This even affected many of the most courageous supporters of the peace process; see J. Cohen, *Dear Chief Rabbi: From the Correspondence of Chief Rabbi Immanuel Jakobovits* (Hoboken, NJ: Ktav, 1995), p.35f.
54 See Y. Leibowitz, 'Heroism', in A. Cohen and P. Mendes-Flohr (eds.), *Contemporary Jewish Religious Thought* (New York: Touchstone, 1988), p.303ff.

of the Faithful') – was created to settle the newly-captured areas, inspired by the 'prophetic' leadership of Zvi Yehudah Kook, accused by leading moderates of twisting the legacy of his father, Abraham Isaac.

Historically, leaders of the 'Right-wing' of the National Religious bloc have sought to bolster their political position, faced with incessant attacks from the 'non-Zionist' parties, by adopting a fierce and anti-Arab 'nationalist' high ground – many, for instance, reading the passage from *Tanchuma* quoted at the beginning of this paper in the light of a negative stereotype of Arabic culture as deeply violent and cruel.[55] A vocal but small strain within the National Religious bloc supports 'solutions' to the threat posed by their Arab neighbours that would curtail Arab rights to the point of their 'transfer' outside the region, or holds some sympathy with small 'underground' groups of extremists such as 'Kach'. This fringe includes prominent maverick rabbis, such as Shlomo Aviner, lambasted by figures in the moderate wing of the Religious Zionist camp for their appropriation of the teaching attributed to Shimeon bar Yochai, 'The best of the gentiles you shall kill', in a literal sense.[56] Faced with enemies they have largely seen as implacably hostile, prominent figures within the Religious Zionist military rabbinate have also sought to construct a military ethics which will withstand what they believe to be the situation. The first Chief Rabbi of the IDF, Shlomo Goren, thus stirred controversy within the religious Zionist community by arguing that the limitations in war imposed by Deuteronomy 20 are only possible before the actual outbreak of hostilities – war by nature being wild, lawless, and uncivilized.[57] Drawing on rabbinic sources, Goren nevertheless turned the thrust of the earlier texts outlined above on its head.

From the 1970s, a disaffected wing within the Religious Zionist movement attempted to combat the growing influence of the religious parties which had taken an increasingly hawkish approach to relations with the Arab world. The *OzveShalom-Netivot Shalom* movements failed to generate enough political momentum to make any measurable impact until the beginning of the peace process of the 1990s, when the Meimad Party was formed. Whereas *OzveShalom* – like its largely non-Orthodox counterpart *Shomrei Mishpat*/Rabbis for Human Rights – has centred its attention on issues of peace and human rights, Meimad, with evident success, has located these issues in the context of a campaign against the 'Iranian'-style involvement of religious leaders in political and military decision-making. Both movements have advanced a religious basis for a rational defence of the 'land for peace' process, which rests primarily on the contention that

55 See, e.g., E. Shochetman, *He Who is Compassionate to the Cruel will Ultimately Become Cruel to the Compassionate: Contemporary Lessons from an Ancient Midrash*, Ariel Center Policy Paper 14, 2001.

56 S. Schwarzschild, 'The Question of Jewish Ethics Today', *Sh'ma*, vol.7, no.124, 24 December 1976.

57 Discussion in Rabbi Mordecai Tendler, 'Exchanging Territories for Peace', lecture of 2 March 2000:
www.yu.edu/faculty/emayer/riets_notes/ notes_pages/contemphalakha_sp00.doc.

saving life is always more important in Judaism than defending land, even within the frameworks laid down by Nachmanides and the elder Rabbi Kook.[58]

Despite a brief period in the early 1990s when the rabbinic councils of the main Ashkenazi and Sephardi political parties ruled that a 'land-for-peace' deal was technically permissible, *Haredi* leaders have shown little sustained commitment to the peace negotiations, arguing that *halakhah* mandates trading land only if it is known that this will secure lasting peace.[59] Overwhelmed by the urgency of the defence of Jews in Israel, the most evident tendencies amongst the leading rabbis of both Zionist and non-Zionist factions is that which has privileged arguments from classical commentaries in favour of humane standards in conditions of low military threat, but for a permissive approach to conduct in a truly defensive war. The task for those who seek to assess contemporary shifts in Jewish 'just war' literature thus turns all the more on judgments of the international context and of relations with neighbouring Arab populations, rather than on straight interpretations of distinctive halakhic typologies or categories of war.

---

58 See regularly updated discussions at:
www.netivot-shalom.org.il and www.meimad.org.il.

59 See, e.g., Aveizer Ravitsky, *Messianism, Zionism and Jewish Religious Radicalism* (Chicago: University of Chicago Press, 1997); Also Rabbi Mordecai Tendler, 'Exchanging Territories for Peace', lecture given on 2 March 2000, www.yu.edu/faculty/emayer/riets_notes/notes_pages/contemphalakha_sp00.doc, and Prof. T. Groner, 'A Response to the Halakhic Ruling Against the Return of Territory', www.netivot-shalom.org.il/judaism/halter.php.

Chapter 2

Catholicism and the Just War Tradition: The Experience of Moral Value in Warfare

Paul Dearey

The ethics of just war is a part of the social doctrine of the Roman Catholic Church. It appears sometimes in a robust form, that is with the familiar *jus ad bellum* criteria, which, if satisfied, suspend the strong presumption against the use of force: these include the criteria of just cause, comparative justice, legitimate authority, last resort, and probability of success. And together with these, making up the traditional doctrine of just war, appear the *jus in bello* criteria, those which, if satisfied, curb the violence of war by imposing moral standards on the conduct of armed conflict: these include the criteria of right intention, proportionality, and non-combatant immunity. Furthermore, one finds occasional exhortations of the Catholic faithful to become more familiar with the principles of just war as part of the life-long task of understanding and applying in good conscience the Church's teaching on war and peace.[1]

It would be mistaken, however, to assume for these reasons that Roman Catholic social teaching is conclusively in favour of the ethics of just war. Indeed, the most authoritative teaching of the Roman Catholic Church on peace and war, found in the Second Vatican Council's *Pastoral Constitution on the Church in the Modern World*, considers the matter differently, calling for a 'completely fresh reappraisal of war'.[2] The reason this reappraisal is needed is the development of weapons of mass destruction, which, according to a footnote reference to the encyclical *Peace on Earth* of Pope John XXIII, makes war an improper way to obtain justice for violated rights.[3]

1   See for example the National Conference of Bishops, *The Harvest of Justice is Sown in Peace*, 1993, http://www.usccb.org/sdwp/harvestexr.htm.
2   Vatican Council II, *Pastoral Constitution on the Church in the Modern World* (1965), para. 80, http://www.vatican.va/archive/hist_councils/ii_vatican_council/documents/vat-ii_cons_19651207_gaudium-et-spes_en.html.
3   Pope John XXIII, *Peace on Earth* (1963), http://www.vatican.va/holy_father/john_xxiii/encyclicals/documents/hf_j-xxiii_enc_11041963_pacem_en.html.

One may reason – although these documents do not explicitly say as much – that other social and cultural conditions make a straightforward application of just war ethics inconsistent with Roman Catholic moral theology: that there are reasons why the just war tradition should not be applied as a set of mechanical criteria to justify political conclusions on resort to and the use of force. For instance, the application of just war criteria in political decision-making must involve public debate, which in turn presupposes a developed public understanding of the criteria, an understanding that in fact may not exist. And if public understanding is lacking at the level of political decision-making, it seems likely that it is still more deficient in the scrutiny of military planning, training and command systems. Moreover, in the absence of a commitment to respect for life – something which Pope John Paul II has remarked about contemporary culture in his encyclical *The Gospel of Life* – it is difficult to expect that any application of the just war tradition will enact a commitment to the deepest needs of human solidarity, to what the Roman Catholic Church calls the 'common good', rather than to some other purpose.[4]

Although the relation between just war ethical theory and conscientious practice is uncertain, it must be considered that the application of just war principles requires a way of moral reasoning that is recognisably catholic. Minimally, this means a way of moral reasoning that respects people of good will who nonetheless come to different conclusions about the use of force by public authorities. It means a way of moral thinking that is prudent, yet at the same time courageous in criticizing either advocates or opponents of the use of force who employ the just war tradition to promote their own political positions. A still more adequate interpretation of the appearance of just war ethics in Roman Catholic social teaching would stress that it is informed by the beliefs and values of Catholicism. It would insist that apart from the catholic experience of morality, apart from the experience of what is good and what is evil – as for example in ethical systems which identify the starting point of ethics in a given individual, in a given social situation, or in abstract reason – apart, that is, from the way of moral reasoning that Catholicism fosters, there cannot exist within the Church's social doctrine a meaningful commitment to the ethics of just war.

The status of just war doctrine within Roman Catholicism is dependent upon a certain connection of values, disputed positions, and doctrinal reforms. More specifically, its status depends upon, firstly, the ethics of peacemaking; secondly, the mediation of two positions on warfare, namely non-violent resistance and just war; and thirdly, the consensus that exists among the universal episcopate on the ethically justifiable use of force by public authorities. Let us consider each of these circumstances in turn, before giving our attention to the experience of moral value when confronting warfare.

4   Pope John Paul II, *The Gospel of Life* (1995),
     http://www.vatican.va/holy_father/john_paul_ii/encyclicals/documents/hf_jp-
     ii_enc_25031995_evangelium-vitae_en.html.

The Ethics of Peacemaking

A primary moral obligation of all Catholics, not only when confronted by violent conflict but at all times, is to meet the challenges of peacemaking. Indeed this is at the heart of the Catholic faith, since God's desire for peace for all people is fulfilled in Christ, in whom all humanity is redeemed and reconciled. The work of peacemaking is lived out in every possible way: by doing good, by loving enemies, by spreading the gospel of peace, by openness to the grace of God's healing and Christ's redemption. This penetrating gift of peace transforms everyday life and the world. It consists of sharing the goodness of life together, and not merely in the absence of war. Pope John Paul II has written in this encyclical *On Social Concern* that 'The goal of peace, so desired by everyone, will certainly be achieved through putting into effect social and international justice, but also through the practice of the virtues which favour togetherness and which teach us to live in unity so as to build in unity, by giving and receiving a new society and a better world'.[5]

The virtues of sharing together what is good, virtues which are required for an enduring peace, are fostered by communities whose faith and hope is doubtless tried by the violence of contemporary culture and the growing contempt for human life. It is with courageous perseverance that the search for peace is moved to action. The Roman Catholic Church has encouraged this effort by laying out a visionary framework for a peaceful world. Pope John XXIII proposed, in his encyclical letter *Peace on Earth*, a political order adequate to satisfy the needs of the universal common good. In keeping with this encyclical, Roman Catholic social ethics upholds a number of principles:

1. The primacy of the common good for political life.
2. Social and economic development as the necessary conditions for justice and for peace.
3. The need for solidarity between affluent and poorer developing nations.

According to this vision of a peaceful world, all political authority has as its end the promotion of the common good. Insofar as this applies to the defence of large numbers of people whose fundamental rights are at risk, it means that governments individually and collectively have a right and a duty to defend, promote and realize the human rights of all people. Failure to address the fundamental problems of individual governments is a failure to exercise sovereignty in the service of all peoples. Moreover, there is a collective responsibility for promoting the economic and social development of all peoples. In a memorable phrase from Pope Paul VI's encyclical *On the Development of*

---

5   Pope John Paul II, *On Social Concern* (1987), para. 39,
    http://www.vatican.va/holy_father/john_paul_ii/encyclicals/documents/hf_jp-
    ii_enc_30121987_sollicitudo-rei-socialis_en.html.

Peoples, development is the new name for peace.[6] Citing this very idea, the present Pope has written in the encyclical *The Hundredth Year*,

> Just as there is a collective responsibility for avoiding war, so too there is a collective responsibility for promoting development. Just as within individual societies it is possible and right to organize a solid economy which will direct the functioning of the market to the common good, so too there is a similar need for adequate interventions on the international level. For this to happen, a great effort must be made to enhance mutual understanding and knowledge, and to increase the sensitivity of consciences. This is the culture which is hoped for, one which fosters trust in the human potential of the poor, and consequently in their ability to improve their condition through work or to make a positive contribution to economic prosperity. But to accomplish this, the poor – be they individuals or nations – need to be provided with realistic opportunities. Creating such conditions calls for a concerted worldwide effort to promote development, an effort which also involves sacrificing the positions of income and of power enjoyed by the more developed economies.[7]

At the root of war there are usually real grievances to do with injustice, poverty and the exploitation of desperate people. Cooperation in development is necessary in order that such people have peaceful means to improving the conditions of their lives.

A further imperative that contributes greatly to lasting peace is solidarity. At the heart of solidarity is the idea of community. Solidarity requires thinking and acting out of obligation to members of the global community, in respect for the equal dignity of others with whom is shared the goodness of life. It is expressed not by a vague compassion or distress at the misfortunes of so many people, but by individual and collective acts of social charity, as well as by public contributions to the common good. It extends to global relations through economic reform, development assistance and institutions designed to meet the needs of the hungry, refugees and the victims of war.

Non-Violent Resistance and Just War

The Roman Catholic Church's social teaching on the morality of force is strictly conditional upon the diversity of beliefs that exist about the justification of warfare. It is most important to observe this diversity, which is so revealing about the application of the just war tradition. Since the Christian tradition possesses two ways of addressing conflict, namely non-violence and just war, it is to be assumed that differences of belief and opinion among people of good will on the morality of

---

6   Pope Paul VI, *On the Development of Peoples,* para. 79,
    http://www.vatican.va/holy_father/paul_vi/encyclicals/documents/hf_p-
    vi_enc_26031967_populorum_en.html.
7   Pope John Paul II, *The Hundredth Year,* para. 52,
    http://www.vatican.va/holy_father/john_paul_ii/encyclicals/documents/hf_jp-
    ii_enc_01051991_centesimus-annus_en.html.

warfare are complementary rather than opposed. Consequently, the just war criteria are to be understood with equal and respectful regard for the ethic of non-violent resistance. Indeed, the application of just war criteria should advance the aims of non-violent resistance, namely to reduce the amount of violence in the world, since this is the common goal of both ways of addressing conflict within the Christian tradition: the outstanding issue being whether the reduction of violence is best brought about through peaceful or violent conflict.

At a time when the peaceable virtues are held in contempt and weaponry is developed that is capable of mass destruction, the option of non-violent resistance must not be neglected in enunciating and applying the hard tests of the just war tradition, since it is the larger tradition of the Catholic faith that mediates both positions in relation ultimately to the Christian God. Neither position is reduced to or nullified by the Church's preparation for the reign of God, a kingdom of true justice, love and peace; rather each is conserved and affirmed as an integral aspect of peacemaking. The person of Christ is ontologically prior to all endeavours at earthly peace, be they violent or non-violent, since it is in Christ's own person that hostility is killed.[8] Earthly peace is the image and fruit of the peace of Christ, the messianic 'prince of Peace'.[9]

However, despite this fundamental convergence between a non-violent ethic and a just war ethic, there is not one right way to act. Many within the Roman Catholic Church recognize that force may be necessary in a sinful world, and that just war thinking restrains war by placing strict moral limits on the use of force. Others object to the just war tradition on principle, because they believe the use of force always to be wrong; or because just war criteria have been shown to be ineffective in preventing or regulating wars. Indeed the devastation wrought upon civilian populations by war in recent decades reinforces the strong presumption against the use of force. On the other hand, the moral meaning of a total commitment to non-violence in an unjust world is also unclear in important respects. The moral responsibility to actively resist and confront evil and serious injustice may sometimes fail except in the form of military force. In such circumstances it is right that the Church teaches the ethical conditions for the use of force by public authority.

To be passive about grave injustices to others is always incompatible with the Catholic understanding of non-violent resistance. In situations of conflict, the Church's constant commitment is to strive for justice through non-violent means, and particularly, in consideration of its own standing as a major global institution, to realize the power of organized, public non-violence; for example, through dialogue, negotiations, protests, strikes, boycotts, civil disobedience and civilian resistance. However, when sustained attempts at non-violent action fail to protect the innocent against fundamental injustice, when all styles of preventative diplomacy and conflict resolution have been explored and failed, then legitimate political authorities are permitted as a last resort to employ limited force if there is

---

8   *Ephesians* 2:16, cf. *Colossians.* 1:20-22.
9   *Isaiah* 9:5.

a reasonable expectation that it will re-establish justice without causing greater injustice.

Consensus among the Universal Episcopate

The balance between violence and non-violence, and the simultaneity of different views on warfare, can both be conceived as aspects of ecclesiology. That is to say, there are ecclesial structures that mediate different evaluations of justice and violent conflict. Indeed, the mediation of differences on this topic is, theologically speaking, a reflection of the greater synthesis between Christology and Pneumatology in ecclesial existence. We look to conciliarity above all, that is, to the view of the general episcopate on peace and justice, for true guidance on moral action, not because the bishops are any less susceptible to the effects of war which distort moral judgement, but because the episcopate has, in its ecclesial existence, affirmed the validity of the moral law at all times, particularly in times of war. The theological *raison d'être* of conciliarity is to be found in the idea that communion is an *ontological* category in ecclesiology, i.e., communion is the Church's way of existing, its very being. The true nature of conciliarity can be understood only as implying communion. Therefore, the institution which expresses the unity of the Church – even when the Church is divided on grave matters of moral importance – must be an institution which expresses *communion*. No institution of the Roman Catholic Church derives its authority from anything but the event of communion; nor is any institution of the Church self-sufficient or self-justifying prior to the event of communion. At the same time, any institution of universal unity must involve a ministry that safeguards the oneness which communion expresses, which is to say the episcopacy, and particularly the episcopal council.

The episcopacy remains an expression of communion even in circumstances of war. It would be incorrect to say that just and lasting peace is what this communion aims for, since that would imply that communion is somehow for the Church's well-being, whereas in fact it is the very being of the Church. Therefore, what the existence of the episcopacy expresses is prior to just and lasting peace; so that justice and peace must be expressed through the episcopacy. And it pertains even amid war that the general episcopate affirms the moral law. Indeed, the just war doctrine is only invoked subject to an absolute affirmation of the moral law. So we find in the *Catechism of the Catholic Church* that rather than being affirmed the traditional elements of the just war doctrine are merely enumerated.[10] By contrast, what is affirmed is the prudential judgement of these elements, particularly when exercised by those with responsibility for the common good.[11] This is clearly something less than an assertion of the just war tradition, since those with responsibility for the common good are said to include international authorities, public authorities, the Church, and human reason, which is to say

---

10 The Vatican, *The Catechism of the Catholic Church*, no.2309,
    http://www.vatican.va/archive/ccc/index.htm.
11 Ibid.

informed conscience,[12] none of which assumes necessarily the machinations of national sovereignty.

The role of conscience is properly a part of the Church's doctrine on peace, justice and warfare. This leads us to consider the experience of morality in warfare. For the task of peacemaking requires both just structures and informed consciences. Policies and structures of peace will reflect the integrity of the individuals who design and participate in them.

Distortions of Moral Experience

It is abundantly clear that war distorts moral experience. Various forces associated with warfare prevent recognition of good and evil, free will, and responsibility: the dangers of totalitarianism, propaganda, the attraction of weapons, the cult of nation, economic and political ambition – each of these distorts the reception of love and justice in a broken world; each distorts the reception of truth and love by humankind. The idea that sacred Scripture and traditional ethical principles teach us about peacemaking is too often superseded by the generalization that religion causes war, that by its very nature religion is a source of conflict, or even that war is often a religious act. Regrettably this is commonly reinforced by those who would attribute the extreme militancy of a few to some religious faith as a whole. While the notion that religion is a warring ideology, an epiphenomenon of time and place, is easily answered in principle, this notion has the effect of eliminating from society and from people's hearts the influence of religions for peace.

It is wrong to use religion as an explanation of conflicts that have political, economic or ideological causes. It compounds the wrong when extremists themselves justify their violence and hatred in the name of a religious tradition, since in addition to the greater evil of causing death, injury, destruction and terror, they are distorting their professed faith. Profanity is wrong and should not be ignored, even in circumstances when it is the lesser of evils. It should not be ignored, because the world's religious traditions and the witness of people of faith to peace and justice are what offer the most effective responses to pseudo-religious justifications of violent attacks.

A deeper appreciation of the role of religion in peacemaking, in protecting the fundamental rights of people, and in defending the common good, tells us that peace is a matter of the heart: it tells us that war is a symptom of humanity's resistance to the Spirit that gives life. To reason in this way about war and peace is not by any means to evade the question of the justified and careful execution of military force, but rather to reflect upon repentance and forgiveness as constructive attitudes towards enduring peace; and also upon the virtues of courage and compassion that motivate respectful regard and even love of one's enemies.

From the point of view of ontology, war consists of a rupture between truth and neighbourly love, and ultimately between truth and communion with God. War is a refusal to make being dependent upon communion and a symptom of the decisive

12 Ibid., no.2308.

importance given to the notion of individuality in ontology. Regarding the being of things as ultimate and prior to communion commits one to the view that everything that exists posits its own being as something 'given': the world appears ultimately to consist of a fragmented existence in which beings are particular before they can relate to each other. In moral terms, this role of the individual in ontology is connected with the challenge that nature ultimately represents for human freedom, namely that each of us dies. War distorts moral experience to the extent that it makes this truth repulsive to us. It compels people to submit to the truth of *being*, to acknowledge only created existence, and thereby to acknowledge an impasse in terms of their own freedom. War distorts moral experience because it makes people repel the truth of Christian morality, which, with its message of salvation, accepts not the priority of being over communion, but challenges the rupture between truth and neighbourly love that is symptomatic of war.

Another consequence of associating truth with the individual existence of things – an ontology to which war testifies most eloquently – is that we are persuaded that it is within our power to *obtain just peace*, rather than and even without entering into neighbourly love and communion. In the circumstances of warfare, the other – whether it be in the form of a 'person', a 'thing', or a future state in which hostilities have ceased, retribution made, and peace permanently established – is only present as an object before any relationship of communion can take place. Knowledge and ambition then precede communion, when a dichotomy is created between love and knowledge, person and nature, thought and action in the very heart of human existence. If the possibilities of peace in war exist first of all as something known or anticipated by one side to a conflict, then it becomes possible to act independently of communion, to dissociate peace from love, and thus to falsify truth. Humanity, as we know, has the capacity for such hypocrisy.

The falsification of truth at the ontological level has tragic consequences, for it presents the absurdity of being-into-death. When nature becomes the ultimate reference point of existence, then what is called 'truth' subjects all existence, the whole cosmos, to death. Death is connected with truth in existence precisely through the identification of truth with individualized, fragmented nature. This absurdity is not to be avoided or ignored. Humanity and creation requires deliverance from it, and it is for this purpose that God draws near. As far as this concerns war, we need to understand war in terms of salvation history, that is in terms of God's approach to created existence and to humanity especially. To be saved from war means that life should be something true, something undying. It is for this reason that the Fourth Gospel identifies life without death, i.e. eternal life, with truth and knowledge. But this application of truth to existence becomes possible only if the individualization of nature is transformed into communion, so that life and not death becomes identical with being. It is in this way that the problem of war should be described, not humanity in terms of violence and injury, nor existence in terms of death.

Indeed, to describe humanity by its experience of violent conflict, and moral existence by the reality of death, is the most fundamental misapprehension caused by war. It is as inevitable as it is unacceptable. War must be understood in the history of salvation. More particularly, the just war theory must be understood as an exhortation to live in the truth, and therefore as a profession of faith in the Spirit of life. It is a way of moral reasoning with ontological and pneumatological dimensions. War occurs always in the context of God's remaining close. In this context it is the manifestation *par excellence* of resistance and opposition in human reality to God's approach.

Peacemaking as Encountering the Person

By contrast, the spiritual gifts known in Roman Catholic moral theology to describe the human person are, remarkably enough, nowhere apparent in the theory of justified war: love, joy, kindness, goodness, gentleness, self-control, and peace. These personal qualities describe human nature and the manner of its redemption even in the face of war, for they affirm a personal way of being that transcends the natural demise of each individual, a way of being in which the dignity of the person has priority over acts that destroy and are contemptuous of human life.

Personal being, not being-into-death, is the ontological condition of moral experience in Roman Catholic thought, and therefore a presupposition of thinking on just war. A personal being is capable of loving someone more than their own nature, more than their own life. The person, that is to say, the image of God in humanity, is humanity's freedom with regard to his or her nature: it is the fact of being freed from the domination of nature, and being able to determine oneself freely. This truth of the person transcends all conditioning. Even though each individual is conditioned by their temperament and character, heredity and social ambiance, their very historicity, their personal dignity consists of transfiguring their nature in God. Being a person is fundamentally different from being an individual or a 'personality', for a person cannot be imagined in him/herself, but only within his/her relationships. A person is not identical with the 'self' or the 'personality' of the self, which is to say with all the qualities and experiences that the self possesses. On the contrary, the identity that defines a person is that between personal existence and truth.

This identity between personal existence and truth, which seems at first sight to represent two things simultaneously that are in contradiction, precedes all moral evaluations. Catholicism understands the person to be a horizon within which the truth of existence is revealed. The person is not a simple nature, but an image of the catholicity of being. To subject a person to individualization or fragmentation, or indeed even to comprehension, is in fact to deny the mystery of personal being, i.e., to deny that otherness and communion coincide in a person's life. Catholicism understands the moral experience of the person in terms of *otherness*, but not in terms of *division*. This identification of otherness and personhood is incompatible with categories of natural existence according to which individuals seek to dominate and possess being. Rather than implying the unity and permanence of being that critics of Christian metaphysics have called 'ontotheology' – which is a way of existing in which the 'other' becomes an enemy – truth in personal existence leads to the affirmation of otherness in and through love. The Catholic understanding of love reflects the fact that a person is a revelation of truth.

How then is it possible to experience the person and his or her dignity? How is the dignity of a person known through experience? In order to apply the ontology of the person to the ethics of just war, it is necessary to understand that a person's dignity is revealed by moral experience: i.e., that there is a moment of insight into, or experience of, the person. In Catholic thought the person is the bearer of moral value. It is by his or her manner of living that moral values are known.

Moral value is differentiated from all other kind of value because it appeals to someone's character as a person. Therefore, at the basis of morality is a person. The experience of moral value enables us to encounter a person as possessing a dignity that distinguishes him or her from all other creatures. In this sense, every person as such has an innate dignity that must be recognized and respected.[13] 'Person' and 'dignity' are not identical terms, however, since, according to the Thomistic tradition, a person also has an acquired dignity that is attained by developing their human possibilities. It is for this reason that the morality of the act gives us an insight into the world of the person. The morality of the act reveals the dignity of the person whom we are obliged to treat according to his or her fullest possible development.

In warfare, the action that discloses the dignity of the other person in accordance with their fullest possibilities is peacemaking rather than violence. Violence distorts the experience of the person even when it is justified, since violence promotes attitudes which degrade the person. Opposed to such attitudes is love, which not only gives to the person what is owed because of their dignity, but more than this is a giving of oneself, whereby the subject of love is more fulfilled.[14]

In human love, however, selfishness remains, and so we need to ask, on behalf of those weak and innocent whose rights are trampled upon in so many ways, for particular proofs of love's extension and original depth. The values that are necessary for the development of the person in his or her wholeness must become real and effective. Included among these values is the value of life itself, and also of health, education, employment, community, and religion. These values contribute to a proper way of living together, i.e., living for oneself through a sincere gift of self. In whatever way we apprehend the truth of this social doctrine, for example in the case of the family (although even here the possible pathology of family life must be observed), its application is an immense challenge. We may understand that for a family, its common good is found in a concrete, unique and unrepeatable way in each person that belongs to it. However, it is not obvious to say that, albeit to a different degree, a person is also the common good of other social institutions, for example of the state of which she is a citizen. By far the more prevalent perception today is to regard an individual as part of an aggregate of humanity, rather than as *this unrepeatable person* with the right to fulfil herself

13 Cf. Saint Thomas Aquinas, *Summa Theologica*, I, q. 29, a. 3; I, q. 29, a. 3, ad 2.
14 Vatican Council II, *Pastoral Constitution on the Church in the Modern World* (1965), para. 24.

on the basis of her dignity. But it is the second attitude that Roman Catholic social doctrine encourages, namely that the dignity of a person establishes her place among all others, so that she may exist for herself.

The Roman Catholic Church teaches with conviction the truth about human love, aware of its many complexities and contradictions. It has identified sources of serious opposition to this teaching, particularly in Pope John Paul II's encyclical *The Splendour of Truth*, which argues that within the Christian community itself there is a separation of human freedom from its 'essential and constructive relationship to truth'.[15] How it is that responsibility for the common good, in which is included the good of every person, is effectively realized at the level of societies and states is certainly difficult to explain, not least because its moral hermeneutic is contentious.

Nonetheless, the need for a renewal of social and political life that will ensure justice, solidarity, honesty and openness is understood by vast numbers of people who feel their rights as citizens or as human beings are held in contempt. One need only recall the activities of protest movements across the globe in recent years to appreciate this point. Undoubtedly, this moral sense of outrage is rooted in diverse issues of culture. What characterizes the Roman Catholic interpretation of these affairs is that it understands morality to be rooted and fulfilled in a religious sense. Pope John Paul II wrote in the encyclical *The Hundredth Year*:

> Man is understood in a more complete way when he is situated within the sphere of culture through his language, history, and the position he takes towards the fundamental events of life, such as birth, love, work and death. At the heart of every culture lies the attitude man takes to the greatest mystery: the mystery of God. Different cultures are basically different ways of facing the question of the meaning of personal existence. When this question is eliminated, the culture and moral life of nations are corrupted.[16]

The religious sense of morality is that the truth of humanity meets the truth of God, the Creator and Redeemer, and it is this truth that makes possible the authentic freedom of the person in society.[17] Translating the moral experience of the person into the renewal of social and political life, especially when faced by serious forms of injustice and corruption affecting entire peoples and nations, depends upon this religious sense of morality.

Western cultures are resistant to assertions of absolute moral values. Moreover, the essential relationship between freedom and objective truth is often dismissed in whatever ways it manifests itself, whether in ideas or art, politics or economics, morality or religion. Social and cultural existence is no longer explained in such terms. From the critique of social and political ideology has developed a more expansive philosophical hermeneutic that is suspicious of explaining human existence in essential terms. Both materialist philosophies and spirituality are

---

15 Pope John Paul II, *The Splendour of Truth* (1993), para. 4,
     http://www.vatican.va/holy_father/john_paul_ii/encyclicals/documents/hf_jp-
     ii_enc_06081993_veritatis-splendor_en.html.
16 Pope John Paul II, *The Hundredth Year*, para. 24.
17 Pope John Paul II, *The Splendour of Truth,* para. 99.

equally suspect from this point of view: particularly the teaching that a person achieves their full identity in obedience to a transcendent truth, since such a doctrine appears merely to frustrate and undermine values that are supposed to guarantee just relations between people, namely tolerance, pluralism, and dialogue. The judgement of the present Pope that such aspirations – insofar as they fail to affirm, or may even deny, the transcendent dignity of the human person – will inevitably succumb to the force of power, that they in fact promote the self-interests of individuals, classes or nations without regard for the rights of others, represents a contentious political interpretation.[18]

At the same time, the doctrine of a mutual relationship between freedom and truth is an extremely significant moral hermeneutic for the life of persons in the social, economic, and political spheres. The Church's presentation of commandments governing specific kinds of behaviour and concrete acts in these spheres aims to articulate the truthfulness of relations and functions within nations and states. It is the Church's view that it must remain possible to acknowledge truth as a reference point for moral life, if the religious yearnings of the human heart are to be respected as such.[19] The alternative is a scandal to democratic life and a danger to world peace, namely that religious convictions are manipulated for political reasons.

Openness in truth to freedom, and openness to freedom founded upon truth: these attitudes render an important translation of the commandment of love into the language of politics and philosophical ethics, and an indispensable service to the common good of society in which the development of each person is valued. They represent what a person would be like who is capable of loving his or her neighbour, and precisely in this way a radical interpretation of what it is to be a person in contemporary society.

Interpreting social life with reference to neighbourly love validates the authenticity of both selfhood and community. The tension between the essential question of human being and the complexity of its social and cultural manifestations means that interpretation is always a priority for understanding. The hermeneutical condition of self-consciousness is widely understood today, although mostly on the model of signifiers and meaning-bearing items, rather than in terms of the neighbour's relevance. Yet neighbourly love makes friendly, forgiving relationships possible, even though one is estranged from the world, its consumption of signs, and its desires. Love of neighbour that is also love of God, which is to say *caritas*, addresses the habituation of desires to the community and to the creativity of each moral act.

In the quest to renew society and politics, the command of love presents the neighbour's relevance as an answer to our reasoned understanding of human possibilities. It reminds us that sound knowledge of what is good cannot be assumed, but rather involves care for a concrete person and their fullest possibilities. It reminds us too that any social theory of just war is fraught with dangers, since the killing of large numbers of people can not only be justified, but

18 Ibid.
19 Ibid., para. 101.

regarded even as a praiseworthy service to progressive, rational, social goals. Ethical judgement is broadened and deepened by Catholic social doctrine, which consistently exposes and condemns the achievements of progress which are founded on sin and transgression, and on the denial of the value of personhood. It does so with an invitation to the primary free human act, namely to give fully of oneself, and by this life-affirming act to oppose irrational antagonism with joy, kindness, and goodness. Such creative, freely chosen actions as bring us to life depend upon the grace of the Holy Spirit, who is 'the giver of life'.

The question of a mutual relationship between freedom and grace is addressed not only to Christian believers, but to all people who desire to think philosophically about the violation of fundamental human rights and the possibility of joyful freedom. For the Christian philosopher, of course, it is the language of 'grace' that protects personal freedom in its full measure, making it relevant and comprehensible to contemporary thought. At the same time antagonists of freedom bring freedom low when claiming 'humble obedience' to a higher will. Worst of all is when evil is done in the name of a religious faith. But it is fundamentally wrong also to construe the invitation of the divine will as a denial of freedom, or as anything less than preserving freedom and personal autonomy in their inviolability, for God requires but one kind of response, namely a free response from the depths of autonomous selfhood.

The Pope has put it this way in his World Day of Peace message in 2002:

> Terrorism is often the outcome of that fanatic *fundamentalism* which springs from the conviction that one's own vision of the truth must be forced upon everyone else. Instead, even when the truth has been reached – and this can happen only in a limited and imperfect way – it can never be imposed. Respect for a person's conscience, where the image of God himself is reflected (cf. *Genesis* 1:26-27), means that we can only propose the truth to others, who are then responsible for accepting it. To try to impose on others by violent means what we consider to be the truth is an offence against human dignity, and ultimately an offence against God whose image that person bears. For this reason, what is usually referred to as fundamentalism is an attitude radically opposed to belief in God. *Terrorism exploits not just people, it exploits God:* it ends by making him an idol to be used for one's own purposes.[20]

Peace, Justice and Forgiveness

To understand Roman Catholic thinking about war, it is necessary to understand its prior commitment to certain conditions of peace, and especially to the moral value of the person. The fundamental principle of thinking about war and peace is that one is more fully a person who makes a gift of himself or herself to others. Just war ethics does not confirm this morality, but it must conform to it. After the

---

20 Pope John Paul II, Message for the Celebration of the World Day of Peace 2002, *No Peace Without Justice, No Justice Without Forgiveness,* para. 6, http://www.vatican.va/holy_father/john_paul_ii/messages/peace/documents/hf_jp-ii_mes_20011211_xxxv-world-day-for-peace_en.html.

attacks of 11 September 2001 this is a trying condition, for it means nothing less than to offer forgiveness as a condition of peace.

How can forgiveness be a source and condition of peace at this time? Responding to this question, Pope John Paul II has remarked that what is under assault today by international terrorism is precisely *the peace that is born of justice and forgiveness*.[21] The basis of true peace has been shattered and now requires restoration, brought about 'by justice and that form of love which is forgiveness'.[22] Terrorism is contemptuous of human life and a crime against humanity. There is a right to defend oneself against terrorism, a right which can be exercised in accordance with the moral and legal limits on the means and ends of violence.[23] Justice requires that the guilty be correctly identified and defeated. It requires also that culpability be not extended beyond the persons involved in terrorism, particularly to ethnic or religious groups to which the terrorists may belong. But justice must soon be joined to forgiveness, as international cooperation in the fight against terrorist activities includes commitments to relieving the causes of poverty, oppression and marginalization that facilitate the designs of terrorists. Prior injustices facilitate tolerance of terrorism, even though they do not excuse acts of terrorism. In this awareness, the justice that is sought and demanded after the recent terrorist slaughter must be fulfilled and completed in the tranquillity of order that is the basis of peace, which is more either than a cessation of hostilities or restoration of the *status quo*, but is 'the deepest healing of the wounds which fester in human hearts'.[24] Justice with forgiveness is essential to such healing.

In this way of reasoning, both justice and forgiveness make the moral value of the person a condition of true peace. Justice does so when it ensures full respect for rights and responsibilities, and the just distribution of benefits and burdens. It is not merely an abstract or a legal concept, but more a way of life to which individuals, families, communities and nations are called.[25] Justice is rooted in merciful love. It expresses the human need for reconciliation. It is primarily an active and life-giving virtue, promoting the dignity of every human person and concerned for the common good.[26] Concerning the causes of international disharmony, justice is shown in respect for human rights;[27] also in showing solidarity amid processes of vast geo-political changes involving especially the globalization of free markets and international finance.[28] The globalization of economics brings opportunities for social and political progress, but also new

---

21 Ibid., para. 4.
22 Ibid., para. 2.
23 Ibid., para. 5.
24 Ibid., para. 3.
25 Pope John Paul II, Message for the Celebration of World Day of Peace 1998, *From the Justice of Each Comes Peace for All*, para. 1,
     http://www.vatican.va/holy_father/john_paul_ii/messages/peace/documents/hf_jp-ii_mes_08121997_xxxi-world-day-for-peace_en.html.
26 Ibid.
27 Ibid., para. 2.
28 Ibid., para. 3.

inequalities between rich and poor, contrasts that are an affront to the dignity of the human person.[29]

In these and other ways justice conforms to the moral dignity of the person, but in this respect it is forgiveness that is the primary condition without which there is no peace. An ethics and a culture of forgiveness must prevail before forgiveness is expressed in politics and laws, and therefore before justice has a more human character.[30] At the same time, respect for the truth is a prerequisite for forgiveness, since lies and falsehood, corruption and ideological manipulation, breed suspicion and division.[31] Forgiveness requires that evil which has been done is acknowledged and corrected, and therefore that the truth regarding crimes is ascertained. Pope John Paul II has said:

> Forgiveness therefore, as a fully human act, is above all a personal initiative. But individuals are essentially social beings, situated within a pattern of relationships through which they express themselves in ways both good and bad. Consequently, society too is absolutely in need of forgiveness. Families, groups, societies, States and the international community itself need forgiveness in order to renew ties that have been sundered, go beyond sterile situations of mutual condemnation and overcome the temptation to discriminate against others without appeal. The ability to forgive lies at the very basis of the idea of a future society marked by justice and solidarity.[32]

In consideration of war particularly, forgiveness presupposes a number of practical measures: stopping the growth of arms production and arms trafficking;[33] that the duty of governments and the international community be done; that the efforts of regional and even local organizations for promoting peace be supported; and that the religions, in speaking out against war, draw upon the genuine patrimony of their traditions to engender a sincere desire for peace.[34]

This last point is particularly noteworthy, for it is the religions that understand the encounter with forgiveness, however difficult, to be liberating, since it is a form of love which has its first source in God who is Love. The common witness of the religions to the truth that the deliberate murder of the innocent is always and without exception a grave evil will give to people and to the international community the sound moral knowledge that is essential for pursuing just peace. This common witness to the healing power of love, particularly in the form of forgiveness, leads to understanding, respect and trust. In his 2002 World Peace Day message, the Pope said this:

---

29 Ibid., para. 4.
30 Pope John Paul II, *No Peace Without Justice, No Justice Without Forgiveness*, para. 8.
31 Pope John Paul II, Message for the Celebration of World Day of Peace 1997, *Offer Forgiveness and Receive Peace*, para. 5,
    http://www.vatican.va/holy_father/john_paul_ii/messages/peace/documents/hf_jp-ii_mes_08121996_xxx-world-day-for-peace_en.html.
32 Pope John Paul II, *No Peace Without Justice, No Justice Without Forgiveness*, para. 9.
33 Pope John Paul II, *Offer Forgiveness and Receive Peace*, para. 4.
34 Ibid.

In this whole effort, religious leaders have a weighty responsibility. The various Christian confessions, as well as the world's great religions, need to work together to eliminate the social and cultural causes of terrorism. They can do this by teaching the greatness and dignity of the human person, and by spreading *a clearer sense of the oneness of the human family*. This is a specific area of ecumenical and interreligious dialogue and cooperation, a pressing service which religion can offer to world peace.[35]

---

35 Pope John Paul II, *No Peace Without Justice, No Justice Without Forgiveness*, para. 12.

Chapter 3

Justifiable War in Eastern Orthodox Christianity

Fr. Alexander F.C. Webster

Introduction

The justifiable war tradition seems to be facing a frontal assault, or is, at least, under siege, by a growing cadre of Eastern Orthodox bishops and theologians. Although it enjoys an unbroken continuity from its origins in Old Testament Israel – precursor of the Church – through two millennia of Orthodox moral reflection and praxis as an aretaic (or virtue) tradition, justifiable war has been recast as a mere concession to human weakness and sin, a 'lesser evil' than the alternative failure to resort to such unsavoury military means in pursuit of justice. This has, in turn, created the spectacle of highly respected religious leaders of one of the venerable Christian communities advocating what may be charitably dismissed as a 'lesser morality'.

The Orthodox proponents of the 'lesser evil' approach to war do, indeed, constitute a formidable phalanx of notables. In May 1989, the forty Orthodox theologians who gathered in Minsk (then in the U.S.S.R.) under the auspices of the politically left-wing World Council of Churches declared: 'The Orthodox Church unreservedly condemns war as evil. Yet it also recognizes that in the defence of the innocent and the protection of one's people from unjust attack, criminal activity and the overthrowing of oppression, it is sometimes necessary, with reluctance, to resort to arms'.[1] On 7 March 1991, when the decisive victory of the U.S.-led alliance in the Persian Gulf War was only a week behind them, the otherwise cautious, generally conservative Holy Synod of Bishops of the Orthodox Church in America (OCA) issued a surprising statement on that military operation. The OCA bishops insisted that what they called the 'just war theory' (instead of the more common 'justifiable war tradition' originally proposed by the late Princeton theologian, Paul Ramsey) 'does not reflect our theological tradition', because war

---

1 'Orthodox Perspectives on Justice and Peace,' in G. Limouris (ed.), *Justice, Peace and the Integrity of Creation: Insights From Orthodoxy* (Geneva: WCC Publications, 1990), pp.17-18.

may never be 'theologically justified'. And yet they hastened to add, '[A] lesser evil must sometimes be chosen to resist a greater evil'.[2]

Nor is the 'mother' church of the OCA immune from such moral confusion. In a comprehensive statement on *The Basis of the Church's Social Concept* issued in August 2000, the Moscow Patriarchate offer a mixed message. First, they concede the following: 'While recognizing war as evil, the Church does not prohibit her children from participating in hostilities if at stake is the security of their neighbours and the restoration of trampled justice. Then war is considered to be a necessary though undesirable means'. But then they make moral room for the measured pursuit of justice in war: 'The Christian moral law deplores not the struggle with sin, not the use of force towards its bearer and not even taking another's life in the last resort, but rather malice in the human heart and the desire to humiliate or destroy whosoever it may be. In this regard, the Church has a special concern for the military, trying to educate them for the faithfulness to lofty moral ideals'.[3] However, one must ask how can soldiers be educated in this way if their vocation is fundamentally evil?

Finally, the most esteemed Orthodox moral theologian in the last century has, by his own admission, experienced a profound metamorphosis in his moral reflections on the problems of war and peace. In an influential article published as a book chapter in 1981, Fr. Stanley S. Harakas, dean emeritus of Holy Cross Greek Orthodox School of Theology near Boston, declared, 'The just war theory holds that war is an evil and seeks to make it less so'.[4] Five years later, he elaborated on this theme of war as 'a necessary evil' in an essay entitled, 'The Teaching of Peace in the Fathers'. The Church Fathers in the Christian East, he contended, 'rarely praised war, and to my knowledge, almost never called it "just" or a moral good'. Following their example, then, the Eastern Orthodox Churches 'cannot speak of a "good war", or even a "just war"'. What Harakas termed the 'peace ideal', though not absolute pacifism, 'continued to remain normative and no theoretical efforts

---

2   Complete text in *The Orthodox Church* (monthly newspaper of the OCA), vol.27, nos 5-6 (May-June 1991), p.4.

3   *The Basis of the Church's Social Concept* (Moscow: Jubilee Bishops' Council of the Russian Orthodox Church, 13-16 August 2000), VIII.2, VIII.4. (available online at: http://www.incommunion.org/resources/orthodox_church_and_society.asp). There is, to be sure, a surprising precedent for this statement. In a small but influential pamphlet published in the middle of the First World War entitled, *The Christian Faith in War* (Reprint edition; Jordanville, N.Y.: Holy Trinity Monastery, 1973), pp.11-12, Metropolitan Antony (Khrapovitsky) of Kiev and Galich also conceded, 'War is an evil, but in the given case, and in the majority of Russian wars, a lesser evil than declining war and surrendering to the power of the barbarians either our holy homeland or the other Orthodox nations who are our brothers'. That bishop's fundamental moral perspective was, however, uncharacteristically at once utilitarian and parochial: '[I]n such situations the following question must be asked: which choice will produce the least harm and the greatest good for the Orthodox faith and one's native people?'

4   S.S. Harakas, 'The Morality of War', in J.J. Allen (ed.), *Orthodox Synthesis: The Unity of Theological Thought* (Crestwood, N.Y.: St. Vladimir's Seminary Press, 1981), p.75.

were made to make conduct of war into a positive norm'.[5] In his most recent contribution on this issue in the aftermath of the terrorist attacks in September 2001, Harakas expresses an extreme hostility toward military operations as thoroughly immoral and detestable, though sometimes necessary. He confidently proclaims that 'Jesus' teaching regarding the Kingdom of God excludes the idea and practice of war among nations', owing, in particular, to 'the awful killing, maiming, destruction, horror and evil which is war'. The task of the Church is 'to constantly and persistently remind civil leaders that war – and terrorist war in particular – is an unacceptable alternative in international relations'. And yet, he balances this quixotic advice by allowing realistically for the 'necessary evil' of war 'sometimes'. When a nation such as the United States of America cannot influence an aggressive enemy through peaceful means 'to deal with us righteously', the 'most which we can do ... is to defend ourselves without seeking to harm the other beyond what is necessary to stop the attack'. To fail 'to defend the innocent,' Harakas concedes, is 'paradoxically consenting and contributing to their extermination'. But he mitigates the value of that insight by adding that 'war can never be our goal, [sic] it can only be a falling away from our goal for which repentance is the only appropriate response'.[6] Again, one must ask how can a nation conduct defensive military operations without having war – especially military victory – as a 'goal'?

These quotations highlight the lack of moral clarity and consistency that besets contemporary Orthodox bishops and theologians in their reflections on the morality of war – or, to be sure, the *immorality* of war according to an emerging consensus.[7] This is what any Orthodox moral theologian must overcome who would argue that war may be engaged and conducted as a virtuous or righteous act, or at least as a 'lesser good' instead of a lesser or necessary evil. The textual evidence is, however, so abundant that the task before us is hardly daunting.

The Orthodox Justifiable War Trajectory in Outline

Eastern Orthodox teaching on the morality of some wars forms one of only two 'trajectories' through the entire multi-millennial history of the Church, beginning

5 Reprinted in S.S. Harakas, *Wholeness of Faith and Life: Orthodox Christian Ethics: Part One – Patristic Ethics* (Brookline, MA: Holy Cross Orthodox Press, 1999), pp.154, 157, & 155.
6 S.S. Harakas, 'Thinking About Peace and War as Orthodox Christians', *Praxis* (Quarterly Journal of the Department of Religious Education, Greek Orthodox Archdiocese of America), vol.3, no.1, January, 2002, pp.28-9.
7 As a point of honour, I hasten to add that the errant notion of war as a 'lesser evil' or always 'unholy' in Byzantium or Orthodox Christianity in general appears in several of my own previous works, most recently A.F.C. Webster, *The Pacifist Option: The Moral Argument Against War in Eastern Orthodox Theology* (Lanham, MD: Rowman & Littlefield Publishers [International Scholars Publications imprint], 1998), p.86. The present essay is thus intended as, at once, a correction and an initial public atonement!

with the experience of ancient Israel as recorded in the Old Testament. The other trajectory is absolute pacifism, which a previous volume has explored in detail.[8] The justifiable war trajectory may be traced in the six types of textual sources that the Orthodox moral tradition comprises: Holy Scripture (that is, the complete Bible of the Church in the fourth century CE, including the 'Septuagint' Greek version of the Old Testament – which remains normative for the Orthodox, though not Protestant Christians or Jews – and, of course, the New Testament); the writings of the Church Fathers from the first century through the entire Byzantine era that ended in 1453 CE with the conquest of Constantinople by the Ottoman Turks; canon law; hagiographic literature and the associated icons of the saints as narrative theology 'in colour and form'; devotional literature, which includes liturgical and hymnographic texts and a special type of spiritual writing focusing on ascetical or mystical themes; and the works of modern theologians and literary authors. We shall provide in this essay only a few representative examples of how each of these components contributes to a moral perspective on some wars as a 'lesser good'.[9]

Holy Scripture

Orthodox Christians, like other Christians, as well as observant Jews, of course, and Muslims who respect the Bible, cannot avoid the disturbing presence of 'holy wars' in the Old Testament.[10] Whether intended as a sacrifice of non-Hebrews to ensure Yahweh's aid in battle or to purify the Hebrew community by eradicating injustice and evil beyond the Jewish community, the 'ban' (*herem* in Hebrew) enjoined Israel to kill all human beings – irrespective of age, sex, or non-combatant status – in its numerous wars of conquest and survival in Canaan. But the Old Testament, especially in the Septuagint version that extends the revelatory history of Israel to the first century BCE, is a rich tapestry of religious and moral traditions. Careful, critical, methodical exegesis can unravel from the original strands of the 'ban' – epitomized in the extreme divine command that appears in Deuteronomy 20 – limitations on the means and targets of violence. This progressive moral tightening suggests a dynamic trajectory through ancient Israel's

---

8   For an explanation of the concept of trajectory, see Webster, *The Pacifist Option*, pp.59-62.

9   A greatly expanded version of the present essay with more numerous examples of texts from the six components of Orthodox moral tradition is scheduled for publication in the next volume of *St. Vladimir's Theological Quarterly*.

10 The best recent study of the holy war tradition of the Old Testament is S. Niditch, *War in the Hebrew Bible: A Study in the Ethics of Violence* (New York: Oxford University Press, 1993). For useful summaries of the various types of 'ban,' see especially pp.28, 35, & 77. Elsewhere I have argued that Eastern Orthodoxy has rejected the possibility of the 'holy war' or 'crusade' as intrinsically immoral. See Webster, *The Pacifist Option*, pp.84-87, and, more recently, A.F.C. Webster, 'Between Western Crusades and Islamic "Crescades"', in J. Figel (ed.), *Byzantine Christianity and Islam* (Eastern Christian Publications, 2001), pp.149-66. All biblical quotations in this essay are taken from the Revised Standard Version (RSV).

history. According to this 'salvation history', God leads His people from the primitive barbarism of the captivity in Egypt to the more complex ethical civilization after the return from exile in Babylon (late sixth century BCE) and during the Maccabean period (second and first centuries BCE) and on to the perfect holiness revealed by Jesus Christ in the New Testament gospels.

The later texts found in 1-3 Maccabees (Septuagint) mark the zenith of the progressive Old Testament trajectory. The book of 1 Maccabees (*ca.* 140 BCE) contains seven episodes that place additional limits on the conduct of war by Israel. 1 Maccabees 2:29-48 allows the Jews to engage in righteous self-defence even on the Sabbath; 1 Maccabees 5:28, 35, & 51 relate the killing of every male enemy, but not their women; 1 Maccabees 5:55-62 enunciates a proto-principle of 'legitimate authority' by making it clear that only the Hasmonean dynasty is called by God to lead Israel in battle; 1 Maccabees 5:67 depicts the personal defeat of some brave Jewish priests who fight unwisely and without proper divine sanction; and 1 Maccabees 13:43-48 reveals how Simon the high priest and commander of the Jews (d. 134 BCE) spared and exiled all of the survivors of the siege of Gamara (Gaza in Greek).

Perhaps the most dramatic instance of war as a moral good in the Maccabean era occurs in 2 Maccabees 15:11-16. Confronting a powerful army of the Seleucid King Demetrios I Soter led by the treacherous Nicanor, Judas Maccabeus (d. 160 BCE), the most celebrated hero of the Hasmonean dynasty founded by his father Mattathias, tells his fellow Jews a dream, 'a sort of vision', [2 Maccabees 15:11] to inspire them in the coming battle:

> What he saw was this: Onias, who had been high priest, a noble and good man, of modest bearing and gentle manner, one who spoke fittingly and had been trained from childhood in all that belongs to excellence, was praying with outstretched hands, for the whole body of the Jews. Then likewise a man appeared, distinguished by his gray hair and dignity, and of marvellous majesty and authority. And Onias spoke, saying, 'This is a man who loves the brethren and prays much for the people and the holy city, Jeremiah, the prophet of God'. Jeremiah stretched out his right hand and gave to Judas a golden sword, and as he gave it he addressed him thus: 'Take this holy sword, a gift from God, with which you will strike down your adversaries'. [2 Maccabees 2:12-16]

In a scene reminiscent of the English at Agincourt after King Henry V's St. Crispin's day soliloquy in Shakespeare's play, the narrative then describes the effect of this amazing story on the Jewish warriors: 'Encouraged by the words of Judas, so noble and so effective in arousing valour and awaking manliness in the souls of the young, they determined not to carry on a campaign but to attack bravely, and to decide the matter, by fighting hand to hand with all courage, because the city and the sanctuary and the temple were in danger' [2 Maccabees 12:17].

Turning to the New Testament, we find the justifiable war trajectory much more difficult to detect amidst an abundance of texts that clearly reflect an absolute pacifist perspective.[11] We ought to resist the temptation to mimic the popular use of a number of passages that are too vague or incidental to accommodate theories of the nature of war or the soldier's profession. For example, the reply of St. John the Baptizer to the soldiers who come to him for advice [Luke 3:14] need not imply an acceptance of their profession, especially if, as seems probable, they were Gentiles for whom the Jewish law was not binding. The use of military imagery is common in the epistles of St. Paul, but caution is advised lest we read too much into such literary conceits. Texts such as 1 Thessalonians 5:8 and Ephesians 6:10-17 employ predominantly defensive armour – helmet, breastplate, shield, etc. – as metaphors for exhorting the Christians either to withstand the onslaughts of the devil or to continue in love and hope of salvation. The analogy in 2 Timothy 2:3-4 to the priorities of the conventional soldier may reflect approval of his profession, but it may be little more than a device for stressing the similar sense of priorities expected of Christians. Jesus Himself appears to sanction the use of swords by His disciples in two rather perplexing passages. In Matthew 10:34 (RSV), Jesus' words seem plain enough: 'I have not come to bring peace, but a sword'. But the presence of the word 'division' in lieu of 'sword' in the parallel passage in Luke 12:51 suggests that both versions were intended as metaphors: instead of an endorsement of violent warfare, the statement probably alludes to the adverse consequences that the disciples will experience from the world as a result of their faith and love.[12] The other gospel text is even more problematic. The two swords that Jesus deems sufficient in Luke 22:35-38 are undoubtedly symbolic of a deeper truth, but what is that truth? Although the two swords may signify approval of the use of force by the disciples in self-defence,[13] the sheer inadequacy of two swords for proper resistance by a band of disciples leaves this interpretation without firm support.

Patristic Writings

The only Church Father of the ancient Church to achieve celebrity status as an original thinker on issues of war and peace among contemporary Western religious and secular scholars is St. Augustine of Hippo (d. *ca.* 430 CE).[14] The contribution of this North African bishop was indeed profound but his impact on Eastern Orthodoxy has been minimal, since Orthodoxy relies more heavily on the

---

11 Webster, *The Pacifist Option*, pp.133-42.

12 Ignio Giordani, *The Social Message of Jesus*, trans. A.I. Zizzamia (Boston: Daughters of St. Paul, 1977), pp.340-41.

13 E.A. Ryan, 'The Rejection of Military Service by the Early Christians', *Theological Studies*, no.13, 1952, pp.4-5.

14 The secondary literature about St. Augustine's perspectives on the morality of war is quite extensive. The best attempt by a modern ethicist to evaluate his contribution remains the second chapter of P. Ramsey, *War and the Christian Conscience: How Shall Modern War Be Conducted Justly?* (Durham: Duke University Press, 1961). For a briefer analysis also see A.F.C. Webster, 'Just War and Holy War: Two Case Studies in Comparative Christian Ethics', *Christian Scholar's Review*, vol.15, no.4, 1986, pp.347-50, & 364-66.

patrimony of the Greek Fathers and those from the Near East. Let it suffice here to cite merely two passages from his voluminous writings, which sound a keynote for his nuanced view of justifiable war. In his magnum opus, *The City of God*, the Latin Father avers, 'The "wise man", if he remembers that he is a human being, ... will rather lament the fact that he is faced with the necessity of waging just wars; for if they were not just, he would not have to engage in them, and consequently there would be no wars for a wise man. For it is the injustice of the opposing side that lays on the wise man the duty of waging wars'.[15] But victory in war providentially still goes to the 'juster' side, and St Augustine does not shrink from assigning the moral description of 'good' to that result: 'Now when the victory goes to those who were fighting for the juster cause, can anyone doubt that the victory is a matter for rejoicing and the resulting peace is something to be desired? Those things are goods and undoubtedly they are gifts of God'.[16]

Two Greek Fathers may be cited here as representative of the justifiable war trajectory both before and after Emperor Constantine the Great's Edict of Milan (313 CE) legalized the Church and rendered participation in the Roman military a morally acceptable occupation.

First, Clement of Alexandria, toward the end of the second century, clearly accepts the active involvement of Christians in military life as a meritorious enterprise. In the *Pedagogue* he proposes the soldier, the sailor, and ruler as models for the modest dress of 'the self-restrained man' and later comments on Luke 3:12-13 by observing that God 'commands soldiers, through John, to be satisfied with their pay and nothing besides'.[17] In his *Exhortation to the Heathen*, Clement may be encouraging military converts to remain in their profession instead of abandoning it, as his pacifist colleagues would have insisted: 'Has knowledge [i.e., *gnosis*, or the unique Christian revelation] taken hold of you while engaged in military service? Listen to the commander, who orders what is right'.[18] In an entire chapter in the *Stromata* (or 'Miscellanies'), he certainly expresses fondness for Moses' skill as a military leader in Old Testament Israel. In that same context, Clement also praises the virtues of military command in general, which Moses exemplified:

> Now, generalship involves three ideas: caution, enterprise, and the union of the two. And each of these consists of three things, acting as they do either by word, or by deeds, or by both together. And all of this can be accomplished either by persuasion, or by compulsion, or by inflicting harm in the way of taking vengeance on those who ought to

---

15 *De Civitate Dei* 19:7. ET: Augustine, *Concerning the City of God Against the Pagans*, trans. H. Bettenson (Baltimore: Penguin Books, 1976), pp.862.

16 *De Civitate Dei* 15.4 (ET: 600).

17 *Pedagogue* 3.12.91. ET: Clement of Alexandria, *Christ the Educator*, trans. S.P. Wood (New York: Fathers of the Church, Inc., 1954), p.268.

18 *Exhortation to the Heathen* 10:100.2. ET in A. Roberts and J. Donaldson (eds.), *The Ante-Nicene Fathers*, vol.2 (American Reprint of the Edinburgh Edition; Grand Rapids, MI: Wm. B. Eerdmans Publishing Company, 1975), p.200.

be punished; and this either by doing what is right, or by telling what is untrue, or by telling what is true, or by adopting any of these means conjointly at the same time.[19]

Second, St. Basil the Great (d. 379 CE) stands out among the many post-Constantinian Church Fathers who endorsed war, at least on occasion. In one brief letter to a soldier written a year before he died, the renowned bishop of Caesarea in Cappadocia offers encouragement and blesses the young man's vocation:

> I have many reasons for thanking God for mercies vouchsafed to me in my journey, but I count no blessing greater than the knowledge of your excellency [*arete*, or 'virtue,' in Greek], which has been permitted me by our good Lord's mercy. I have learnt to know one who proves that even in a soldier's life it is possible to preserve the perfection of love to God, and that we must mark a Christian not by the style of his dress, but by the disposition of his soul. It was a great delight to me to meet you; and now, whenever I remember you, I feel very glad. Play the man; be strong; strive to nourish and multiply love to God, that there may be given you by Him yet greater boons of blessing. I need no further proof that you remember me; I have evidence in what you have done.[20]

Canon Law

Eusebios of Caesarea, a fourth century Church historian and champion of Emperor Constantine the Great, foreshadowed the dual canonical standard that would later prohibit all clergy from killing any human beings (in war or otherwise), while regulating the conditions under which laymen might serve in the military. In his treatise, *Demonstration of the Gospel*, Eusebios continues:

> Two ways of life were thus given by the law of Christ to His Church. The one is above nature, and beyond common human living; it admits not marriage, childbearing, property nor the possession of wealth, but wholly and permanently separate from the common customary life of mankind, it devotes itself to the service of God alone in its wealth of heavenly love! And they who enter on this course, appear to die to the life of mortals, to bear with them nothing earthly but their body, and in mind and spirit to have passed to heaven. Like some celestial beings they gaze upon human life, performing the duty of a priesthood to Almighty God for the whole race ... Such then is the perfect form of the Christian life. And the other more humble, more human, permits men to join in pure nuptials and to produce children, to undertake government, to give orders to soldiers fighting for right; it allows them to have minds for farming, for trade, and the other more secular interests as well as for religion; and it is for them that times of retreat and instruction, and days for hearing sacred things are set apart. And a kind of secondary grade of piety is attributed to them, giving just such help as such lives require,

---

19 *Stromata* 1.24. ET in *The Ante-Nicene Fathers*, 2:337.
20 *Epistle* 106. ET: *A Select Library of Nicene and Post-Nicene Fathers of the Christian Church*, vol.8, P. Schaff and H. Wace (eds) (2nd ser.; New York: The Christian Literature Company, 1895), p.186.

so that all men, whether Greeks or barbarians, have their part in the coming of salvation, and profit by the teaching of the Gospel.[21]

We could not ask for a more explicit statement of the pursuit of justifiable war – albeit by Christian laymen alone – as a 'lesser good.'

The rich canonical corpus of the Orthodox Church contains three canons and a *novella* (or 'new law') of Emperor Justinian the Great (d. 565 CE) that allude briefly to Christian laymen in military service, as well as three canons that address the issue more directly.[22] Two of those canons are profoundly significant in Orthodox moral tradition.

Tucked almost inconspicuously in the body of canon 1 of St. Athanasios the Great (d. 373 CE) is a remarkable argument in defence of the exceptional nature of killing in war. To be sure, the renowned archbishop of Alexandria sent this letter to the monk Amun in 354 CE to help him deal with certain problems pertaining to sexual purity. But the small passage in question, intended obviously as an analogue to his argument, has endured far beyond its original context and is rendered here in full:

> It is not lawful to murder, but in war [it is] both lawful and worthy of approval to destroy the adversaries. Thus at any rate, those who are bravest in war are also deemed worthy of great honours, and monuments of them are raised proclaiming their successes; so that the same thing, on the one hand, is not lawful according to some circumstances and at some times, but, on the other hand, according to some other circumstances and opportunely it is permitted and possible.[23]

21 Eusebios of Caesarea, *Demonstration of the Gospel* 1.8. ET in *The Proof of the Gospel Being the Demonstratio Evangelica of Eusebius of Caesarea*, vol.1, trans. W.J. Ferrar (London: S.P.C.K., 1920), pp.48-50.

22 These canons number several hundred and include those produced by the bishops assembled at the seven Ecumenical Councils of the ancient Church between 325 and 787 CE, in addition to those approved at a subsequent council in the imperial capital of Constantinople in 861 CE (the so-called First & Second Constantinople Council) and those canons of earlier regional councils and those culled from the writings of various esteemed Church Fathers that were ratified at a special council that convened in AD 690 in Constantinople. The original Greek texts may be found in G. A. Ralles and M. Potles (eds.), *Syntagma Ton Theion kai Ieron Kanonon* ('The Order of the Divine and Holy Canons'), 6 vols (Athens, 1852). Also useful is the widely used ET known as *The Rudder* [*Pedalion* in Greek], which contains valuable interpretations of each canon by St. Nikodemos of the Holy Mountain, an eighteenth century Greek Orthodox monk: Agapius and Nicodemus (eds. and comps.), *The Rudder*, trans. D. Cummings (Chicago: The Orthodox Christian Educational Society, 1957). The canons pertaining to the laity are analyzed in detail in A.F.C. Webster, 'The Canonical Validity of Military Service by Orthodox Christians', *Greek Orthodox Theological Review*, vol.23, nos 3 & 4, Fall/Winter 1978, pp.271-6.

23 The ET is my own based on the Greek original in Ralles and Potles, *Syntagma* 4.69.

The Rudder contends that St. Athanasios proffers this counsel as an example of how the same thing can be sometimes 'good' and sometimes 'evil'.[24]

The other canon worth noting here looms even larger in Orthodox moral tradition. Canon 13 of St. Basil the Great (actually his *Epistle* 188.13 to Amphilokios around 374 CE) reads as follows: 'Our fathers did not reckon as murders the murders in wars, it seems to me, giving a pardon to those who defend themselves on behalf of moderation and piety. But perhaps it is well to advise that they abstain from the [holy] communion for only three years, since their hands are not clean'.[25] Unlike his fellow bishop in Egypt, St. Basil explicitly provides a particular condition for the traditional justification for killing in war – or what we now term a 'right intent' – that shapes the morality of the act. Further, the suggested penance – and it is, as *The Rudder* observes, only 'an advisory and indecisive suggestion'[26] – entails refraining from receiving the 'holy mysteries' (or 'sacrament' in Western Christian parlance) of the Body and Blood of Christ, but not expulsion from the Church altogether or reduction to the status of catechumen (or novice learner). Nevertheless, the twelfth century Byzantine canonists John Zonaras and Theodore Balsamon regard this penance, respectively, as excessive and irrelevant. Zonaras views even a three-year excommunication from the holy mysteries – in contrast to twenty years for murder and even ten for having or performing an abortion – as unfairly burdensome and an unbearable punishment for Christians who perform so noble a service as defence of faith and empire. For Christian soldiers, particularly the bravest, would never be able to partake of the most precious thing in Orthodox liturgical life throughout their entire military careers, owing to the frequency of wars.[27]

Hagiography

The stylized written accounts of the lives (*vitae* in the scholarly community's preferred Latin) and activities (*acta* in Latin) of the thousands of Orthodox saints proclaimed officially by the Church constitute a fourth source of the Orthodox moral tradition of war as a 'lesser good'. A previous study has analyzed the moral significance of those 'exceptional saints' who offer an absolute pacifist witness. But their company is easily exceeded by the number of saints who engage in or bless certain military operations as righteous or good acts.[28]

Among the dozens of ancient military martyrs who served as Christian soldiers in the pagan Roman army until faced with the dilemma of openly professing paganism or their faith in Christ, two warrant special attention here. St. George, a

---

24 *The Rudder*, p.762.

25 The ET is my own based on the Greek original in Ralles and Potles, *Syntagma* 4.131.

26 *The Rudder*, pp.801-802.

27 Ralles and Potles, *Syntagma* 4.131-2.

28 For the Orthodox pacifist saints, see Webster, *The Pacifist Option*, 183-95. For a more comprehensive analysis of Orthodox warrior saints, see A.F.C. Webster, 'Varieties of Christian Military Saints: From Martyrs Under Caesar to Warrior Princes', *St. Vladimir's Theological Quarterly*, vol.24, no.1, 1980, pp.3-35.

Syrian Christian from birth and a tribune (equivalent to a modern lieutenant colonel) of a famous regiment, was, because of his courage in battle, promoted to the rank of general by Emperor Diocletian toward the end of the third century. Only when he was certain that the emperor's new purge of Christians could not be stopped by other means did he take the dramatic step of resistance that led to his execution. He refused to sacrifice to the pagan gods and was summarily imprisoned, tortured, and killed.[29] He is, like the other soldier saints, popularly regarded by Orthodox Christians as a fervent intercessor before the throne of God and a supernatural protector in time of war. In one miracle story, the great martyr is invoked by Leontios, a soldier whose son George is about to fight in the Byzantine army against the Bulgarians after war had begun in 913 CE. The prayer of Leontios before an icon of St. George is probably prototypical of the invocations that were (and still may be) addressed to other soldier saints as well: 'To thee, Great Martyr Saint George, we entrust our only son, whom we called by thy name out of love for thee! Be to him a guide on the way, a guardian in battle, and return him to us safe and sound, so that, having been blessed by thee according to our faith, we may by many good works ever glorify thy solicitude and care for us'.[30]

According to the *acta* of St. Demetrios of Thessalonike, a favorite saint of the Greek Orthodox, the soldier pretends to be an idolater until Emperor Maximilian names him *stratelates* ('general') of the armies of Thessaly at the beginning of the fourth century. Thereafter, General Demetrios openly professes his Christianity and suffers imprisonment for his witness. The immediate cause of his death is, however, most unusual even for *acta* or *vitae* with presumably little historical content. He blesses a certain Nestor (also later canonized as a saint) in his jail cell, who, despite his diminutive size, manages to defeat a pagan giant named Lyaios by killing him in combat in the arena. (The parallel to the boy David slaying the giant Philistine Goliath was not lost on the ancient Orthodox.) The emperor orders Demetrios put to death, when he learns that his general was instrumental in the death of his champion.[31] What commends this popular hagiographic narrative to generations of Orthodox faithful is precisely the captivating drama of the saint's personal moral decision. When compelled, at length, to choose between fidelity to Christ and loyalty to the pagan emperor whom he previously served without question, Demetrios the Roman general casts his lot with the 'soldiers' of Christ and consequently forfeits his command and his life. And yet he maintains his vocation as a combatant against injustice – by proxy, to be sure, but in an unmistakably violent setting. The great soldier-martyr of Thessalonika is often depicted in icons astride a horse while lancing an enemy soldier lying prostrate

---

29 A standard legendary version of his *vita* may be found in an ET of a Russian *menologion* (collection of *vitae* arranged by month of celebration*): The Passion and Miracles of the Great Martyr and Victorious Wonderworker Saint George* (Jordanville, N.Y.: Holy Trinity Monastery, 1976), esp. pp.2-4.

30 *The Passions and the Miracles of the Great Martyr and Victorious Wonderworker Saint George*, p.26.

31 ET of text in M.J. Fochios (trans.), *For the Glory of the Father, Son and Holy Spirit: History of Eastern Orthodox Saints* (Baltimore: Phanari Publications), pp.17-19.

near his horse (unlike his counterpart St. George, whose icons have him slaying a serpent or dragon-like beast). That an act of such violence can adorn a sacred image leaves no doubt that the Church regards Demetrios' profession – and his role in particular – as worthy of veneration.[32]

Perhaps the most familiar example of an unabashed exhortation to military victory by an Orthodox Christian saint appears in an early fifteenth century *vita* by Epiphanius the Wise entitled, *The Life, Acts, and Miracles of Our Blessed and Holy Father Sergius of Radonezh* (d. 1392 CE). When the Grand Duke Dmitrii discovers that another invasion of Russia by Khan Mamai of the Muslim Tatars is imminent, he consults the holy Russian ascetic, who, 'bestowing on him his blessing, and strengthened by prayer, said to him, "It behooveth you, lord, to have a care for the lives of the flock committed to you by God. Go forth against the heathens; and upheld by the strong arm of God, conquer; and return to your country sound in health, and glorify God with loud praise"'. Later, shortly before the forces of Dmitrii and the Khan clash, a courier arrives in the camp of the Russian commander with a new message of assurance from St. Sergius: 'Be in no doubt, lord; go forward with faith and confront the enemy's ferocity; and fear not, for God will be on your side'.[33] The eventual victory by the Russian army certainly helped St. Sergius' reputation as a prophet and national saint –indeed, the patron saint of Russia – and it also served to implant firmly in the memory of the Russian Orthodox Church the decisive encouragement and support for the Grand Duke and his army that the saint had provided at a crucial moment in the nation's history. This spectacular episode was, however, only the latest in a long series that validated, according to George Fedotov, an emerging Russian commitment to 'the idea of a just war'. That entailed a specific focus on causation: 'Defensive war is always justified, and to defend one's "heritage" is not only the right of a prince but also his duty towards the inhabitants of his lands'.[34]

Devotional Texts

The rich hymnographic and liturgical traditions of Orthodox Christianity[35] have, from its inception in the New Testament Church, informed and shaped Orthodox

---

32 Often depicted in icons in full Roman armour and bearing swords or lances is St. Michael the Archangel as the 'captain of the heavenly host' in the war against Satan and his minions (according to Revelation 12:7-9) and protector of Christians (as he was of ancient Israel, according to Daniel 12:1), as well as the Old Testament prophet and military commander, Joshua, and numerous other ancient soldier-martyrs and warrior princes of Russia, Serbia, and Romania.

33 ET in S.A. Zenkovsky (ed. and trans.), *Medieval Russia's Epics, Chronicles, and Tales* (2nd ed.; New York: E.P. Dutton & Co., Inc., 1974), p.284.

34 G.P. Fedotov, *The Russian Religious Mind*, vol.2 (Cambridge, Mass.: Harvard University Press, 1966), p.175.

35 It has become a commonplace for Orthodox Christians to define 'Orthodox' etymologically as a compound of two ancient Greek words: the adjective *orthos* ('correct') and either the noun *doxa* ('glory' or 'worship') or the infinitive *dokein* ('to think') – hence 'correct worship' or 'correct thinking.'

theological and moral doctrine at least as much as the converse. That experience yields some weighty evidence for the justifiable war trajectory as a lesser good.

The same liturgical texts in which appeals for 'peace' abound also include a petition (repeated several times) on behalf of the head of state (emperor, king, or president), the government (or civil or public authorities, depending on the translation), and 'our armed forces everywhere'. In the variable hymns that adorn the various feasts and seasons of the church year, we find a surprising amount of militaristic imagery often juxtaposed with word images of peace, mercy, humility, suffering, and martyrdom. For example, the hymnography for the Feast of the Exaltation of the Holy Cross on 14 September is redolent of such military typologies. In its original Greek text, the *troparion* hymn – the key signature hymn of the day – prays for the victory of the Byzantine emperor over the 'barbarians'. Here is how that hymn would be translated into English: 'O Lord, save thy people, and bless thine inheritance. Grant victories to the emperor [*basileus* in Greek] over the barbarians, and preserve thy habitation with thy Cross'. To be sure, the post-imperial era has witnessed a spiritualizing of that text, so that now it usually implores the Lord to grant victories to 'the Orthodox Christians over their adversary' – that is, Satan. But other hymns from the office of the Holy Cross retain their original bellicosity. Moses and Joshua are depicted as antitypes of Christ on the Cross immediately before their military victories against the Canaanite enemies of Israel. The second *sticheron* hymn at the lamp-lighting psalms for great vespers begins: 'Moses prefigured thee, O precious Cross, when he stretched out his hands on high and put Amalek the tyrant to flight'.[36] A sessional hymn after the *megalynarion* during matins begins: 'In times past Joshua, the son of Nun, stretched out his arms crosswise, O my Saviour, mystically prefiguring the sign of the Cross: and the sun stood still until he had defeated the enemy that resisted Thee, O God'.[37] The first canticle for matins attributes the Emperor Constantine's military triumphs to the Cross: 'Heaven showed the Cross as a sign of victory to Constantine, the holy king and defender of the faith. Through it the proud insolence of his enemies was cast down, deceit was overthrown, and the divine faith was spread to the ends of the earth. Therefore let us sing to Christ our God, for He has been glorified'.[38] And the *kontakion* hymn for the feast (or second signature hymn) extends this martial spirit to the present: 'Make the Orthodox people [originally 'our faithful kings' or 'emperor' in Greek] glad in Thy strength, giving them victory over their enemies: may Thy Cross assist them in battle, weapon of peace and unconquerable ensign of victory'.[39]

Unmistakable in their sanctioning of things military are the specific prayer services in time of war and the liturgical rites of blessing for military personnel and weapons. In the section on 'general calamities' in the *Book of Needs* (a prayerbook

---

36 Text in *The Festal Menaion*, trans. Mother Mary and Archimandrite Kallistos Ware (London: Faber & Faber, 1977), p.133. Hereafter cited as FM. The biblical event is narrated in *Exodus* 17:10-14.

37 Text in FM, p.142. The biblical event is narrated in Joshua 10:12-13.

38 Text in FM, p.145.

39 Text in FM, p.148.

for the Orthodox clergy), there is a 'Molieben to the Lord God Sung in Time of War Against Adversaries Fighting Against Us'. The hymns in the *canon* of canticles refer repeatedly to Old Testament military victories by Moses, Joshua, David, and Samson over the enemies of Israel as precedents for the Lord now to 'grant victory to them that govern us over all adversaries who have risen against us'. In one set of petitions the deacon calls upon the Lord, obviously without mincing words, to let 'the nations who have fallen against Thine inheritance and defiled Thy Holy Church ... be assailed by Thy tempests and shake them with Thy wrath; fill their faces with dishonour; let them be put to shame and troubled forever; let them be disgraced; and by the power of Thy judgment let their pride be destroyed'. Finally, a long prayer recited by the priest toward the end of the service reprises the hostility toward the enemy: 'Rise up to our help and set to naught the evil counsels purposed against us by the evil ones. Judge them that affront us and defeat them that war against us, and turn their impious boldness into fear and flight'. Then the prayer immediately accentuates the positive: 'But grant unto our godfearing armies that hope in Thee great boldness and courage to drive onward and overtake them, and to defeat them in Thy Name. And unto them that Thou hast judged to lay down their lives for Faith and Country, forgive them their trespasses, and in the day of Thy righteous reckoning grant them incorrupt crowns'.[40] The crowns are a standard image for the heavenly rewards of faithful and holy martyrs.

Another text has drawn the ire of the Orthodox Peace Fellowship (OPF), a mostly pacifist, international association based in The Netherlands. A recent documentary collection compiled by two OPF activists, Hildo Bos and Jim Forest, includes an English translation of a service for the blessing of weapons that appears in a Serbian edition of the *Book of Needs* published in Kosovo in 1993. After the usual preliminary prayers, the rubrics call for the bishop or priest to read the following prayer 'over the weapons':

> Lord our God, God of powers, powerful in strength, strong in battle, you once gave miraculous strength to your child David granting him victory over his opponent the blasphemer Goliath. Mercifully accept our humble prayer. Send your heavenly blessing over these weapons (naming each weapon). Give force and strength that they may protect your holy Church, the poor and the widows, and your holy inheritance on earth, and make it horrible and terrible to any enemy army, and grant victory to your people for your glory, for you are our strength and protection and we sign praise to your glory, Father, Son and Holy Spirit, now and ever, and to the ages of ages. Amen.

The bishop or priest then sprinkles the weapons with blessed water, invoking the blessing of the Triune God 'upon these weapons and those who carry them, for the protection of the truth of Christ'. Finally, the bishop or priest blesses 'the soldiers carrying the weapons' and exhorts them to 'Be brave and let your heart be

---

40 Text in *The Great Book of Needs (Expanded and Supplemented)*, vol. 4: *Services of Supplication (Moliebens)* (South Canaan, PA: St. Tikhon's Seminary Press, 1999), pp.130-50, esp. 132, 135, 140, 145, & 149. This collection is called *Euchologion* in Greek and *Trebnik* in Slavonic.

stronger and win victory over your enemies, trusting in God, in the name of the Father, Son and Holy Spirit'. The concluding rubrics – 'This is the way to bless sword and sable' – lead the OPF activists to concede that this text, though not usually included in contemporary editions of the *Book of Needs* published by the various Orthodox Churches in the world, seems to reflect an ancient usage and 'an established ecclesiastical custom'.[41] What the OPF activists find so disquieting, however, the mainstream Orthodox justifiable war trajectory deems quite compatible with morality and worthy of a blessing.

Modern Theology and Literature

The final component of Orthodox moral tradition, though the least authoritative for a religious community that generally prefers the time-tested wisdom of the 'ancients' over the opinions of the 'moderns,' provides additional textual testimony for justifiable war as a moral good instead of an evil.

Recently canonized Serbian Orthodox bishop St. Nikolai Velimirovich (d. 1956 CE) reflected his nation's martial spirit in many of his writings. In a Russian Orthodox émigré periodical published in Paris in 1929, he offered the following thoughts:

> War is one of the tools in the hands of God, as well as peace.
> War is a poison, which kills, but which at the same time cures and heals.
> It is better to have one great and mighty river than many small streams which easily freeze in frost and which are easily covered with dust and filth. A war which gathers an entire people for a great cause is better than a peace which knows as many tiny causes as it knows people, which divides brothers, neighbours, all human beings, and which hides in itself an evil and hidden war against all.
> We have to wish those, whom we love, both a good life and a good death. To die in the struggle for a great common cause is a good death.[42]

Like most Serbs, St. Nikolai admired his saintly predecessor, Tsar Lazar, battlefield commander of the ill-fated Serbian army that lost the decisive Battle of Kosovo Polje against the Ottoman Turks in 1389 CE. In another popular work entitled *The Serbian People as a Servant of God*, St. Nikolai marveled at Tsar Lazar's 'holiness and righteousness', primarily because 'he laid down his life on the field of Kosovo for the venerable cross and golden freedom. For this the Serbian people have cherished him and praised him in verse, and God has glorified

---

41 H. Bos and J. Forest (eds.), *'For the Peace From Above': An Orthodox Resource Book on War, Peace and Nationalism* (Bialystok, Poland: Syndesmos, The World Fellowship of Orthodox Youth, 1999), pp.120-21. In the Byzantine era, according to A. P. Kazhdan (ed.), *Oxford Dictionary of Byzantium*, vol.2 (New York: Oxford University Press, 1991), p.1373, 'the blessing of standards and weapons' was one of the 'prebattle rituals', together with mutual forgiveness, fasting, holy confession, and partaking of the holy mysteries of the Body and Blood of Christ.

42 ET of text in Bos and Forest (eds.), *For the Peace From Above*, p.67.

him by making him a saint and crowning him with a double crown, as His servant and as His martyr'.[43]

Many modern Russian Orthodox writers have also affirmed the possibility of war as at least a 'lesser' good. St. Philaret, Metropolitan of Moscow, exhorted the faithful after Napolean's invasion of Russia in 1812: 'If you avoid dying for the honour and freedom of the Fatherland, you will die a criminal or a slave; die for the faith and the Fatherland and you will be granted life and a crown in heaven'.[44] The enigmatic philosopher and theologian Vladimir Soloviev offered his own views on war and peace through 'Mr. Z', one of five fictional Russian characters in his 1899 dialogue entitled, *War and Christianity from the Russian Point of View: Three Conversations*. Mr. Z responds to a Tolstoyan's pacifism by insisting that 'war is not an unconditional evil, and that peace is not an unconditional good ... [I]t is possible to have a good war, it is possible to have a bad peace'.[45] St. Tikhon, Patriarch of Moscow (d. 1925 CE) issued a letter on 26 October 1918 (new style) to the Bolshevik government's Council of People's Commissars, in which he denounced them for dishonouring the role of the Russian soldier in their haste to conclude an extremely disadvantageous treaty with Imperial Germany: 'You have taken from our soldiers everything for which they fought splendidly in the past. You have taught those, who not long ago were still brave and invincible, to abandon the defence of the motherland, to run from the battlefields. You have extinguished in their hearts the conscience that "greater love has no man than this, that a man lay down his life for his friends"'.[46]

And there is the great Nobel laureate and Orthodox layman, Aleksandr Solzhenitsyn. Arguably the most profound and complex Russian writer since the mid-twentieth century, he served in the Soviet Army as a captain, but was arrested in February 1945 by the Soviet military counterintelligence agency and charged with having written derogatory statements about Stalin in his personal correspondence. As a result of this 'offence', Solzhenitsyn endured eight years in *gulags* and three more years in domestic exile. The mystical bond with his homeland and his advocacy of its defence that Solzhenitsyn has maintained throughout his turbulent citizenship is dramatically evident in *August 1914*, the first in his five-part 'wheel' of historical novels pertaining to the end of the tsarist empire and the beginning of the Soviet era. In that novel in the grand Russian tradition, Isaakii (or 'Sanya') Lazhenitsyn, a pacifist follower of Tolstoy, resolves to join the army at the outset of the First World War. His reason is as simple as it

43 N. Velimirovich, *The Serbian People as a Servant of God*, vol.1: *A Treasury of Serbian Orthodox Spirituality*, trans. T. Micka and S. Scott (Grayslake, Il: The Free Serbian Orthodox Diocese of America and Canada, 1988), pp.36-7.

44 *The Basis of the Church's Social Concept*, II.2.

45 V. Solovyof, *War and Christianity from the Russian Point of View: Three Conversations* (London: Constable, 1915), p.9.

46 ET of text in Bos and Forest (eds.), *'For the Peace From Above'*, p.66.

is profound: 'I feel sorry for Russia', he says to his fellow student Varya.[47] This kind of melancholy compassion is assuredly not the triumphalist or nationalistic kind. Sanya is not moved by an unbridled, militant patriotism. As Fr. Alexander Schmemann of blessed memory perceived, Sanya determines to fight for Russia simply 'because Russia *is*, and because she, and not another country, is his motherland, granted him like the sun and the air; because she is his home and body, and no one can be without these'.[48] The worst has come to pass – war with Germany and Austria – and so one must fight. Thus, to the proverbial inevitabilities of death and taxation, Solzhenitsyn has added nations and war. Sanya neither extols war nor condemns it, since both of those attitudes ignore the grim reality and necessity of war. But war, when engaged, ought to be conducted efficiently and successfully. For the individual, war is nevertheless a severe challenge. In Schmemann's estimation, the task confronting Solzhenitsyn's Sanya 'is a test of the entire man, bringing out the best or the worst in him; it measures his relation to life, and his capacity for sacrifice and selflessness'.[49]

In Sanya we are offered Solzhenitsyn himself. Just as Sanya responds to the call to serve in the army of Imperial Russia in 1914 (as did Solzhenitsyn's father), so the young Solzhenitsyn sought to defend his homeland (and, less happily, its Soviet regime) against the Germans in 1941.[50] If there is any planned, universal, Orthodox Christian application of Sanya's decision, it would be that the Christian ought to serve his country in time of war regardless of who happens to be governing the homeland at the time. For the exigencies of birth have located him in that particular place and it is the only country he has. Such service will most likely be a tragic, bittersweet endeavour, a moral necessity and a virtuous activity, but in no way a joy.

Conclusions

The moral proposition that runs through the various biblical, patristic, canonical, hagiographic, liturgical and hymnographic, and modern theological and literary texts presented above is really quite simple. We may call it a 'teleology of justice'.

This particular teleology, like other forms of this moral or ethical perspective, entails a proportionality of morally good (or at least, in some circumstances, morally 'neutral') means to morally good ends (that is, purposes, intentions, goals,

47 A. Solzhenitsyn, *August 1914*, trans. M. Glenny (New York: Bantam Books, 1972), pp.10-11.
48 A. Schmemann, 'A Lucid Love,' in J.B. Dunlop, R. Haugh, and A. Klimoff, *Aleksandr Solzhenitsyn: Critical Essays and Documentary Materials* (2nd rev. ed.; New York: Collier Books, 1975), p.389.
49 Ibid., p.390.
50 The identity of author and character is suggested in P. Blake, 'Solzhenitsyn and the Theme of War,' in K. Feuer (ed.), *Solzhenitsyn: A Collection of Critical Essays* (Englewood Cliffs, N.J.: Prentice-Hall, Inc., 1976), p.87.

or *teloi* in Greek). The internal debate within Orthodox ecclesiastical circles (and perhaps also more widely in other religious and scholarly communities) concerns the issue of means. Setting aside the views of the absolute pacifists, for whom any violence against human beings is precluded *a priori*, we may sharpen the question further to whether the resort to war for a good end is itself an evil or a good means to that end. The Apostle Paul provides an important moral prescription in Romans 12:17 ('Repay no one evil for evil, but take thought for what is noble in the sight of all'.) and a few verses later in Romans 12:21 ('Do not be overcome by evil, but overcome evil with good'). The defining moment of St. Paul's own teleological approach to morality occurs earlier in the same epistle. In Romans 3:8 the Apostle asks rhetorically: 'And why not do evil that good may come? – as some people slanderously charge us with saying. Their condemnation is just'. Oxford philosopher John Finnis has dubbed this biblical rejection of evil means to good ends the 'Pauline principle'.[51] Further, a sweep of patristic literature would fail to detect even one Church Father who gives moral permission to commit an evil act, lesser or otherwise. An intrinsic evil may be defined precisely as an unholy, unrighteous, or sinful offence against God, another human being, or oneself, which, irrespective of the particular circumstances, intention, or anticipated consequences, may not be freely and knowingly chosen.

In the mediaeval Christian West, St Thomas Aquinas crystallized this fundamental biblical and patristic insight in his forceful argument in the *Summa Theologiae* that the object of one's moral decision (that is, the action that is chosen as the means to one's end) must itself be morally good, or at least not intrinsically evil.[52] How then, may any Christian countenance a course of action – such as war – that he freely and knowingly concedes is 'evil', albeit a 'lesser' enormity than permitting, through inaction, an aggressor to subvert justice and wreak havoc among his or any people? If all war or any particular war is deemed an evil, a Christian nation or people may not elect to go to war, even as a last resort. The logical contra-positive also holds. If a particular war can be justified morally, it must be a good – or at least a morally neutral – act: perhaps a 'lesser good' than diplomatic persuasion or nonviolent, nonresistant suffering in full imitation of the 'higher' self-sacrificing love of Jesus Christ, but a good nonetheless.

The key to the problem is how to frame the moral decision properly – specifically how to define accurately and correctly both the means and the end in question. To the familiar refrain among anti-consequentialists that ends do not justify the means, we might offer the flippant rejoinder: If the ends do not justify the means, at least in part, then what else does? The act of cutting human flesh, for example, may be good or evil, depending on the identity of the agent (the person cutting), his intention, and, above all, how he goes about his business. An armed robber assaulting his victim with a switchblade obviously commits an intrinsically

---

51 J. Finnis, *Fundamentals of Ethics* (Washington, D.C.: Georgetown University Press, 1983), p.109.
52 See, for example, the brilliant section on the moral analysis of an act in St. Thomas Aquinas, *Summa Theologiae*, 1a-2ae.6-17.

evil act, but a skilled cardiac surgeon operating on a patient may be engaged in a good act. To be sure, the immediate slicing of skin and muscle tissue and the cracking of ribs to get at the heart might, in itself, appear to be cruel or violent, but it may also be the only way the surgeon can perform a life-saving operation; in addition, the good surgeon cuts and breaks only the bare minimum of human flesh and bones, thereby safeguarding the life of the patient and treating the entire body with respect and the person with reverence.

In the admittedly much rarer cases when war may be justified in accordance with the Orthodox justifiable war trajectory elucidated above, the specific acts of harming, wounding, or killing enemy soldiers must similarly be evaluated in the context of a teleology of justice. Orthodox Christian soldiers and other military personnel duly authorized by a legitimate political authority (such as the Byzantine emperor or, currently, internationally recognized governments that do not pose an immediate threat to the Orthodox community, or, to be sure, any other religious community) to defend and protect their Church or homeland from an unjust aggressor such as an invading force (whether a conventional military transgression of internationally recognized borders or lethal violence in the more contemporary form of international terrorism), and who utilize minimal force in direct proportion to the clearly – in their own minds and the expressed will of their constituency – intended restoration of the *status quo ante* (instead of conquest or other kinds of unwarranted aggrandizement), may, in good conscience, engage in warfare as a lesser good.[53]   Such limited or proportionate warfare in pursuit of just ends becomes a function of justice. Since justice is one of the four 'cardinal' virtues introduced by Plato, acknowledged in the Septuagint (Wisdom 8:7), and amplified through the entire patristic tradition, justice in war – both as an end and the means to that end – may also be virtuous and hence morally good.[54]   This is the ineluctable conclusion to which the scores of texts adduced above give rise. Whenever the Holy Scriptures, Church Fathers, canons, lives of the saints, liturgical and hymnographic texts, and modern theologians and literary authors speak of military activity in terms of right or righteousness or nobility or valour or heroism, their individual and collective impact alike is the same: a justification of

---

53 A longer outline of these moral conditions, which do rather closely parallel the more familiar and more systematic Western just war tradition, appears in A.F.C. Webster, 'Just War and Holy War: Two Case Studies', pp.358-61. Please see note 7 above, however, concerning my disavowal of the use of the 'lesser evil' approach in that article and other previous works.

54 P. Ramsey, *War and the Christian Conscience*, pp.xxviii, made a strong case for the primacy of 'the norm of Christian love, and not natural justice only' in the Western justifiable war tradition since St. Augustine. But the textual sources of the Eastern Orthodox justifiable war trajectory, aside from Latin Church Fathers such as St. Augustine, focus primarily on justice or righteousness. The virtues of love (whether *agape* in the New Testament era or *philanthropia* in the patristic era after the second century) and mercy govern those texts that constitute the absolute pacifist trajectory in Eastern Orthodox moral tradition. See, for example, my conclusions on this dichotomy in *The Pacifist Option*, pp.256-9.

such activity as a moral good and of the soldiers who serve as its agents as virtuous warriors.

Whence the lesser morality that seems to have displaced this Orthodox justifiable war tradition? What has caused so many Orthodox hierarchs and theologians to veer off the mainstream trajectory? To be sure, there are occasional glimpses in the historical sources of a 'lesser evil' or 'necessary evil' approach to the question. One text that proponents of the lesser morality like to trot out is an anonymous treatise on Byzantine military strategy dating from the reign of Emperor Justinian the Great in the sixth century, which concedes that 'war is a great evil and the worst of all evils'.[55] But that comment is remarkable for its extreme rarity among the texts. The likely influences of the modern revisionism in Orthodox thinking on war are external to Orthodox tradition and have, beginning in the first quarter of the twentieth century, infiltrated Orthodoxy as a result of a flurry of ecumenical contacts with Western Christians and accelerated emigration of Orthodox Christians to Western Europe and North America.

First, there is the enduring legacy of one of the fundamental anthropological claims of the Protestant Reformation in the sixteenth century – namely, the inherent sinfulness and depravity of all of mankind after the Fall from grace. To summarize the views of Martin Luther and many Anabaptists, for example, the human will was so corrupted by Adam's sinful rebellion that every moral choice – unaided by divine grace – is fraught with danger.[56] In fact, one can only elect evil of one kind or another, lest, through his self-justification through ostensibly good works, he fool himself into thinking that he has grounds to boast before God and render the atoning sacrifice of Christ irrelevant or superfluous. The most for which one might hope in this vale of tears is to minimize but not overcome his sinful tendencies: to choose an evil assuredly lesser than its more grievous alternatives. Such a dim view of human nature in its present fallen state has little in common with the essential patristic heritage of Orthodoxy Christianity.

The second suspect is contemporary Roman Catholic 'proportionalism'. Pope John Paul II himself took square aim at this movement in his monumental encyclical *Veritatis Splendor* ('The Splendor of Truth') in 1993. In Europe and North America, in particular, the proportionalists, or 'mixed teleologists' as they are also known, greatly outnumber the more traditional Thomist or neo-Thomist moral theologians. The proportionalists withhold moral judgment of particular acts until they can calculate the likely proportion of good and evil effects of the alternative choices; for them, *contra* St. Thomas Aquinas and the Church Fathers, personal intent and particular circumstances have at least equal weight to that of the specific means. Indeed, the proportionalists generally maintain that it is impossible to establish moral absolutes that prohibit certain behaviour at all times and everywhere. Through a remarkable ethical sleight-of-hand, they manage to

---

55 ET of text in G. Dennis, S.J. (ed.), *Three Byzantine Military Treatises* (Dumbarton Oaks Texts, no. 9; Washington, D.C.: Dumbarton Oaks, 1985), p.21.
56 Luther's moral evaluation of the Christian soldier and his work was, however, more complex and difficult to fathom, much of it hinging on a sharp distinction between the office and the personal agent.

absolve persons who, it would appear *prima facie*, violate universal negative norms (such as those prohibiting lying, premarital sex, or military violence against civilian noncombatants) by elevating their 'good' intentions and the presumably 'good' consequences of their decisions, while downplaying the 'evil' quality of the act itself considered objectively. Such a seeming evil is not really intrinsic, but rather only 'physical', or 'ontic', or 'premoral,' or even 'nonmoral'. Sometimes the evil is of a 'lesser' magnitude than the presumed alternatives and hence acceptable.

Finally, Darrell Cole of Drew University, whose own research in the various Western Christian moral traditions complements the thesis of the present paper, has identified the kind of 'Christian realism' popularized by Reinhold Niebuhr and his many academic and ecumenical disciples in the middle of the last century as the primary cause of the preoccupation with war as a 'lesser evil' among Protestants and Roman Catholics.[57] (Apparently the contagion knows no geographical or ecclesiastical bounds!) On Cole's view, Niebuhr, prescinding from his interpretation of the gospel ethic as a 'pure ethic of love' – an ideal toward which men and women must strive if they hope to act morally, especially as individuals – conceded that the perfect morality modelled by Jesus Christ is not practical in human society and must be moderated by a pragmatic or realistic ethic of responsibility that requires a choice of lesser evils on behalf of justice for the community. The fatal flaw of this approach, according to Cole, is the self-evident moral incongruity of Niebuhr's logic: 'Jesus's ethic of love impels us to do vicious things'. Specifically in terms of war, Niebuhrian realism creates a slippery slope that could facilitate a slide into total or unlimited warfare: 'Once we begin to believe that we are acting viciously by the very nature of the case, then the temptation becomes to be a little more vicious and guarantee victory'.[58] That kind of consequentialism has not been nicknamed the 'dirty hands' approach in vain.

Niebuhrian and other early twentieth century varieties of Christian or secular ethical realism may be unsurpassed in their impact on the revisionist Orthodox proponents of the lesser morality. In chapter four of this book, Paul Robinson demonstrates convincingly that Ivan Il'in, for example, was such a relentless realist. Author of a controversial 1925 treatise, *On Resistance to Evil by Force*, Il'in categorically rejected any association of justice or good with war and endorsed some wars as 'an *unsinful* (!) perpetration of injustice' that may, nevertheless, be 'morally and religiously *necessary*'.[59]

Il'in and his ilk, as it were, furnish, unwittingly to be sure, a *reductio ad absurdam* of the embrace of the 'lesser evil' or 'necessary evil' approach to the moral problem of war. It is a counterfeit of the genuine, mainstream Orthodox justifiable war trajectory. Orthodox Christians and those who desire to know and

---

57 D. Cole, 'Good Wars,' *First Things*, no.116 (October 2001), pp.27-31. See also the more detailed argument in D. Cole, 'Virtuous Warfare and the Just War: A Christian Approach' (Unpublished Ph.D. Dissertation, University of Virginia, 2001).

58 Cole, 'Virtuous Warfare', pp.104 & 112.

59 Paul Robinson, 'The Justification of War in Russian History and Philosophy', see below, Chapter 4.

understand the Orthodox moral tradition on war and peace should accept no substitutes.

Chapter 4

The Justification of War in Russian History and Philosophy

Paul Robinson

In a recent television interview, one of the most senior clerics of the Russian Orthodox Church, Metropolitan Kirill of Smolensk and Kaliningrad stated that the United States had the right to use force in response to the terrorist attacks of 11 September 2001, because the conditions of war met the criteria for a just war laid down by St. Augustine.[1] In this way, the Metropolitan placed his weight fully behind the standard Western just war formula. Indeed Russians often use the term 'just war'.[2] However, it would be a mistake to believe that standard Catholic just war doctrine is part of Russian tradition, or that its precepts are widely understood or adhered to in Russian thought and practice. Certainly just war theory as understood in the West contains no specifically Russian input, while in Russia philosophers and theologians have never developed a systematic just war tradition of their own. Russian thought on the justification of war has followed a number of diverging paths, some of which reflect similar ideas in the Western world, and others of which are more uniquely Russian.

One of the problems of analyzing Russian thought on the justification of war, and on the limits to the use of force, is that Russian philosophers and theologians have rarely devoted much attention to the subject. The absence of any systematic thinking of the issue of war in Russian thought can in part be explained by the traditionally mystical nature of Orthodox Christianity, which at times seems to deliberately distance itself from the problems of the real world. The traditional subordination of the Church to secular authority has exaggerated this characteristic in Russia. Under both the Tsars and the Soviets, the Russian state expected the Church to restrict itself to purely spiritual matters, and not to interfere in the state's sphere of responsibility. This expectation clearly limited the Church's ability to comment on matters such as when the state had a right to wage war and what methods it could use. According to Paul Valliere, until the mid-nineteenth century, conservative clergy 'viewed the mingling of secular and ecclesiastical affairs with

---

1 *Pol'nyi tekst teleinterv'iu mitropolita Smolenskogo i Kalingradskogo Kirilla programme 'Zerkalo'*, broadcast on RTR, 22 September 2002, available on the internet at: http://www.orthodox.org.ru/nr109262.htm.

2 In Russian, 'just war' is either *spravedlivaia voina* or *pravednaia voina*. The two terms are entirely interchangeable.

alarm. ... Monks were expected to avoid controversy'.[3] Reliance on patristic texts hampered creative thought: 'theological scholarship was a series of footnotes on patristic tradition'.[4]

Only in the mid-nineteenth century did the situation change, when thinkers such as Aleksandr Bukharev began for the first time to move 'beyond the Fathers' and address the problems of the contemporary world. Other thinkers such as the novelists Leo Tolstoy and Fedor Dostoyevsky also began to tackle modern political and social issues. Russian philosophy briefly flourished as never before. But this 'silver age' then came to an untimely end with the advent of Bolshevik rule in 1917. Russian philosophy fled abroad into exile, where it gradually withered on the grapevine. By the mid-1940s most of the pre-revolutionary generation of Russian philosophers had died, and Russian theology once again turned its back on the contemporary world, coming under the dominating influence of the 'Neopatristic school'. According to Valliere, 'By the middle of the twentieth century, the ascendancy of the Neopatristic school was secure. Almost no one in the Orthodox world talked any longer about going "beyond the fathers"'.[5]

Since the Soviet authorities did not tolerate independent, non-Marxist, thought within the Soviet Union, this history indicates that if one is to find any systematic thinking on the subject of war, one is only likely to find it in a period spanning roughly 80 years, from about 1860 to about 1940. Indeed it is in this period that three Russian philosophers did address the issue of violence. The first was Leo Tolstoy, who became the most famous Russian proponent of pacifism. He expounded his views on non-resistance to evil in his 1894 book *The Kingdom of God is Within You*.[6] Six years later in 1900, Russia's most eminent philosopher, Vladimir Soloviev (sometimes described as 'the Pushkin of Russian philosophy'),[7] rebutted Tolstoy's pacifism in his book *Three Conversations on War, Progress and the End of World History, with a Brief Tale of the Anti-Christ*.[8] Finally, in 1925 the émigré philosopher Ivan Il'in published his book *On Resistance to Evil by Force*.[9] Together these three works constitute practically the entire canon of written Russian ideas on the justification or non-justification of violence outside of the Soviet era. Given the paucity of such works, it is hardly surprising that Russians do not have a systematic just war doctrine.

This does not mean, however, that there is no independent Russian thought on issues concerning war, or that Russians have to rely entirely on Western ideas.

---

3   P. Valliere, *Modern Russian Theology: Bukharev, Soloviev, Bulgakov: Orthodox Theology in a New Key* (Edinburgh: Eerdmans, 2000), p.22.
4   Ibid., p.29.
5   Ibid., p.5.
6   L.N. Tolstoy, *The Kingdom of God is Within You* (New York: Charles Scribner's Sons, 1917).
7   Georgii Gachev, quoted in Valliere, op. cit., p.149.
8   Translated into English as V. Solovyof, *War and Christianity from the Russian Point of View: Three Conversations* (London: Constable, 1915).
9   I.A. Il'in, *O soprotivlenii zlu siloiu* (Berlin, 1925). Republished, with a commentary by P.N. Poltoratskii: London, Ontario: Zaria, 1975.

Merely it means that one can speak only in terms of what Fr. Alexander Webster calls 'trajectories'. This is useful term as it rightly indicates that Russian philosophy has not developed any systematic doctrine with regard to war, but rather contains a number of trends and general directions (or 'trajectories') of thought, none of which have ever been fully systematized.

Fr. Webster identifies three trajectories of thought regarding war. These are 'holy war' or 'crusade', which identifies war as a positive good, and sees the warrior as an instrument of God's will; 'just' or 'justifiable' war, which permits war but sets certain rules restricting its use; and pacifism, which rejects war totally.[10] Philosophers often place just war theory in the middle ground between the other two – justifying war in a way pacifism cannot, but simultaneously limiting its use in a way that holy war will not. To these three trajectories, some philosophers add another – Realism. This is the ideology associated with names such as Thucydides, Machiavelli, and Morgenthau. Realism places war outside of the moral sphere, and thus, like Holy War, can be seen as likely to permit excess in the name of national or personal interest. Just war again occupies the middle ground between pacifism and Realism,[11] permitting war as Realism does, but restraining its excesses in a way Realists do not see as necessary.

I would add to these four trajectories a fifth, which emerges clearly from Russian thought on the subject of war. I call this the 'necessary war' trajectory. It clearly distinguishes some Orthodox and especially Russian philosophy from Western thinking. Citing a 1989 meeting of Orthodox Church leaders in Minsk, as well as the opinion of the Holy Synod of Bishops of the Orthodox Church in America, Fr. Webster shows in chapter three of this book that this line of thought has some considerable support in Orthodox circles (although he disagrees with it himself). The language of the 'necessary war' trajectory speaks not of justice or of a right to wage war, but rather of necessity and obligation. War is in certain circumstances permissible, but it is never 'just'. One fights because in certain situations one has no other practical or moral choice. As the philosopher Nikolai Berdyaev noted, 'In the evil condition of our world, war may be the lesser of two evils',[12] in which case one has an obligation to participate in it. But the lesser of two evils is never a good, and war is never 'just'.

The 'necessary war' argument, resting on the concept of war as a 'lesser evil', forms an independent 'trajectory' of thought with no obvious parallels in Western thinking. To illustrate this point more completely, I will now describe the various trajectories of Russian thought on the justification of war in more detail.

---

10 A.F.C. Webster, *The Pacifist Option: The Moral Argument Against War in Eastern Orthodox Theology* (San Francisco: International Scholars Publications, 1998), p.82.

11 G. Reichberg, 'Just War or Perpetual Peace?', *Journal of Military Ethics*, vol.1, no.1, 2002, p.16.

12 From *The Divine and the Human* (1947), cited in D.A. Lowrie, *Christian Existentialism: A Berdyaev Anthology* (London: George Allen & Unwin, 1965), p.303.

Pacifism

Russian pacifism dates back to the earliest era of Russian Christianity. The first saints of the Russian Church were the Princes Boris and Gleb. When their brother Sviatopolk usurped the throne, they refused to resist him, and when he sent assassins to kill them, they meekly awaited the assassins' arrival and quietly accepted their deaths. Their martyrdom has been described as 'a witness on behalf of the redemptive value of innocent suffering and the transformative power of non-resistance to evil'.[13] The violent nature of Russian history suggests that pacifism never took deep root in Russia, although after the schism of the Church in the seventeenth century, various dissenting groups, such as the Dukhobors and the Molokans, did adhere to ideas of non-resistance to evil. Non-conformists who came to Russian to flee persecution in the West, most notably the Mennonites, supplemented these dissenting groups. Their example then helped to inspire the most famous of all Russian pacifists, Leo Tolstoy.

Tolstoy laid out his philosophy of non-resistance to evil in his 1894 book, *The Kingdom of God is Within You*. He argued that evil comes from within men's souls, and that violent resistance of evil merely tackles the external manifestations of evil, while magnifying the hatred in men's hearts that created evil. Violence therefore merely perpetuates evil. Interestingly, although Russian dissenters had some influence on Tolstoy, the main influences on him were Western. R. V. Sampson argues that Tolstoy's pacifism 'emerged ... out of a slowly developing tradition of European thought',[14] and it is noticeable that the sources cited by Tolstoy in *The Kingdom of God is Within You* are primarily American, demonstrating a powerful influence on the author by American Quakers. Tolstoy's pacifism did not, therefore, represent a peculiarly Russian philosophy.

Such a philosophy does exist, in the form of Russian *kenoticism*, which, on the basis of the Passion of Christ, teaches that it is a noble act to suffer undeservedly. This concept requires 'meekness, self-abasement, voluntary poverty, humility, obedience, non-resistance, acceptance of suffering, and death, in imitation of Christ'.[15] Despite their separate intellectual roots, in the late nineteenth century, Tolstoyan ideas acquired a certain degree on popular support, especially among the Russian peasantry, by tapping into the peasantry's long-standing understanding of the kenotic principle. According to Peter Brock and John Keep, the rejection of violence 'had authentic popular roots'.[16] An example is the village teacher Yevdokim Nikitich Drozhzhin (1866-1894), who was imprisoned for refusing to serve in the army. A fellow conscientious objector, N. Z. Iziumchenko, described Drozhzhin in his memoirs as joyfully accepting the humiliations heaped on him by

---

13 A.F.C. Webster, *The Pacifist Option*, p.194.

14 R.V. Sampson, *Tolstoy: The Discover of Peace* (London: Heinemann, 1973), p.xviii.

15 Webster, *The Pacifist Option*, p.220.

16 P. Brock & J.L.H. Keep (eds), *Life in a Penal Battalion: The Tolstoyan N.Z. Iziumchenko's Story* (York: William Sessions Ltd, 2001), p.xiv.

his captors, while forgiving them for what they did. Eventually, Drozhzhin died of tuberculosis while still in prison.[17]

Such examples make it clear that pacifism has a well-established place in Russian thought. Nonetheless, it has never been fully accepted, and non-resistance to evil, or alternatively non-violent resistance to evil, have been the exceptions rather than the rule in Russia's distinctly violent history. It is noticeable that most Russian philosophers denounced Tolstoy, and that the Russian Orthodox Church excommunicated him. While pacifism is one of the trajectories in Russian thought, it is clearly not the most important.

Holy War

The same may be said of 'holy war'. One may define the holy war trajectory as one which sees the waging of war as the execution of God's will, or in secular terms as the righteous pursuit of some higher moral value. In the language of holy war, the waging of war acquires positive moral overtones, while enemies acquire the status of morally inferior persons whom one may treat almost as one pleases.

At times, Russians have without doubt adopted the language of holy war. The war against Turkey in 1877-8 was one such example. The Second World War (or Great Patriotic War, as it is known in Russia) is another. The Great Patriotic War acquired the status of a crusade against the evils of fascism in the contradictory names of communism, patriotism, and God. It is not surprising that the communist regime should have adopted the language of holy war (albeit in a secular guise), but it is slightly more surprising that the Russian Church did likewise. According to Fr Webster, the Orthodox Church was 'overcome by an excessive crusader mentality'.[18] It sponsored military units (e.g. the Dmitrii Donskoi tank battalion), and in 1941 Metropolitan Aleksei of Leningrad said that 'War is a holy thing for those who are forced to fight – in defence of righteousness and their country. Those who take up arms in such cases perform a feat of righteousness, and ... follow in the footsteps of the martyrs to win unwaning and eternal crowns'.[19]

Nonetheless, in general terms holy war and crusading are not central to Russian tradition. This can be illustrated by reference to the attitude of Muscovite Russia to the Mongols. One might have expected the Russian state and Church to declare holy war against the Mongol invaders, but in fact they did not, if only because both the state of Muscovy and the Orthodox Church were keen collaborators with Mongol rule. Muscovy came to dominate the other Russian states in part because the Mongols allowed it to do so, in return for the zeal with which the Grand Dukes of Muscovy collected tribute. Mongol rulers exempted the Orthodox Church from taxes and tribute, and in consequence the Church prospered under Mongol rule.[20]

---

17 Ibid., pp.3-63.
18 Webster, *The Pacifist Option*, p.85.
19 A.F.C. Webster, *The Price of Prophecy: Orthodox Churches on Peace, Freedom, and Security* (Washington, DC: Ethics and Public Policy Center, 1993), p.211.
20 R. Pipes, *Russia under the Old Regime* (London: Penguin, 1995), p.226.

It had no interest in preaching war against the Mongols, and instead urged submission and non-resistance.[21]

It is true that several Russian saints of this period of history were warriors. However, in general the Church canonized them not for their military achievements but for other virtuous acts. For instance, St. Aleksandr Nevskii is best known for defeating the Teutonic Knights at the battle on the ice of Lake Peipus, but was not canonized because of this famous victory. Rather he was celebrated for making peace with the Mongols, despite the fact that the peace he signed was humiliating for Russia. Clearly the Church regarded a humiliating peace, which saved Russia from further destruction, as more worthy than military victory over the non-Orthodox.

To some degree, the situation changed in 1380, when Prince Dmitrii Donskoi defeated the Mongols at the Battle of Kulikovo. Orthodoxy prohibits clergymen from participating in war, but before the Battle of Kulikovo, St. Sergius of Radonezh blessed two monks, Peresvet and Oslyabiya, and permitted them to fight in Dmitrii's army.[22] From then on, the Church increasingly gave its blessing to Russian wars of conquest. Ivan the Terrible justified his attack on Kazan as a war against 'godless people' fought 'to defend Orthodox Christianity',[23] while in the late seventeenth century Tsar Alexis portrayed his war against Poland as a holy crusade to rescue Orthodox Ukrainians from Catholic rule. During the siege of Smolensk, the Metropolitan and other priests marched around the city, icons aloft, in support of the Russian forces.[24]

Nonetheless, it would be a mistake to views these as 'holy wars', since in truth the campaigns of Ivan and Alexis were traditional secular wars of conquest given a religious gloss by a thoroughly complaisant Church. Furthermore, some Russians resisted the trend to give religious sanction to war. For instance, a sixteenth century priest, Maxim Grek, wrote various works dealing with the ethics of foreign policy, in which he cautioned against 'useless' foreign conquests.[25] Prince Andrei Kurbskii, chided by Ivan the Terrible for burning churches and fighting against him alongside the heathen Lithuanians, responded, 'Consider, O Tsar, the Scriptures, how even David was compelled because of Saul's persecution to wage war on the land of Israel together with a pagan King'.[26]

All together, the prevailing opinion among Russian religious leaders seems to have been that one should not describe war as a moral good. At best it is only a

---

21 J. Fennell, *A History of the Russian Church to 1448* (London: Longman, 1995), p.97.

22 G.P. Fedotov, *The Russian Religious Mind*, vol.2 (Cambridge, Mass: Harvard University Press, 1966), p.160.

23 *The Correspondence between Prince A. M. Kurbsky and Tsar Ivan IV of Russia*, edited by J.L.I. Fennell (Cambridge: Cambridge University Press, 1963), p.63.

24 P. Longworth, *Alexis: Tsar of all the Russias* (London: Secker & Warburg, 1984), pp.94-9.

25 W.E. Butler, 'P.P. Shafirov and the Law of Nations', preface to P.P. Shafirov, *A Discourse Concerning the Just Causes of the War between Sweden and Russia* (Dobbs Ferry: Oceana, 1973), p.5.

26 *The Correspondence between Prince A. M. Kurbsky and Tsar Ivan IV of Russia*, p.207.

'lesser evil'. For instance, in during the First World War, one of Russia's leading clergymen, Metropolitan Antonii of Galicia and Kiev, wrote a pamphlet justifying the waging of war, but in limited terms. In his pamphlet, he wrote that 'war is an evil, but in the given case, and in the majority of Russian wars, a lesser evil than declining war and surrendering to the power of the barbarians'.[27] Such statements suggest that although elements of holy war thinking have long been present in Russian minds, on the evidence of Russian history Orthodox commentators are right to conclude that holy war is 'non-normative in Orthodox moral tradition'.[28]

Realism

In truth, moral considerations do not seem to have been of great importance in determining the behaviour of combatants and would-be combatants in Russian history. Dynastic and state interest have been the overwhelming criteria controlling decisions regarding when to wage war and how to wage it. In this regard, Russia is probably no different from most other nations of the world. One might, therefore, expect Realist assumptions to lie behind Russian behaviour. In practice this would appear to be the case.

One can observe the lack of moral considerations in Russian thinking on war in the work of Petr Shafirov, one of the leading diplomats of Peter the Great. In 1717, Shafirov wrote a book entitled *A Discourse Concerning the Just Causes of the War between Sweden and Russia*, which has been described as 'an isolated and lonely monument, unemulated by another Russian work of comparable scope or originality for many decades'.[29] Shafirov's argument was that Russia was entitled to declare war against Sweden for the simple reason that Sweden's Baltic territories were historically Russian.[30] As William Butler points out, 'there is no suggestion by the author that sovereigns are in any sense obliged to settle their disputes by peaceful means'.[31]

It would appear, therefore, that the Russian ruling classes viewed the matter of war in classic Realist ways, as being outside the moral sphere. In the nineteenth century Russian socialist revolutionaries adopted a similar attitude with regard to revolutionary violence. Sergei Nechaev (1847-1873) was one of the founders of modern terrorist methodology, and adopted a ruthless approach to violence, according to which any means were appropriate if they furthered revolutionary goals. According to Nechaev, 'Rejecting all morality, the revolutionary must be ready "to destroy everyone who stands in his way"'.[32]

27 Metropolitan Antony Khrapovitsky, *The Christian Faith and War* (Jordanville: Holy Trinity Monastery, 1973), p.11.

28 Webster, *The Pacifist Option*, p.84.

29 Butler, 'P.P. Shafirov', p.39.

30 Shafirov, *Discourse*, p.241.

31 Butler, 'P.P. Shafirov', p.10.

32 O. Figes, *A People's Tragedy: The Russian Revolution* (London: Jonathan Cape, 1996), p.133.

Another revolutionary Petr Tkachev developed Nechaev's concepts further, and both Nechaev and Tkachev then had an important influence on Vladimir Lenin and through him on Soviet thinking on violence and war. According to Soviet thinkers, 'the division of wars into just and unjust is of extremely great importance', but they determined the division between the two on political rather than moral grounds, seeing no distinction between them.[33] According to Julian Lider:

> It is important to note that the terms just and unjust do not have a purely moral sense in Marxism-Leninism, for the criterion of justness is essentially the same as the criterion of progress, namely whether the object serves the interests of the working class. ... all which is good for the revolution is good for man, and is therefore moral. Thus the ethical character of war is related to a set of moral values that are not purely moral because they are connected with a socio-political cause and its carrier.[34]

In practice, what this meant was that any war fought by the Soviet Union and its allies was automatically just, as the Soviet Union was the arm of 'progress'. By contrast, wars fought by 'reactionary' capitalist states were automatically unjust. 'It appears therefore, that although the division of wars into just and unjust remains, and its importance is still stressed, it is in fact the classification according to political characteristics that provides the basis for scientific analysis'.[35]

Little has happened in post-communist Russia to supplant such modes of thought. Despite some resistance to the First Chechen War (1994-1996), Russians have not engaged in any serious debate about the justification of war in recent years, and the Second Chechen War (1999 to the present) has almost universal support among Russians. Although post-Soviet Russia has decisively turned its back on communist philosophy, 70 years of communist rule have left their mark on Russian minds and left a void in many areas of philosophy in which Western thinkers have been applying themselves for the past century. We must, therefore, not be surprised that Russians do not have much by way of philosophical alternatives to supplant the crude Realism of communist thought regarding war. It is likely that simple appeals to state interest will dictate practical attitudes to war for the immediate future.

Just War

This does not mean that Russians have no comprehension of the moral dimension of war. However, there is a distinct lack of work laying out any sort of equivalent of 'just war theory'. To find such a work, one has to look back to the year 1900, when the philosopher Vladimir Soloviev published his book *Three Conversations*. This is one of the most approachable books on the ethics of war in any European

---

33 V. Izmaylov, cited in J. Lider, *On the Nature of War* (Farnborough: Saxon House, 1977), p.227.
34 Lider, op cit., pp.216-7.
35 Ibid., p.221.

language, for the simple reason that Soloviev wrote it in the form of a conversation between five characters, rather than as a dense philosophical treatise. This fact makes the book easy to read and follow, while not depriving it of philosophical depth.

Before Soloviev, there had been no equivalent work of Russian philosophy. Louis Swift has noted that differences emerged between Western and Eastern writers on the subject of war as early as the fourth century, and that 'the moral limits surrounding the *ius belli* and *ius in bello* were never serious topics of interest in the minds of eastern writers'.[36] The idea of just war does, however, have a long heritage in Russia. In the eleventh century, for instance, St. Theodosius of the Caves resolved the dilemma caused by the need to protect the weak from attack and Christ's apparent rejection of violent methods by saying, 'Live peacefully not only with your friends, but also with your enemies; but only with your own enemies, and not with God's enemies'.[37] Similarly in the nineteenth century, Metropolitan Philaret said 'Love your enemies, beat the enemies of the Fatherland, treat God's enemies with disdain'.[38]

These quotations appear to permit violence in defence of others, but forbid it in self-defence. If someone beats you, you must turn the other cheek. But if they beat others, you must defend them, using force if necessary. This is the reverse of the position which came to dominate Western thinking in the twentieth century, namely that the only just cause for war is self-defence. The Russian line of thinking is similar to that proposed by St. Ambrose, who argued in the fourth century that fighting for others was much more praiseworthy than fighting for reasons of individual self-defence.[39] More recently Archimandrite Tikhon, Father Superior of the Sretenskii Monastery and Confessor to President Vladimir Putin, has stated:

> To not resist evil, directed personally toward you, is the highest form of self-denial ... It is absolutely different, when a Christian confronts the evil directed towards his neighbour or the whole of society. Here he not only may, but must do everything to confront this evil.[40]

In *Three Conversations*, Vladimir Soloviev made a similar argument. Four of the five characters in the book represent different trajectories of thought regarding war. The fifth, The Lady (perhaps because of her sex), offers no personal opinions. Of the other four, The Prince represents Tolstoyan pacifism; The General to some extent represents the idea of 'holy war', arguing that military service 'is and will be to the end of the world, a great honourable and holy doing';[41] The Politician

36 L.J. Swift, *The Early Fathers on War and Military Service* (Wilmington, Delaware: Michael Glazier Inc., 1983), p.96.
37 Il'in, *O soprotivlenii*, p.134.
38 Cited in *The Interview of the Archimandrite Tikhon to 'Profile' Magazine*, available online at http://www.pravoslavie.ru/english/intarchimtikhon.htm.
39 Swift, *The Early Fathers*, p.97.
40 *The Interview of Archimandrite Tikhon*, op cit.
41 Solovyof, *War and Christianity*, p.32.

represents the Realist perspective; and Mr. Z. (who represents the voice of the author) articulates the 'justifiable war ethic'. Thus The Politician states that 'everyone always knew that war was evil and the less of it the better, and, on the other hand, wise people know now that it is a kind of evil which cannot yet be removed'.[42] By contrast, Mr. Z says that 'I am absolutely convinced ... that war is not an unconditional evil, and that peace is not an unconditional good, or speaking more simply, it is possible to have a *good war*; it is also possible to have a *bad peace*'.[43]

Mr. Z concludes the book with what is to modern eyes an extremely bizarre story concerning the Anti-Christ. The point of the story is that the Anti-Christ, when he comes, will not be obviously evil. On the contrary, he will seem to be good. The danger will come not from 'unbelief or negation or materialism and such like', but rather from 'imposture' – evil masquerading as good.[44] After Mr Z tells his story, which ends with the exposure and defeat of the Anti-Christ, The Prince, who represents Tolstoy, mysteriously vanishes from the stage. The insinuation is that Tolstoyism is, like Soloviev's Anti-Christ, an imposture – an evil masquerading as a good. It is the seeming goodness of pacifism, Soloviev is implying, that will undermine the will of the Western world to defend itself, and thus lead to the victory of evil forces.

Necessary War

Soloviev died shortly after writing *Three Conversations* in 1900. His ideas were, however, very influential and traces of them can be found in the next Russian work to address the issue of war. This was the book *On Resistance to Evil by Force*, written by the philosopher Ivan Il'in in 1925. Il'in was an opponent of the Bolsheviks, who deported him to Germany in 1922. He wrote his book primarily to attack the principles of Tolstoyism. Indirectly thereby, he was also justifying the armed struggle of the White Armies against the Bolsheviks in the Russian Civil War. His conclusions are intriguing. On the one hand, he was quite insistent that armed struggle against evils such as Bolshevism was not merely permissible but actually obligatory, while on the other hand, he refused to call such struggle 'just'.

In *On Resistance to Evil by Force* and an earlier essay entitled *The Basic Moral Contradiction of War*,[45] Il'in argued that the moral demands of war are contradictory. In certain circumstances one may be obliged to wage war, but doing so involves carrying out actions normally considered unjust, such as killing. He therefore argued that war involves the use of means which are 'necessary in all

---

42 Ibid., p.5.
43 Ibid., p.11.
44 Ibid., p.98.
45 I.A. Il'in, 'Osnovnoe nrastvennoe protivorechie voiny', in I.A. Il'in, *Sobranie sochinenii*, vol.5 (Moscow: Russkaia Kniga, 1996), pp.7-30.

their injustice'. It is an '*unsinful* (!) perpetration of injustice', the use of which requires 'spiritual compromise'.[46]

If these expressions seem contradictory, that is deliberate. Il'in argues that moral use of force requires a recognition that its use involves moral contradictions. Only by facing up to the moral imperfection of what one does can one avoid the worst moral pitfalls of violence.

Il'in reaches this conclusion by arguing that the imperfection of the world creates situations in which one has no choice but to use force. He wrote that, 'He who does not resist evil, concedes to it, and joins its retinue; he who does not fight off its attacks, becomes its weapon and perishes from its craftiness'.[47] Il'in concluded that 'physical coercion can be the straightforward religious and patriotic obligation of man'.[48]

These points show that Il'in considered that the issue is not so much whether force is 'permissible' or 'justifiable', but whether it is 'necessary'. It can be necessary in two senses – in the sense that sometimes one has to use force because there is no other way of protecting others, and in the sense that in such circumstances it is obligatory to act. 'Resistance to evil with the sword is *permissible*', he writes, 'not when it is possible, but when it is *necessary*; but if it in fact necessary, man does not have a "right", but a "duty" to follow this path'.[49]

Nonetheless, Il'in insists that 'the way of the sword is an unjust path',[50] 'what the swordbearer does in the fight with evildoers is not perfect, not holy, not just … it is an *unsinful* (!) perpetration of injustice'.[51] This is because the actions of the enemy which justify your action are partly your fault, and there is always something more you could have done to prevent them.

In making this point Il'in borrows some ideas from Russian kenoticism. In Dostoevsky's novel *The Brothers Karamazov* the character Father Zossima, who was modelled on the archetype of Russian kenoticism, St. Tikhon of Zadonsk, states:

> If the evil-doing of men should arouse your indignation … go at once and seek suffering for yourself just as if you were yourself guilty of that villainy. Accept that suffering … and you will understand that you, too, are guilty, for you might have given light to the evil-doers, even as the one man without sin and you have not given them light.[52]

In a similar vein, Il'in argues that even a war of self-defence cannot be considered 'just' because everybody is in some way responsible for the external environment which has created the situation where he has to fight a war of self-

46 Il'in, *O soprotivlenii*, pp.195, 190, & 203.
47 Ibid., p.156.
48 Ibid., p.54.
49 Ibid., p.195.
50 Ibid., p.201.
51 Ibid., p.190.
52 F. Dostoyevsky, *The Brothers Karamazov* (Harmondsworth: Penguin Classics, 1985), p.379.

defence. Since everybody is at least *partially* responsible for any war they fight, Il'in says that, 'every war without exception is *a morally guilty act*'.[53]

Il'in also draws on another strand of thought which has influenced Russian pacifism. As Fr. Webster has pointed out, anger and other negative passions 'were viewed universally by the Church Fathers in the Orthodox East as foreign to the rational self, destructive of equilibrium, and consequently requiring extirpation'.[54] War excites these passions, and must therefore be avoided. Il'in shares the view that war will excite the passions and so undermine the moral equilibrium of those who wage it, but he does not share the conclusion that this problem should make one avoid war. Rather he argues that there is a way to avoid this problem. The solution is to recognise the pitfalls of what one does in using violence, to reject the idea that war is just, and instead to admit that what one is doing, though necessary, is unjust. If one does this, and undergoes a continual process of 'penitential self-purification', one can prevent one's moral condition being undermined by war, and can thereby avoid the worst excesses that often accompany violence.[55] In short the solution to waging war in a moral manner depends on a recognition of the contradictory moral nature of war. This is an original and incisive conclusion without clear parallels in Western thought

The originality of Il'in's ideas inevitably created opposition. A large number of Russian intellectuals lined up to denounce his views on the use of force. Leading the charge was the philosopher Nikolai Berdyaev, who denounced Il'in's conclusions as 'a nightmare'. Yet deep down, Berdyaev and most of his colleagues agreed with Il'in's central point. For instance, in 1939 Berdyaev wrote that 'There is nothing more monstrous than the blessing of war by Christian churches', but that 'bourgeois pacifism ... may even be a condition lower than war itself'.[56] Similarly in 1940, he wrote that 'war by itself is evil, though it may be the least of all possible evils'.[57] In the same vein, the theologian V.V. Zenkovskii noted that 'war is *always* evil', but that 'the rejection of war, forbidding participation in it, would signify withdrawal from the world'.[58] In short, there appears to have been almost universal agreement among philosophers of the time that war was inherently unjust, but sometimes necessary.

Jus in bello

What is lacking in all these discussions is any mention of *jus in bello*. In so far as Russian philosophers have concerned themselves with the issue of violence, it has been to discuss whether it can ever be right to use force. The limits to force have

---

53 Il'in, 'Osnovnoe nrastvennoe protivorechie voiny', pp.22-3.
54 Webster, *The Pacifist Option*, p.201.
55 I. A. Il'in, 'Koshmar N. A. Berdiaeva', in Il'in, *Sobranie sochinenii*, vol. 5, p.240.
56 From *Slavery and Freedom*, cited in Lowrie, op cit., p.302.
57 From *Put'*, no.61, 1934, cited in Lowrie, op cit., p.300.
58 V.V. Zenkovskii, 'Po povodu knigi I.A. Il'ina', *Sovremennye Zapiski*, no.29, 1926, pp.295 & 297.

never been a subject of discussion. Shafirov's *Discourse* made some complaints that the Swedes had broken the laws of war, but made no effort to define abstract principles regarding the use of force. Discrimination, proportionality, and other concepts from Western *jus in bello* theory are simply absent from Russian writings. The only person even to touch upon the subject was Ivan Il'in, who in a passage in his essay *The Basic Moral Contradiction of War* briefly (but only briefly) discussed the idea of proportionality. He dismissed it as impractical. In the heat of high intensity combat, he argued, soldiers do not have the time to stop and consider whether the force that they are using is proportionate to the value of the target under attack. Were they to do so, they would hesitate at a crucial moment in battle, thus threatening their cause and the lives of their colleagues. To Il'in proportionality made poor military sense.[59]

Apart from this, it is impossible to find any consideration of *jus in bello* in any of the texts mentioned in this chapter. This is a major and quite significant gap in Russian thinking on war. In the Soviet era, Russian thinkers even went so far as to deny that *jus in bello* had any bearing on the question of the justice or injustice of a given war. As Julian Lider noted in 1977, 'In the orthodox Soviet view, the justness of a war is determined by its political characteristics, the actors, and their aims. ... The problem of evaluating means and results was therefore of negligible importance'.[60] One Soviet author stated categorically that 'it would be wrong to confuse the evaluation of war as just or unjust, with its aspects, such as ways, means, and the scale of military operations, which are different questions'.[61] The advent of nuclear weapons made some Soviet thinkers reconsider this position, but the general opinion remained that any means were appropriate in pursuit of a just (i.e. socially 'progressive') cause. Thus I.A. Grudinin wrote in 1966, 'The use by us of nuclear missile weapons would be a forced act and would be the most just means, which would permit the bringing down on the aggressor the superior power of the same sort of weapons with which he will attempt to annihilate our country and other socialist countries'.[62]

One of the leading Russian clergymen of the early twentieth century, Metropolitan Antonii of Galicia and Kiev, pointed out the gap in Russian thinking about *jus in bello*. In a letter to a newspaper he praised the ideas of Ivan Il'in as consistent with Orthodox teaching, but lamented that Il'in had not addressed the question of the limits of force.[63] But the Metropolitan's comments stand out precisely because his concern for the limits of force is so unique. No Russian philosopher or spiritual leader has ever made a serious effort to define them.

Given that most contemporary Russian political and military leaders learnt their trade during the Soviet era, we must not be surprised at their willingness to use what seems to Western eyes to be excessive force against rebels in Chechnya. One must wonder whether there is a link between Russia's history of excessive violence

---

59 Il'in, 'Osnovnoe nrastvennoe protivorechie voiny', p.10.
60 Lider, *On the Nature of War*, p.221.
61 Ibid., p.221.
62 Ibid., p.228.
63 Metropolit Antonii, 'O knige I. Il'ina', in Il'in, *Sobranie sochinenii*, vol. 5, pp.272-3.

and lack of restraint in war on the one hand, and the absence of any systematic just war thinking on the other. Russians have occasionally considered the justification of war, but not in anything like the depth that Western peoples have. Russians have, moreover, failed entirely to address the problem of the limits of force. It is not clear how these deficiencies are related to what is, even by the bloody standards of Europe, a particularly bloody history. Perhaps the lack of thinking on war explains the lack of restraint so often shown by Russians. Perhaps it is a product of a culture which does not consider any such thinking necessary. But whatever the answer, it seems likely that the two matters are connected in some intimate fashion, and it is clear that Russia, while in many respects a truly European state, in other respects has followed a cultural path uniquely its own.

Chapter 5

War, Peace and the Imperatives of Justice in Islamic Perspective: What Do the 11 September 2001 Attacks Tell Us about Islam and the Just War Tradition?

John Kelsay

Since 11 September 2001, discussion has moved along several lines with respect to ideas about Islam. In the United States, at least, we began with a kind of 'all or nothing' approach, in which some people argued that Islam had nothing to do with the attacks, while others argued just the opposite. Both cited the Qur'an and other Islamic sources; neither took us very far.

The all or nothing discussion continues; but people did move to another set of questions, along lines of placing those responsible for the attacks, especially Usama bin Ladin, in the history of Islamic thought. Here, attention turned, for example, to 'Wahhabi Islam'.[1] The interest and importance of these issues seem obvious, but I think that we are ready for another kind of inquiry. In both the all or nothing and the historical location discussions, various participants quoted snippets of two important documents in which Usama bin Ladin and his colleagues stated their grievances, their goals, and articulated their understanding of the duties Muslims have regarding armed struggle with the United States and its allies. We are ready for a more extended analysis of these documents. In this chapter, I shall

1 See, most recently, Stephen Schwartz, *The Two Faces of Islam: The House of Saud From Tradition to Terror* (New York: Doubleday, 2002). Gilles Kepel views Wahhabism as a relevant but not final factor; for him, bin Ladin and al-Qa'ida are examples of something distinctive which he terms 'jihadist-salafist' Islam. See his *Jihad: The Trail of Political Islam* (Cambridge, Mass.: Harvard University Press, 2002), especially p.219ff. I review Kepel's book, along with Bernard Lewis, *What Went Wrong? Western Impact and Middle Eastern Response* (Oxford: Oxford University Press, 2002) and John Esposito, *Unholy War: Terror in the Name of Islam* (Oxford: Oxford University Press, 2002) in 'Speaking of Islam', *The Christian Century*, vol.119, no.19, 11-24 September 2002, pp.34-38. Like Kepel, each of these authors has a distinctive take on the 'historical location' question, as do Steven Simon and Daniel Benjamin in *The Age of Sacred Terror* (New York: Random House, 2002) and Michael Scott Doran in 'Somebody Else's Civil War', *Foreign Affairs*, vol.81, no.1 January/February 2002, pp.22-42.

focus on the more recent of them, the so-called 'Declaration' of the World Islamic Front regarding the duty of 'struggle against Jews and Crusaders'. I will have occasion to refer back to the earlier document, sometimes called 'Bin Ladin's Epistle'. But that will mainly be to sharpen our sense of points made in the more recent document, for example by way of showing a progressively greater sense of what can only be called the emergency facing the Muslim community.[2]

I begin with an exposition of the text. I then move to some comments assessing the status of the text in terms of normative Islamic thinking. Finally, I want to say something about attitudes of Muslims and others with respect to the ongoing military campaign in Afghanistan.

Exposition

On 23 February 1998 a London paper, *al-Quds al-Arabi*, published a document under the headline *Text of a Declaration by the World Islamic Front with respect to Jihad against the Jews and the Crusaders*. Five people are associated with the document. All are known from movements involved with armed resistance. One is Usama bin Ladin. None of the signers is a recognized scholar of Islam, though Ayman al-Zawahiri, an Egyptian physician, is from a family with scholarly credentials.[3] This lack of credentials is important. As one often hears, Islam has no formal clergy. Nevertheless, from a very early period the Islamic community recognized a class of religious specialists. The issuing of authoritative opinions regarding Islamic practice was understood to be the duty of certain members of this class, following upon the obtaining of appropriate scholarly credentials. Modern Islam illustrates some change in this historic practice, with the end result that on occasion, 'ordinary' Muslims can and do give opinions. If these opinions are followed, this is often for reasons tied to personal charisma rather than to broad or deep learning.

Despite this lack, the *Declaration* speaks in authoritative terms. It identifies norms relevant to the behaviour of Muslims, particularly with respect to fighting the U.S. and its allies. The language suggests that sincere Muslims should read, discuss the reasoning of the text, and (the authors hope) follow its directives.

2   A translation of the *Declaration* produced by the Foreign Broadcast Information Service is appended at the end of this chapter. Like the *Epistle,* it is available in a number of places. See, for example, http://www.washingtonpost.org, among others. By now the *Declaration* has in fact been discussed, though not to the extent offered here, in a number of places. A pre-September 11 analysis was given by Bernard Lewis in 'License to Kill: Usama bin Ladin's Declaration of Jihad', *Foreign Affairs*, vol.77, no.6, November/December 1998, pp.14-24; more recently, see James Turner Johnson, 'Jihad and Just War', in *First Things*, no.124, June/July 2002, pp.12-14; for my own brief comments, see 'Bin Laden's Reasons', in *The Christian Century*, vol.119, no.5, 27 February-6 March 2002, pp.26-9.

3   For a very interesting and readable account of al-Zawahiri's pilgrimage to radicalism, see Lawrence Wright, 'The Man Behind Bin Laden', *The New Yorker Magazine*, 16 September 2002.

The *Declaration* begins with a pious recitation.

> Praise be to God, who revealed the Book, controls the clouds, defeats factionalism, and says in His Book: 'But when the forbidden months are past, then fight and slay the pagans where you find them, seize them, beleaguer them, and lie in wait for them in every stratagem' [Qur'an 9:5]; and peace be upon our Prophet, Muhammad Bin 'Abdallah, who said: 'I have been sent with the sword between my hands to ensure that no one but God is worshipped, God who put my livelihood under the shadow of my spear and who inflicts humiliation and scorn on those who disobey my orders'.[4]

In the normative tradition of Islam, the goal is to comprehend divine guidance. That is the meaning of the term Shari'a, which is usually translated 'Islamic religious law'. The term implies the belief, crucial to Islamic practice, that there is an ideal way to live; a way that will make for happiness in this world and the next.[5]

God, the merciful and compassionate Creator and Lord of all, provides his creatures with guidance pertaining to this ideal way of life. The world is filled with 'signs' that indicate such guidance. But the surest of the signs of God, the best sources for those who would walk the straight path which God favours, are the Qur'an and the example of the Prophet. Thus the authors of the *Declaration* begin with the invocation of the two basic sources of Shari'a, the Book of God 'wherein is no doubt' and the example of the Prophet, given as mercy to humankind.

They then continue:

> The Arabian Peninsula has never – since God made it flat, created its desert, and encircled it with seas – been stormed by any forces like the crusader armies spreading in it like locusts, eating its riches and wiping out its plantations. All this is happening at a time in which nations are attacking Muslims like people fighting over a plate of food.[6] In the light of the grave situation and the lack of support, we and you are obliged to discuss current events, and we should all agree on how to settle the matter.

Here, the authors further establish the connection of their *Declaration* with Islamic tradition. One who reads traditional biographies of Muhammad will be

---

4   Throughout I refer to the translation appended to this chapter, which is by the Foreign Broadcast Information Service. I have made some alterations in the translation to fit my sense of the Arabic original.

5   For many years the standard introductions to Islamic law have been the works of Joseph Schacht. See, for example, his *Introduction to Islamic Law* (Oxford: Clarendon Press, 1964). This and other works by Schacht must now be supplemented by various studies authored by Wael Hallaq. See, for example, *A History of Islamic Legal Theories* (Cambridge: Cambridge University Press, 1997).

6   Here, as elsewhere in the *Declaration*, the authors refer to sources that many Muslim readers will recognize. The notion of a time when the nations will attack Muslims like people fighting over a plate of food refers to a saying of the Prophet which may be found, among other places, in James Robson's translation of the compendium of Prophetic sayings known as *Mishkat al-Masabih* (Lahore: Sh. Muhammad Ashraf, 1981), II: 1115, in the 'Book of Words which Soften the Heart'. Thanks to Michael Cook and James Pavlin for calling this to my attention.

struck by the emphasis on Divine Providence in preparing the way for the last prophet. In such books, the Arabian Peninsula is the site of many of the most important events in world history. Abraham journeyed there; with his son, Ishmael, he built the Ka'ba as the first house of worship. Through his descendants, Ishmael became the father of a great nation, his descendants ultimately attaining status as progenitors of the various tribes of the Peninsula. With a few notable exceptions, the geography of the Peninsula keeps it safe from outside aggression. When the settled ways of the tribes came under stress, during the sixth century CE, leaders of the Quraysh, the most prominent tribe and guardians of the Ka'ba, sponsored initiatives aimed at emphasizing the unity of the sons of Ishmael. They thus unwittingly prepared the way for the Arab Prophet, who came to reemphasize the message of submission – that there is one God, that human beings are responsible to a moral law, and that divine judgment is a reality. By the end of the Prophet's career, he would say that 'Arabia is now solidly for Islam'. The Peninsula, as the land of the two holy places (Mecca and Medina) has ever after been considered by Muslims as an inviolable trust, given to Muslims as a sign and seal of their devotion to the Prophet's message. No land is more holy, no trust more sacred than this.[7]

This passage is thus important as an historical reference. At the same time, it speaks to contemporary Muslims. There have been times of crisis previously, in which the inviolability of Arabia was threatened. But none of these has been more serious than the current crisis, in which the lives and wealth of Muslims are the direct target of a war of annihilation. Greedy and rapacious nations attack Muslims all over the world, and Arabia, with its treasure trove of natural resources, is the grand prize. The next few paragraphs are devoted to delineating how that is so, and to identifying the nation most responsible for the international campaign against Muslims.

'No one argues today about three facts that are known to everyone'. The authors cite the 'occupation' of the Arabian Peninsula by the United States, the ongoing misery of the people of Iraq, and the struggles between Palestinians and Israelis. Of these, the first claim is the most important, in terms of the overall direction of the Declaration. The continuing presence of foreign, especially U.S. troops on Arabian soil since the end of the Gulf War provides a means for plundering the riches of the Arabian Peninsula; 'dictating to its rulers, humiliating its people, terrorizing its neighbors, and turning bases in the Peninsula into a spearhead through which to fight the neighboring Islamic peoples'. The authors note that some people have in the past argued about this – probably a reference to criticisms made of the 1996 'Epistle'. But, they write, 'All the people of the Peninsula have now acknowledged it'.

Establishing the fact of occupation is critical to the argument of the *Declaration*. In this connection, it is useful to recall that Islamic law or Shari'a

---

7   The prime example is that of Ibn Ishaq. See the translation by A. Guillaume as *The Life of Muhammad* (Karachi: Oxford University Press, 1978). Martin Lings combines several traditional biographies for his *Muhammad: His Life Based on the Earliest Sources* (Rochester, Vermont: Inner Traditions International, 1983).

reasoning is best understood as a kind of case or response law. One is always trying to find guidance for the present by connecting the Qur'an, the example of the Prophet, and the wisdom of previous generations of scholars to current situations. In this, the assessment of facts is crucial. One set of facts will suggest a certain kind of normative judgment. Another set of facts will lead in a different direction.

Thus, in 1996, bin Ladin's *Epistle* argued that the facts at that time indicated that the United States and its allies had declared war on God, his messenger, and the Muslims, and that this made it obligatory for Muslims as a community to put aside their differences and contribute to the resistance as they were able.

The 1998 *Declaration* sees things a bit differently. The war against Islam is further along, and thus it becomes obligatory for every Muslim individual to participate in the defense of Islam. This is a very important development, which calls for a brief excursus into the Islamic law of war.

The term *jihad* means struggle or effort. In the Qur'an, it is always joined with the phrase *fi sabil allah*, which means 'in the path of God'. Every Muslim, and really every human being is called to 'command good and forbid evil', or one could say, to defend and establish justice.

One struggles in a variety of ways. Preaching, for example, spreads the word of Islam and calls people to practise justice. If people do not heed the preaching of the word, and in particular if they respond with discrimination or persecution of believers, one continues to struggle in ways that exhibit 'steadfastness'. The example of the Prophet and his companions in Mecca, in the years between 610 and 622, is quite apt. Faced with continual and sometimes violent persecution they remained nonviolent. It was only when things reached the point that God, as a means of protecting the small community of believers, ordered the Prophet to migrate to Medina that this changed. At that time, we are told, Muhammad received Qur'an 22:39-40:

> Permission for fighting is given to those who are victims of aggression. God is powerful in assisting them. These are people wrongly driven from their land for saying 'God is our Lord'. If God did not deter one group of people by means of another, then monasteries, churches, synagogues, and mosques where the name of God is abundantly mentioned would be destroyed.[8]

---

8   When I quote the Qur'an, that is apart from the text of the *Declaration*, I use the translation by Yusuf 'Ali, with my own variations to reflect the sense of the Arabic text. For the sake of readers not well acquainted with Islam, I pause here to note that according to traditional accounts, the Qur'an was given or revealed to Muhammad in a series of revelations over the course of 22 years (610-32 CE). The final text was not arranged chronologically; thus, 22: 39-40 are said to be earlier than, for example 2: 190-191, which also have to do with warfare. For traditional exegesis, knowing the 'occasion' or circumstances of the revelation of a verse or set of verses was an important key in uncovering meaning. Thus, the occasion of 22: 39-40 is presented as the move to Medina and the correlative order given by God to fight in defence of believers' rights.

In Medina, the Islamic struggle took on a military cast, though this was always accompanied by diplomatic, economic, and religious initiatives as well. The point was to create an alliance of tribes in Arabia, and thus to secure the freedom of the Muslims to worship God.

Following Muhammad's death, the Arab tribes, now united under the banner of Islam, pushed out of the Arabian Peninsula and conquered most of the Middle East and North Africa. There are many questions, not only about how they accomplished this, but about the 'why?'[9] For our purposes, the more significant development was scholarly; a class of religious specialists developed a set of judgments about resort to and conduct of war that parallel the mode of thinking Christians and more generally Westerners know as the just war tradition.[10]

The important point in relation to the 1998 *Declaration* is as follows. The scholars who developed the judgments associated with *jihad* did so in the context of an Islamic empire. In that context, they said, the military aspect of *jihad* can be understood in two ways. First, there is a kind of armed struggle in which Muslim troops, under the leadership of an established Muslim ruler, try to secure the borders of an Islamic state. In this kind of struggle, the duty of Muslims is technically described as *fard kifaya*, or a 'collective' duty. This means that the ruler of the Muslims must have a standing army at his disposal, and the community as a whole should provide support. Some Muslims will join the army, others will pay taxes to support it, and so on. Everyone is supposed to do his/her part, but the obligation of defence rests with the community as a whole.

A second kind of struggle is rather different. In this case, we have to imagine that an enemy has invaded the territory of Islam. The enemy's forces are damaging Muslim property. Citizens who have every right to believe that their ruler can and will protect them from attack are being injured or killed. The enemy is violating the rights of Muslims, carrying the campaign into the heart of Islamic territory. The end result is that Islam itself is in danger, in the sense that the Muslim community's capacity to carry out its mission is radically delimited. In the most extreme case, one might fear that this capacity will be eliminated.

In this second kind of struggle, the scholars said that fighting is *fard 'ayn*, an individual duty. This means that every Muslim must fight to defend Islam. The idea is that an emergency exists. The scholars went further, saying that in a true emergency, 'necessity makes the forbidden things permitted'. Under this rubric, they talked about the ordinary lines of authority that make society work, and they argued that these lines did not hold in an emergency situation. So a woman can

---

9   See, for example, the study by Fred Donner, *The Early Muslim Conquests* (Princeton: Princeton University Press, 1981); idem, 'The Sources of Islamic Conceptions of War', in John Kelsay and James Turner Johnson (eds.), *Just War and Jihad: Historical and Theoretical Perspectives on War and Peace in Western and Islamic Traditions* (Westport, CT: Greenwood Press, 1991).

10   Here, see John Kelsay, *Islam and War: A Study in Comparative Ethics* (Louisville, Ky: Westminster/John Knox Press, 1993), as well as James Turner Johnson, *The Holy War Idea in Western and Islamic Traditions* (University Park, Penn: Pennsylvania State University Press, 1997).

fight without obtaining permission from her father or husband, and a young person can fight without obtaining permission from the parents. While this was not much discussed, one could suppose that an emergency would justify groups of ordinary Muslims in organizing a kind of militia for the protection of Muslims – that is, in the absence of an effective central authority, the duty to defend Islam against an invader devolves to the people. In just war terms, one would say that authority to make war devolves to the people, to each and to all.

It is obvious that this kind of emergency provision is open to abuse. Historically, most Islamic reflection has been concerned with the possibility that the emergency provision might be used as a cover for revolutionary or even criminal activity. To my way of thinking, Islamic scholars were quite realistic about the ways religious motivations can, under certain circumstances, lend themselves to the justification of actions that do more harm than good. Muslim authorities usually spoke of this through the symbol of the Kharijites, a group that stood as a prime example of religious zeal leading to excess during the early period of Islamic development. Muslim authorities thus knew the problems with the emergency provision. But they left it on the books, for the rather obvious reason that one cannot rule out the possibility that such situations really do or will exist.

The language of armed struggle as an individual duty stands behind the 1998 *Declaration*. The 'facts' no longer support the judgment that armed resistance to the U.S. and its allies is a communal obligation. Rather, resistance is now an individual duty, in which every Muslim must understand the emergency and do his or her part. The degree of intensity is supported by the authors with a citation from the lawbooks: 'As for fighting to repel, it is aimed at defending sanctity and religion, and all agree it is a duty. Nothing, with the exception of faith itself, is more sacred than repulsing an enemy who is attacking faith and life'.[11]

This leads to the heart of the *Declaration*, which is the ruling that killing (or one could also translate, 'fighting') Americans and their allies, or as the authors write a few lines down, killing (fighting) them and plundering their money, is a matter of individual duty for every Muslim who can, in any country where it is possible. The goal is to move the invading forces 'out of all the lands of Islam, defeated and unable to threaten any Muslim'. That last phrase catches the sentiment that motivates the authors – they believe that fighting the U.S. and its allies constitutes a just response to American attacks on Islam; they further believe that the American attacks have gone far enough that Islam is under an emergency condition. Muslims should fight to defend justice: 'And why should you not fight in the cause of God and of those who, being weak, are ill treated? [Men,] Women and children, whose cry is "Our Lord, rescue us from this town, whose people are oppressors; and raise for us one who will help!"' Fighters, in other words, are the guardians of the weak against the forces of oppression.

---

11 The quote appears to be from Ibn Taymiyya's treatise *al-siyasa al-shari'a*, which is translated by Omar A. Farrukh as *Ibn Taimiyya on Public and Private Law in Islam* (Beirut: Khayat's, 1966), as well as by Henri Laoust as *Le Traite de Droit Public D'Ibn Taimiya* (Beyrouth: Institut Français de Damas, 1948).

Assessment

It has been said that the ruling of the *Declaration* goes beyond the bounds of Islamic law, even with respect to the emergency provision. Some critics focus on issues of authority, others on the scope of armed struggle in Islam, still others on the fact that the document calls for indiscriminate or total war. All of these reflect legitimate questions. I shall address each in turn.

With respect to authority, I have already mentioned that the authors of the *Declaration* lack the credentials to qualify as members of the class of religious specialists. How, then, do they justify issuing a normative statement regarding the duty of Muslims? I think there are two possibilities – and these are not mutually exclusive. The first possibility is that the authors believe that the emergency condition justifies their assumption of the role of a religious specialist. Remember that in the emergency situation, the ordinary lines of authority are suspended. If that is so in the family and in political life generally, perhaps it is so in matters of Shari`a discourse as well.

The second possibility has to do with the basically democratic tendencies of Islam. People say Islam has no clergy. The implication is that nearness to God, and the authority that flows from that, is not the province of any special class of people. The authority of religious specialists was historically supported by a habit of deference. But there is nothing to suggest that such authority is anything more than habitual. Further, according to some legal texts, the criteria for exercising 'independent judgment', and thus for making normative pronouncements, are really quite minimal. Indeed, some even suggest that a person or group of persons can have competence within one area of Shari`a reasoning – for example, the law of war – without obtaining the right to make pronouncements more generally.[12] At most, the question of authority seems to be of this nature: One can argue that bin Ladin and his colleagues 'ought not' to make pronouncements like this. But one would be hard-pressed to say that they 'cannot' do so. The issue is whether anyone listens.[13]

With respect to the scope of armed struggle in Islam, note that the Declaration calls for attacks in any country where it is possible. I do not say this is a direct and clear violation of Islamic norms. But it does involve a stretch. The crucial point of the emergency provision has to do with the defence of Islamic territory which is under attack. Most of those who invoke the emergency provision focus on what we might call 'homeland defence'. That is true, even for most of the radical groups which have invoked the emergency provision in the last twenty years or so. Egyptian Islamic Jihad and Hamas, for example, speak of their campaign in terms of establishing a just and effective Islamic authority in their homelands. In recent history, there is one prominent example of a Muslim force carrying out

---

12 See Mohammed Hashim Kamali, *Principles of Islamic Jurisprudence* (Cambridge: Islamic Texts Society, 1991).
13 On these points, note the very interesting comments made by Richard Bulliett in 'The Crisis within Islam', *The Wilson Quarterly*, vol.26, no.1, Winter 2002, pp.11-19.

'emergency' defence activities far beyond its homeland.[14]	This is the example of Shaykh Umar Abd al-Rahman and the Islamic Group (a kind of splinter from Egyptian Islamic Jihad), who wanted to attack American interests signified by the World Trade Centre – thus the 1993 bombing of the towers, for which Shaykh Umar and others remain in U.S. prisons.	The idea there and also in the 1998 *Declaration* is that the experience of homeland defence shows that Muslim fighters will have to strike not only at oppression close to home.	They will have to strike at those far away powers that support oppression; in particular, they will have to strike at the home front of those far away powers.	Again, I do not say that this is a violation of Islamic norms, but it is a little unusual.	Recalling the worries Muslim scholars expressed about abuses of the emergency provision, one might now consider a new wrinkle: the possibility, that is, that an overzealous group dedicated to armed resistance might strike at targets far from the homeland, and thus bring down on the Muslim lands the wrath of a foreign power – e.g. in Afghanistan.

The more direct violation of Islamic norms in the 1998 *Declaration* has to do with the call for direct and intentional strikes at civilian targets – that is, for indiscriminate or total warfare.	Let there be no mistake about this; Islam is very clear on the matter.	The Prophet said: 'Do not cheat or commit treachery, do not mutilate or kill women, children, or old men'.[15]	In other sayings attributed to the Prophet, these directives are reiterated.	The presupposition is that soldiers fight soldiers.	How then do devout Muslims like the authors of the Declaration justify calling on Muslims to target American civilians?	Readers of a just war text like Michael Walzer's *Just and Unjust Wars* will no doubt already have thought about his famous discussion of 'supreme emergency'.	Here, Walzer argues that in context where defeat is imminent, and where defeat suggests the possibility of annihilation of a people or of a way of life, the ordinary limitations on fighters are temporarily suspended, and moral reasoning is limited to a kind of 'utilitarianism of extremes'.[16]	Perhaps Muslims who, like the authors of the *Declaration*, are convinced that the United States is engaged in a war intended to annihilate Islam might believe that they are justified or excused in attacking civilians under a similar kind of provision.	As I have already indicated, the language of the *Declaration*, and indeed, the very concept of armed struggle as an individual duty, suggests emergency conditions.	Those who fight should understand themselves to be 'repulsing an enemy who is attacking religion and life'.

14	I discuss the reasoning of Hamas and Egyptian Islamic Jihad in *Islam and War*, pp.77-110.	See materials cited there.	Kepel, in *Jihad: The Trail of Political Islam* argues that the Palestinian scholar Abdullah Azzam (d. 1989), who was a noteworthy figure among Arabs who made the journey to fight against Soviet forces in Afhganistan, is the key figure in articulating an 'international' vision in which it would be necessary and justified to strike at targets far away from the Islamic 'heartland'; viz., in Europe and in the US.

15	In my forthcoming article 'Islam and the Justice of War' I show the consistency with which historic interpreters of Shari`a insisted on this point, even in the case of fighting classified as an 'individual duty'.

16	Michael Walzer, *Just and Unjust Wars*, 3rd ed. (New York: Basic Books, 2000).

Further, I have already mentioned that the reasoning associated with armed struggle as *fard `ayn* carries with it the notion that 'necessity makes the forbidden things permitted'. One might reason that, if direct and intentional attacks on civilians are among the forbidden things (which they are), the necessity imposed by emergency conditions permits such attacks.

I cannot rule this out, as a part of the reasoning of the authors of the *Declaration*. Indeed, I am guessing that this is in their minds. However, there is a major problem with such reasoning, given the way Islamic tradition typically thinks about the emergency condition. That is, the maxim by which 'necessity makes the forbidden things permitted' is not taken as an excuse for murder.[17] As mentioned previously, the emergency condition permits action outside normal lines of authority. A woman can take the initiative to fight, without obtaining permission from her father or husband, and so on. But the examples do not include commission of murder. This is a major obstacle to the kind of attacks the authors of the *Declaration* want to encourage. And I find it most interesting that they do not cite any precedents for an exception that would cover such attacks. Indeed, when bin Ladin has been questioned about such matters, he typically answers in two ways. First, he says that the United States has attacked civilians, too. Second, he argues that since all Americans benefit from the oppressive policies of their government (for example, in terms of cheap oil prices), they thus deserve what they get; one who readily accepts gains won by the immoral actions of others can hardly claim to be guiltless.[18]

In either case, the argument is hardly something that the tradition of judgments about jihad using armed force would recognize as compelling. Indeed, it seems the authors of the *Declaration* are in a bad place in terms of Islamic practical reasoning. I do not know of any way to get around it. The idea that there can be an individual duty for every Muslim to participate in armed struggle to defend Islamic territory or values makes good Islamic sense. But the idea that there can be an individual duty for every able Muslim to directly and intentionally kill American or any other civilians does not.

Response

What does the Shari`a tradition suggest be done with people like the authors of the *Declaration*, who seem to think their zeal, and the emergency conditions they confront, justify or excuse them in the commission of acts that are forbidden? In Islamic tradition, Shari`a judgments rest not only on an interpretation of authoritative sources, but on an interpretation of the facts of the matter. In this

---

17 See, for example, the very interesting (though in some ways obtuse) discussion regarding the permissibility of Muslims fighting on the U.S. or allied side in Afghanistan following the 11 September 2001 attacks at www.memri.org, Middle East Media Research Institute 'Inquiry and Analysis Series', no.75, 6 November 2001.
18 For these interviews, see www.pbs.org, where in particular the May 1998 interview with ABC correspondent John Miller is presented.

vein, it is hardly strange that many Muslims have expressed the desire that the United States and its allies would be more forthcoming about the evidence implicating bin Ladin and his colleagues in the attacks of September 11, or that they have further expressed a wish that bin Ladin and his colleagues could have been charged and tried either in an Islamic court or in an international (by which they also mean 'impartial') court.

More fundamentally, however, I think what we need to say is that the problem posed by zealots like the authors of the 1998 *Declaration* is historically a very difficult one in Islam. Over the last twenty years, established authorities, for example, the leadership of al-Azhar has spoken about the problems posed by such people in terms of an analogy with the Kharijites. These stand in the tradition for people who are devout, but overzealous, and who despite their intentions do more harm than good. Historically, Islamic tradition tended to deal with these under the category of 'rebels'. And the scholars thought that, in dealing with rebels, the primary thing to keep in mind is that they are sincere, however problematic their behaviour. The goal of response to them is not elimination, but reconciliation. That does not rule out a military response; it does suggest that any military response to the group should be guided by extremely scrupulous attempts to avoid damage to civilians and their property. Further, one should be more anxious to take the rebel soldiers as prisoners than to kill them, and one should try even in the midst of a campaign to appeal to the rebels as fellow Muslims.[19]

Not all troublesome groups are rebels, however. Some are better thought of as highwaymen, brigands, or just plain thugs. The scholars said that these should be brought to justice. If necessary, they were to be killed. And one ought not feel too badly about the deaths of anyone around them, since such people are prima facie giving aid and comfort to criminals. The main thing is to prevent the thugs from continuing the activities that cause harm. It is best if one can arrest and imprison them, since even a criminal might eventually repent. But the security of people who count on the government for defence is primary, and if killing the thugs is the best way to attain that, then it should be done.[20]

I propose that this distinction between dealing with rebels and dealing with thugs provides a rough grid for understanding some of the differing voices we heard regarding the war in Afghanistan, and regarding the ongoing attempt to capture and/or kill leaders and members of al-Qa'ida. Some Muslims take bin Ladin as a rebel; others see him as a thug. The U.S. and its allies pretty clearly see him as a thug. The interest of those who see him as a rebel is to limit the use of

---

19 See Kelsay, *Islam and War*, pp.81-93; also, Khaled Abou El Fadl, *Rebellion and Violence in Islamic Law* (Cambridge: Cambridge University Press, 2001).

20 Here, see the material translated in Majid Khadduri, *The Islamic Law of Nations: Shaybani's Siyar* (Baltimore: Johns Hopkins University Press, 1966), pp.247-50. Those who are guilty of *hiraba* are sometimes viewed in connection with the Qur'an 5:33: 'The punishment of those who wage war against God and God's messenger, and strive with might and main for mischief throughout the land is: execution, or crucifixion, or the cutting off of hands and feet from opposite sides, or exile from the land. That is their disgrace in this world, and a heavy punishment is theirs in the hereafter'.

force, in line with the goal of reconciliation – if not with bin Ladin himself, at least with some of those associate with him, who may be less committed to his understanding of history, and who might yet be restored as useful members of Islamic and international society. The interest of those who see him as a thug, by contrast, is the prevention of further wrongdoing by people who can only be seen as war criminals.

I do not know any easy way, in terms of Shari`a reasoning, to negotiate the differences between these parties. Surely those arguing for reconciliation must admit that the wrong done on 11 September 2001 is very great, and that bin Ladin and his colleagues have a record of deeds, including statements like the 1998 Declaration, that hardly suggests reconciliation. The Taliban resistance to extradition during the late 1990s, and further resistance to such after 11 September 2001, made legal remedies very difficult, to say the least.

Just as surely, those who see bin Ladin as a thug must admit that there are differences between those who actively supported al-Qa`ida, those who acquiesced in its deeds, and those who were and are simply bystanders. Allied spokespersons tell us that our forces did and are doing everything possible to avoid civilian casualties in Afghanistan, and I for one do not know of evidence to suggest that allied military power has been directly and intentionally aimed at civilians. Even the unintentional deaths of civilians provide reason for regret, however; and for Muslims thinking about the justice of the campaign against al-Qa`ida, such regret may give rise to questions about proportionate means – that is, even though the allied campaign is discriminate in avoiding any direct targeting of civilians, one might ask whether certain types of weaponry or tactics are necessary, or whether there are means available that do less harm to civilian life. Some, for example, expressed concerns about the use of Daisy Cutter and cluster bombs in Afghanistan. It is hard to say that these are unreasonable questions, even if ultimately the answer is that they were the best means available to get at al-Qa`ida's military capacity.

All this suggests the very difficult task before the United States, the United Kingdom and other allies, including Muslim countries, in pursuing justice with respect to al-Qa`ida and related groups. In Islamic terms, as in the criteria of the just war tradition, the point of fighting is to defend the weak, and to establish a balance between peace, order, and justice. The challenge presented by Usama bin Ladin and his colleagues raises difficult questions about the best way to pursue that goal.

Appendix to Chapter 5: *World Islamic Front Statement: Jihad against Jews and Crusaders, 23 February 1998*

Shaykh Usamah Bin-Muhammad Bin-Ladin
Ayman al-Zawahiri, amir of the Jihad Group in Egypt
Abu-Yasir Rifa'i Ahmad Taha, Egyptian Islamic Group
Shaykh Mir Hamzah, secretary of the Jamiat-ul-Ulema-e-Pakistan
Fazlur Rahman, amir of the Jihad Movement in Bangladesh

Praise be to Allah, who revealed the Book, controls the clouds, defeats factionalism, and says in His Book: 'But when the forbidden months are past, then fight and slay the pagans wherever ye find them, seize them, beleaguer them, and lie in wait for them in every stratagem (of war)'; and peace be upon our Prophet, Muhammad Bin-Abdallah, who said: I have been sent with the sword between my hands to ensure that no one but Allah is worshipped, Allah who put my livelihood under the shadow of my spear and who inflicts humiliation and scorn on those who disobey my orders.

The Arabian Peninsula has never – since Allah made it flat, created its desert, and encircled it with seas – been stormed by any forces like the crusader armies spreading in it like locusts, eating its riches and wiping out its plantations. All this is happening at a time in which nations are attacking Muslims like people fighting over a plate of food. In the light of the grave situation and the lack of support, we and you are obliged to discuss current events, and we should all agree on how to settle the matter.

No one argues today about three facts that are known to everyone; we will list them, in order to remind everyone:

First, for over seven years the United States has been occupying the lands of Islam in the holiest of places, the Arabian Peninsula, plundering its riches, dictating to its rulers, humiliating its people, terrorizing its neighbours, and turning its bases in the Peninsula into a spearhead through which to fight the neighbouring Muslim peoples.

If some people have in the past argued about the fact of the occupation, all the people of the Peninsula have now acknowledged it. The best proof of this is the Americans' continuing aggression against the Iraqi people using the Peninsula as a staging post, even though all its rulers are against their territories being used to that end, but they are helpless.

Second, despite the great devastation inflicted on the Iraqi people by the crusader-Zionist alliance, and despite the huge number of those killed, which has exceeded one million ... despite all this, the Americans are once again trying to repeat the horrific massacres, as though they are not content with the protracted blockade imposed after the ferocious war or the fragmentation and devastation.

So here they come to annihilate what is left of this people and to humiliate their Muslim neighbors.

Third, if the Americans aims behind these wars are religious and economic, the aim is also to serve the Jews' petty state and divert attention from its occupation of Jerusalem and murder of Muslims there. The best proof of this is their eagerness to destroy Iraq, the strongest neighbouring Arab state, and their endeavour to fragment all the states of the region such as Iraq, Saudi Arabia, Egypt, and Sudan into paper statelets and through their disunion and weakness to guarantee Israel's survival and the continuation of the brutal crusade occupation of the Peninsula.

All these crimes and sins committed by the Americans are a clear declaration of war on Allah, his messenger, and Muslims. And ulema have throughout Islamic history unanimously agreed that the jihad is an individual duty if the enemy destroys the Muslim countries. This was revealed by Imam Bin-Qadamah in 'Al-Mughni', Imam al-Kisa'i in 'Al-Bada'i', al-Qurtubi in his interpretation, and the shaykh of al-Islam in his books, where he said: 'As for the fighting to repulse [an enemy], it is aimed at defending sanctity and religion, and it is a duty as agreed [by the ulema]. Nothing is more sacred than belief except repulsing an enemy who is attacking religion and life'.

On that basis, and in compliance with Allah's order, we issue the following fatwa to all Muslims:

The ruling to kill the Americans and their allies – civilians and military – is an individual duty for every Muslim who can do it in any country in which it is possible to do it, in order to liberate the al-Aqsa Mosque and the holy mosque [Mecca] from their grip, and in order for their armies to move out of all the lands of Islam, defeated and unable to threaten any Muslim. This is in accordance with the words of Almighty Allah, 'and fight the pagans all together as they fight you all together', and 'fight them until there is no more tumult or oppression, and there prevail justice and faith in Allah'.

This is in addition to the words of Almighty Allah: 'And why should ye not fight in the cause of Allah and of those who, being weak, are ill-treated (and oppressed)? – women and children, whose cry is: "Our Lord, rescue us from this town, whose people are oppressors; and raise for us from thee one who will help!"'

We – with Allah's help – call on every Muslim who believes in Allah and wishes to be rewarded to comply with Allah's order to kill the Americans and plunder their money wherever and whenever they find it. We also call on Muslim ulema, leaders, youths, and soldiers to launch the raid on Satan's U.S. troops and the devil's supporters allying with them, and to displace those who are behind them so that they may learn a lesson.

Almighty Allah said: 'O ye who believe, give your response to Allah and His Apostle, when He calleth you to that which will give you life. And know that Allah cometh between a man and his heart, and that it is He to whom ye shall all be gathered'.

Almighty Allah also says: 'O ye who believe, what is the matter with you, that when ye are asked to go forth in the cause of Allah, ye cling so heavily to the earth! Do ye prefer the life of this world to the hereafter? But little is the comfort of this life, as compared with the hereafter. Unless ye go forth, He will punish you with a grievous penalty, and put others in your place; but Him ye would not harm in the least. For Allah hath power over all things'.

Almighty Allah also says: 'So lose no heart, nor fall into despair. For ye must gain mastery if ye are true in faith'.

PART II
EASTERN RELIGIOUS
PERSPECTIVES

Chapter 6

Buddhism and the Justification of War: A Case Study from Sri Lanka

Elizabeth J. Harris

Hatred is never appeased by hatred in this world; by non-hatred alone is hatred appeased. This is an eternal law. (Dhammapada v. 5)

All tremble at violence, all fear death. Putting oneself in the place of another, one should not kill nor cause another to kill. (Dhammapada v. 129)

A stereotypical view of Buddhism is that there is no place within it for the justification of war. In popular western consciousness, Buddhists, particularly robed members of the monastic community or *Sangha*, lead peace processions or look out at the world from the safe haven of solitary meditation, far from conflict. Immolate themselves, they might, in extreme circumstances, but not sanction the killing of other human beings.[1] The non-violent witness of His Holiness the Dalai Lama since the invasion of Tibet by China acts as a proof text for this view. However, predominantly Buddhist countries do have armies. Buddhists from Sri Lanka and Myanmar fought alongside Britain in World War II. The militarization of Japan in the middle years of the twentieth century did not draw much opposition from the country's Buddhists.[2] And, in more recent years, there has been a vocal Buddhist minority in Sri Lanka that has consistently advocated a military rather than a negotiated solution to the island's long-standing ethnic conflict.

Does Buddhism, therefore, contain within it a Just War theory? Can a set of conditions be found within text or tradition that might sanction the use of force and give guidance on how that force should be used? I shall explore these questions using voices from Sri Lanka's bitter internal conflict. First, I will look at what Buddhist apologists for war are forced to take into account: the normative, essentialist Buddhist critique of violence and war. Then I will describe the

---

1   During the Vietnam War, the venerable Buddhist monk Thich Quang Duc burned himself to death on 11 June 1963. On 16 May 1967, Nhat Chi Mai did the same outside a Buddhist nunnery in Vietnam. See Sallie B. King, 'They Who Burned Themselves for Peace: Quaker and Buddhist Self-Immolators during the Vietnam War', *Buddhist Christian Studies*, vol.20, 2000, pp.127-50.

2   P. Harvey, *An Introduction to Buddhist Ethics* (Cambridge: Cambridge University Press, 2000), p.283.

arguments used by those Buddhists who have supported war in Sri Lanka and ask whether these amount to a Just War theory. Lastly, I will take the words of Sri Lankan Buddhists who have opposed a military solution and will ask what comparative weight these have in the Sri Lankan context. An appendix will give a brief history of the Sri Lanka's ethnic conflict.

Violence Condemned: the Essentialist View

Buddhism is both a view and a path: a view of reality and a path of living. In all schools of Buddhism, the first essential step in the path is *sila*, morality. At the heart of *sila* is the undertaking not to harm any living beings, and this includes oneself. Linked with the twin virtues of loving kindness and compassion, it is an undertaking rooted in an empathetic ability to put oneself in the place of 'the other'. 'Does it harm others? Does it harm oneself? Does it harm both self and others?' are questions all Buddhists are encouraged to ask when deciding on a course of action.[3] If the answer to any of them is affirmative, the action is considered unwholesome (Pali *akusala*).

Perpetrating or sanctioning the violence of war harms both self and others according to Buddhist text and tradition. The harm done to others is obvious. Rare is the war that does not cause death and injury. The harm done to the perpetrators is linked with the Law of Action (Pali *Kamma*, Sanskrit *karma*), which holds that every action, and volition is also considered to be action, has a fruit (Pali *phala*) that will affect self and others. Wholesome action, that which is rooted in non-greed and non-hatred, or to give these words their positive spin – self-forgetting compassion, will give rise to positive fruit. Unwholesome action, that which is rooted in greed, hatred and illusion, can produce only the unwholesome for self and others.

In one Theravada canonical text, a warrior is seen to ask the Buddha whether he will go to a heaven if he is killed whilst fighting energetically in battle, an idea prevalent at the time, linked with the concept of duty, and developed in the Hindu *Bhagavad Gita*. The Buddha, when pressed, condemns the view.[4] A warrior, the Buddha explains, always has within his mind the wish to exterminate the other, in other words anger or hatred, and this can only lead downwards towards hell. Implicit in the text is that the concept of 'duty' cannot mitigate this. The fruit of

---

3   For instance, *Majjhima Nikaya*, I, 414-20 (trans. Oxford: Pali Text Society, 1994). This is a discourse in the Theravada Canon that shows the Buddha in conversation with Rahula. It contains this advice: 'If you, Rahula, are desirous of doing a deed with the body, you should reflect on that deed of your body, thus: "That deed which I am desirous of doing with the body is a deed of my body that might conduce to the harm of others and that might conduce to the harm of both; this deed of body is unskilled, its yield is anguish, its result is anguish"'.

4   E. Harris, *Violence and Disruption in Society: A Study of the Early Buddhist Texts*. The Wheel Publication, no. 392/3 (Kandy: Buddhist Publication Society, 1994), p.19: & Harvey, op cit., p.254.

hatred can be nothing other than negative, unwholesome, anguish-creating.[5] The concept of hatred (*dosa*), here, is key.

Hatred is one of the three 'unwholesome roots' in Buddhism, together with greed (*lobha*) and illusion (*moha*). In other words, it is one of the causes of humanity's dis-ease, its suffering, its spiritual blindness. Enlightenment, that perfect wisdom and perfect compassion which is the goal of the Buddhist path, is possible only when all three have been uprooted from the mind and the heart. To enter a situation fed by hatred, therefore, is to walk away from the goal of the Buddhist path. It is to be in the grip of the unwholesome, for self and society. That war is irrevocably linked with hatred lies at the centre of the essentialist view. In reinforcement of this, the *Vinaya* code of monastic discipline lays down that it is an offence for monks to go to see an army fighting or to stay with an army or even to watch war games. And the Mahayana *Brahmajala Sutra* states that one who has taken the Bodhisattva vow should not take part in war.[6]

Violence Endorsed: a Context-Dependent Morality

How do Buddhists who have supported war tackle this? Just War theories within Christianity have tended to focus on both context and content: in what circumstances war should be accepted as necessary; how war, if deemed necessary, should be carried out. Within this, the pacifist reading of Christian tradition – that one should love one's enemies and do good to those who persecute you – has played a part, as both influence and foil. The same pattern can be seen in Buddhism. The arguments that have been put forward in support of war have had to engage with the arguments against it. The main questions, therefore, that pro-war Buddhists have had to address are: under what conditions can the overwhelming emphasis on *ahimsa*, non-violence, in the Buddhist tradition be superseded or modified? How can such a supercession be justified?

In the Sri Lankan context, I have found three generic types of justification: appeal to a strand within text and tradition that would appear to modify the essentialist reading outlined above; use of utilitarian arguments concerning the greater good – a classical Just War approach; and a contesting of the basic premise that fighting in war must have negative kammic consequences linked with the existence of hatred. Let me illustrate this through an article written by a Sinhala Buddhist, Sarath Weerasekera, in October 2000 to justify the then ongoing war between the Sri Lankan military and the Liberation Tigers of Tamil Eelam (LTTE).[7]

The article was published in *The Island*, one of three major national English newspapers in Sri Lanka, and entitled, *Buddhist Stand on War and its Relevance to the Present Conflict*. Weerasekera begins with the essentialist Buddhist view,

5   *Samyutta Nikaya*, IV, 308-9.
6   Harvey, op cit., p.254.
7   S. Weerasekera, 'Buddhist Stand on War and its Relevance to the Present Conflict', *The Island*, 10 October 2000.

namely that Buddhism is totally opposed to war. He quotes the verse from the Dhammapada with which I have opened this paper (verse 5), and cites the first of the five precepts undertaken by most lay Buddhists, translated by him as, 'to abstain from taking life'. 'Thus we can imagine', he continues, 'how critical he (the Buddha) would have been of indiscriminate killings, deliberate violence and devastation of vegetation in war'. He then refers to the essentialist Buddhist view that war cannot take place without hatred and a mental desire to kill in both aggressor and victim. 'Hence in principle', he concludes, 'Buddhism is opposed to war'.

At this point, however, he changes track, asking:

> But what about the rulers who are drawn into conflict when threatened by aggression for the sole purpose of protecting their citizens? Is a father as the head and the protector of the family not justified in killing a person who has entered the house forcibly to harm the family members? In situations like the above, how far is it relevant or correct to compare the best courses of action with the teachings of the Buddha?

His response to this rhetorical question is reconstruction of the Buddhist tradition rather than a jettisoning of it as irrelevant to political realities. First of all, he appeals to context: one in which the Sinhala people are threatened by 'the most ruthless terrorist organization in the world'. Then, he goes back to the Theravada Buddhist Canon to draw on a textual strand very different from the one previously utilized, a strand that shows the Buddha in dialogue with the ruling powers of his day, the rival kingdoms of Kosala and Magadha. Three textual passages are invoked. All of them show the Buddha using military vocabulary, which, for the author, is in itself an endorsement of the need for a state not only to have an army but to use it in defence of the nation. One of his examples goes further than metaphor:

> King Kosol once approached Buddha and complained that his soldiers join the Order which had resulted in depletion of the army. Buddha immediately incorporated the rule in the formula of ordination that the candidate must not be in the army and, if so, must get the consent of the King to enter the Order.[8]

He continues:

> Buddhism is not very clear as to how far Buddhist principles of non-violence can be followed when it comes to protecting the weak and innocent against aggressors. Buddhism allows the validity of certain worldly necessities which may not be fully

---

8   One version of this story appears in the Mahavagga, part of the *Vinaya Pitaka*, the 'basket' of texts within the Theravada Canon that deals with the discipline of the monastic community. Some warriors within the army of King Bimbisara of Magadha desert and are ordained within the Buddha's community of monks. There is such anger amongst the King's staff about this that violence against the Order of monks is a possibility. King Bimbisara shares this with the Buddha and the Buddha declares ordaining any person who is in the King's service an offence (*Mahavagga*, I, 40).

compatible with the highest ideals of harmlessness and non-violence. The administration of justice itself implies punishment to the offender.

It is at this point that he tackles the classical Buddhist argument concerning hatred and war. Since members of the military are carrying out state duty, he argues, hatred need not be as dominant in the mind as if they were fighting from their own volition. Compassion for the country could even enter. As for the state, it has a primary duty to 'look into the welfare of the people and ensure freedom' so that all can work towards their own 'salvation'. He adds, 'non-violence in the face of violence is not a moral absolute in all circumstances'.

Last of all, he refers to the historical chronicles of Sri Lanka, particularly the narrative in the *Mahavamsa*, which, according to Weerasekera, speaks of Buddhism being saved from domination and destruction by Hindu Tamils from South India. A direct link is made with the present. He ends:

> Our country is in peril. The terrorists are destroying the Buddhist heritage in the North and East. The harmless farmers in the villages affected by terrorism are being massacred. ... In this state of affairs, as patriots, do we fight to eliminate terrorism or ... wait with folded arms allowing terrorists to rule the North and the East?

The following principles can be extracted from Weerasekera's argument:

- Buddhism encourages an ethic of non-violence;
- Non-violence, however, is not a moral absolute and can be overridden if the right conditions are present;
- Primary among these conditions is external aggression that threatens the nation, its religion, culture and identity;
- The proper authority for the use of violence is the State, which has a duty to protect its citizens from aggression;
- Members of the armed forces who act on orders from the State can avoid the fruits of warlike actions since they are acting out of duty and compassion for the country.

When applied to Sri Lanka as it was when Weerasekera penned his article, the argument is this. Both the Sinhala people and Buddhism itself are faced with the threat of annihilation at the hands of terrorists. In this situation, the State has a special responsibility to protect the Sinhala nation and the armed forces, a special duty to cooperate. This accepted, the moral absolute of non-violence encouraged by the Theravada Canon can be overriden, as it was in the Buddha's day. For, if it is not overriden and terrorism is not eradicated by armed force, Buddhism and the Sinhala people of the country could face destruction on an unprecedented scale, beginning with the weakest in society.

The three types of justification already outlined are clearly visible in the article. Their validity in the Sri Lankan context rests on two factors: whether Weerasekera is correct in his assertion there is a context-dependent element within the ethical teaching of the Theravada Canon that could give rise to a Just War argument; and whether, if he is correct, his analysis of the Sri Lankan context can bear the weight of scrutiny.

A Context-Dependent Buddhist Ethic

The Theravada Canon of Buddhism is vast, containing narrative, poetry, high philosophy, down-to-earth ethical teaching, proverbs and scholastic systematization. It is divided into three 'baskets' (*pitakas*). Of these, the *Sutta Pitaka* contains discourses given by the Buddha. Many of them are set in narrative context, which means that they become dialogues as well as 'sermons'. The Buddha is seen in conversation with ordinary members of the public and also with kings. He uses metaphors from everyday speech, metaphors that draw his listeners from the known to the new. Within this, images of violence are not avoided. Records of his conversations with the Kings of Kosala and Magadha reveal images from the worlds of war, punishment and political patronage.[9] Pasenadi, King of Kosala, for instance, emerges in the texts as someone torn between his duties as king, involving a certain amount of ruthlessness, and his concern for spiritual things.[10] At one moment he is seen preparing a sacrifice in which many animals are to be slaughtered and menials beaten and, at another, pondering seriously the dangers of wealth, power and evil conduct. When advising him, the Buddha is shown to meet him where he is. For instance, at one point, Pasenadi asks about the value of gifts and to whom a gift should be given for it to bear good fruit. The Buddha replies using words Weerasekera also quotes:

> A gift bears much fruit if given to a virtuous person, not to a vicious person. As to that, sire, I also will ask you a question. Answer it as you see fit. What think you, sire? Suppose that you were at war, and that the contending armies were being mustered. And there was to arrive a noble youth, untrained, unskilled, unpractised, undrilled, timid, affrighted, one who would run away – would you keep that man?[11]

Not only do such texts make use of military metaphors, they also show an extensive knowledge of the strategies of war and punishment. Graphic descriptions, for instance, are given of battle:

> And again, monks, when sense pleasures are the cause ... having taken sword and shield, having girded on bow and quiver, they leap on to the newly daubed ramparts, and arrows are hurled and knives are hurled and swords are flashing. Those who wound with arrows and wound with knives and pour boiling cow-dung over them and crush them with the portcullis and decapitate them with their swords, these suffer dying then and pain like unto dying.[12]

9   Harris, op cit., pp.4-9.
10 Ibid., p.4.
11 *Sumyutta Nikaya*, I, 97 (part I, para. 97).
12 *Majjhima Nikaya*, 13/1, 86-87 (Sutta 13, vol.1, paras 86-7).

In passages such as this, the State's right to maintain an army might appear to be accepted. That metaphors of war are used, however, does not of necessity mean that war is endorsed by the Buddhist texts or that Buddhism possesses a Just War theory. Mahayana Buddhists might present them as part of the Buddha's 'skilful means', in other words the Buddha's ability to adjust his teaching to meet the needs of his listener.[13] Theravada Buddhists might appeal to the necessity for 'gradual training', the need to draw the learner gradually along the path to truth, a theme present throughout the Canon.[14] And, it must not be forgotten that, in some cases, such imagery is judged 'unwholesome' within the passage itself, as in the case of the above description of war, where it is clearly stated that the violence is caused by 'sense pleasures', the craving for which is seen, within Buddhism, as one of ten fetters (*samyojana*) to liberation.

In a few passages, however, the Buddha is presented as directly addressing the question of war rather than simply utilizing imagery drawn from warfare to illustrate spiritual truth. Sarath Weerasekera refers to one important example when the Buddha seems to protect the armed forces by placing restrictions on those who might want to desert in order to follow him. Another such passage, one which has been much discussed in the context of Buddhism and War,[15] is found in the *Samyutta Nikaya* of the *Sutta Pitaka*.[16] Ajatasattu, a ruler of the Maghadan kingdom attacks the neighbouring kingdom of Kosala in an act of outright aggression. Pasenadi raises an army and defeats him. When told about this by some of his followers, the Buddha's response is this:

> Almsmen, the king of Magadha, Ajatasattu, son of the Accomplished Princess, is a friend to, an intimate of, mixed up with whatever is evil. The king, the Kosalan Pasenadi, is a friend to, an intimate of, mixed up with whatever is good.[17]

It is the aggressor, Ajatasattu, therefore, who is, at this point, condemned as evil. Pasenadi's role as defender of the nation against aggression seems to be linked with 'the good', although he also had mustered an army.[18] The story then

---

13 P. Williams, *Mahayana Buddhism: The Doctrinal Foundations* (London: Routledge, 1989), pp.143-50.

14 Harris, op cit., pp.37-8.

15 See Harris, op cit., pp.18-19; L. Schmithausan, 'Aspects of the Buddhist Attitude towards War', in J. Houben & K. Van Kooij (eds.), *Violence Denied: Violence, Non-Violence and the Rationalization of Violence in South Asian Cultural History* (Leiden, Boston & Köln: Brill, 1999), pp.50-51; Harvey, op cit., pp.250-51; & T. Bartholomeusz, *In Defense of Dharma: Just-war Ideology in Buddhist Sri Lanka* (London: Routledge Curzon, 2002), pp.49-50.

16 *Samyutta Nikaya*, I, 82-5.

17 Ibid., I, 82.

18 In my study, *Violence and Disruption in Society*, op cit., p.18, I wrote that these words of the Buddha accept Pasenadi's role as defender of the nation as 'necessary and praiseworthy'. I would not go as far as this now, having listened to the arguments of colleagues such as Peter Harvey (see, for instance, Harvey, op cit., p.251). But there can be no doubt that this passage avoids condemning Pasenadi's role in war, and links him with that which is good.

continues. In the next battle, Pasenadi is victor. He spares Ajatasattu his life but confiscates his entire army. Again news of this is brought to the Buddha. This time, the tone of his reply changes. There is no discrimination between Ajatasattu and Pasenadi; both are implicitly condemned:

> The slayer gets a slayer in his turn;
> The conqueror gets one who conquers him;
> The abuser wins abuse, the annoyer, fret.
> Thus by the evolution of the deed,
> A man who spoils is spoiled in his turn.[12]

This text does not glorify war or minimize the karmic consequences for the ruler who engages in it. But, in the Buddha's first response, the practical necessity for war in the face of unjustified aggression is not ruled out completely. It could even be argued that if Pasenadi had not, in victory, exacted such a severe penalty the final judgement on him might have been different. I would argue that this is the nearest one can come in the canonical heritage of Theravada Buddhism to a just war theory. The principles that emerge are:

- The higher principles of Buddhism condemn war;
- In some circumstances, war, authorized by the State, to defend a people against external aggression can be justified;
- War to take territory is not justified;
- In war, an ethic of compassion is desirable if the proliferation of war is to be stopped.

Texts such as these point to an empirical, context-dependent element in Buddhist ethics,[19] and I am not the only researcher to have noticed this. Steve Collins has suggested that 'two modes of dhamma' can be detected in the Theravada Canon, defined by the attitude taken towards violence. In the first the 'assessment of violence is context-dependent and negotiable'; in the second, an ethic of absolute values, the assessment is 'context-independent and non-negotiable'.[20] I believe he is right.

The question can still, however, be asked: is this emphasis on context central to Buddhist philosophy? What weight should the contextual be given as opposed to the absolute, the *a priori*? I would argue that context is important within Buddhism, but not to the extent that questions of principle thereby become utterly relative, locked within immediate conditions, untouched by the larger doctrinal picture. Buddhism approaches social phenomena through the doctrine of *paticca samuppada* or dependent origination. In other words, every phenomena is conditioned. Every phenomena has a cause, and if these causes are understood,

---

19 Harris, op cit., pp.10-11.
20 S. Collins, *Nirvana and other Buddhist Felicities: Utopias of the Pali Imaginaire* (Cambridge: Cambridge University Press, 1998), p.420, quoted in E. Harris, *What Buddhists Believe* (Oxford: Oneworld, 2001), pp.206-207.

understanding of the phenomena follows.   Moreover, these causes are to be identified through observation, through gathering empirical evidence.   One consequence of this is that generalizations, stereotypes and statements based on categories of pure reason are suspect, as are standpoints that use inappropriate categories through insufficient observation.[21]   There are a number of examples in the Theravada Canon of the Buddha challenging dogmatically held views with empirical evidence related to causal factors.[22]   His discussion with the warrior cited above is one example.   The *Esukari Sutta* would be another example.   Here, the Buddha is questioned about the role of the one who serves another.   His questioner expects a dogmatic answer: that service is good or that service is bad.   But this is refused.   It all depends on the conditions that are present, the Buddha explains. The crucial conditioning factor in this case is whether the one who serves is better for the service, more moral, wiser.   Moral good is the touchstone and this is not relative, but whether it is present depends on what is empirically observed.

However, this emphasis on conditionality has a sting in its tail.   Discrimination and discernment is needed if the empirical is to be evaluated correctly according to those principles that are not relative, and this is not won easily, according to Buddhist teaching.   Everyone can observe, but to observe is not the same as to 'see' clearly.   It is not the same as being awakened to what is 'the good', to what is linked to the twin Buddhist ideals of wisdom and compassion.

Opposition to War in Sri Lanka: Causal Analysis and the Danger of Clinging to Views

Buddhists who oppose war in Sri Lanka draw on a textual tradition much more consonant with what is generally considered normative for Buddhism.   They refuse, for example, to be drawn into the rhetoric of defending Sinhala identity or Sinhala Buddhism.[23]   Ven Professor Vajira, an influential Buddhist monk in the country, involved in inter-faith peace initiatives, put it this way in a newspaper interview:

> I think the Sangha must continue to play its historic role in guiding Sinhala society and all other communities in the country out of this *vipatha* (wrong way).   We have to help the Sinhalese get a correct understanding of their own history and of their place in the Sri Lankan community.   The Sangha, as an intellectual and inspirational community must enable the Sinhalese to rid themselves of *avijja* (ignorance) – of misconceptions that they are the superior race on the island and that other ethnic groups have to be

21 Harris, *Violence and Disruption in Society*, p.10.
22 See also the *Subha Sutta, Majjhima Nikaya*, 99/2, 197.
23 In this part of the chapter, I draw from two of my previous publications: 'Buddhism and War: A Study of Cause and Effect from Sri Lanka', *Culture and Religion*, vol.2, no.2, pp.197-222; and *What Buddhists Believe*, op cit.   The second brought together material first presented on radio in a BBC World Service series, *The Way of the Buddha*, which I wrote and presented in 1996.   The programme on socially engaged Buddhism included interviews with a number of Buddhist monks who had taken an anti-war stance.

subordinate. Even the insistence by some Sinhalese, both laity and bhikkhu, that Buddhism is superior to other religions is not the right behaviour. The Buddha himself treated all ethnic groups equally and did not condemn any religion.[24]

The points made in the following quotes, also from anti-war members of the Buddhist monastic community are similar:

> We come together not to represent the rights of one chosen nation, one race or one religion. We stand for the rights of all people without any distinctions. We love all people alike. We respect alike the teachings of all religions regarding human love and social justice. This is the Buddhist teaching and vision – the equality of all. (Ven. Uttarananda)[25]

> Buddhism does not make distinctions between people in terms of their ethnicity. Among the animal world and in nature, there are so many species, but Buddhism looks at people as one species and does not recognize ethnicity, caste or any other social division as a basis for conflict or discrimination. (Ven. Vavuniya Wimalasara)

> The solutions are crystal clear in Buddhism. The first step is to ask what caused the war in the North and East. Why did the young people take up arms? The same thing happened in the South. The key to the solution is rooted in this basic question. We must tackle the causes. Now that the conflict in the North and East has spread, we must apply the teachings of Buddhism and other religions as well. The basic message is that war is destructive and the people know this. It is the ordinary people who suffer in war and they want peace. So we must work for it. There is no alternative. (Ven. Delgalle Padumasiri)[26]

Key to all these perspectives are the following: references to *avijja*, ignorance; and analysis of cause. Both are taken from the heart of Buddhist philosophy and are used to challenge the pro-war lobby. The principles of the anti-war lobby, therefore, go something like this:

- The violence perpetrated in war is not consonant with the Buddha's teachings;
- The roots of violence lie in the mind and can be traced back to *avijja*, ignorance, the first cause of human suffering;
- In a conflict situation, resolution will only be possible if a rigorous analysis is made of the causes of the conflict and these causes are addressed.

24 Ven. Vajira, 'Sangha Must Guide Sinhalese on Path to Power Sharing', *Sunday Observer*, 23 May 1999, p.7.
25 Ven. H. Uttarananda Thera, 'Sinhala Buddhist Monks and the Rights of Tamils', *Dialogue*, vol.18, nos 1-3, p.7. Quoted also in Harris, 'Buddhism and War', p.208.
26 The words of Ven. Wimalasara and Ven. Padumasiri are taken from interviews the author did in Sri Lanka for *The Way of the Buddha* in 1995 (see note 23). Extracts were subsequently published in Harris, *What Buddhists Believe*, pp.112-14, & 'Buddhism and War', p.208.

   In analyzing the causes of the Sri Lankan ethnic conflict, those who have opposed war ask this basic question, 'Why did the Tamil youth take up arms in the 1970s to demand a separate state?' The answer they reach is very different from the pro-war lobby, which sees only betrayal and terrorism in the actions of the Tamil militants. For they cite the mistakes of the newly independent nation, Sri Lanka, and see the roots of Tamil militancy in them, and in the ongoing abuse of human rights by state forces. They are more likely to see one of the major causes of the conflict as the failure of the Sri Lankan Constitution to recognize the need of the Tamil people to have substantial control over their own affairs in the North and East of the country. For them, rigorous analysis of cause does not lead to justification of the militancy, but to an awareness of how it arose and how it could be defused. And, as I have shown, they go further than this by turning a Buddhist spotlight on the psyche of the Sinhala people. It is here, I believe, that the most effective critique of a Just War theory enters.

The Legendary Resurrected Tiger

The critique begins with the Buddhist view of consciousness and perception. There are six senses according to Buddhism, including the mind – what could be termed the 'subconscious' mind. Consciousness (*vinnana*) is conditioned by them. It arises as the senses interact with sense objects in the external and internal world, so that the Buddhist texts speak of six forms of consciousness: eye consciousness, ear consciousness and so on. Objective, pure, discriminating thought, therefore, is dependent on the health of the senses and this, according to Buddhism, is where the deepest problem lies. For, in the unenlightened person, the senses are 'programmed' to operate through greed, hatred and delusion, rooted in ignorance (*avijja*), unless the 'doors of the senses' are guarded closely. That, after all, is why Buddhists would say we are born – the ignorance present in our previous life was not uprooted.

   Avijja, ignorance or unknowing, is primarily linked in Buddhism with ignorance of the Four Noble Truths. It is ignorance also of the three marks of existence: unsatisfactoriness (*dukkha*), impermanence (*anicca*) and no-self (*anatta*). The person enslaved by ignorance assumes the impermanent to be permanent. She believes that health, wealth, prestige, youth and possessions will last, and that the most important task in life is to protect and promote the 'I'. With such a predisposition, the feeling (*vedana*) that results when the senses interact with sense objects produces craving (*tanha*), expressed through attraction or aversion, greed (*lobha*) and hatred (*dosa*). And it is this that, in turn, conditions thought.

   Buddhism does not then, on the above analysis, ask people to disregard the evidence of their senses and to submit to an external authority. The importance Buddhism places on the empirical has already been noted. It calls people to break their prison bonds by understanding and then transforming how their senses and their minds work.

To return to the process of perception, at the point when feeling conditions the conceptual process, a further element can enter, according to some Theravada texts: *papanca*, commonly translated as proliferation, the proliferation of concepts. It is a controversial term, but I would like to align myself with the pioneering exploration of it made by Nanananda thirty years ago.[27] Nanananda argues that *papanca* refers to a stage when the conceptual process runs riot, proliferates, hiding the true nature of things. Taking part of the *Madhupindika Sutta* (The Discourse on the Honey Ball),[28] he demonstrates that, at the point when perception and reasoning become *papanca*, deliberate choice vanishes and the perceiver becomes the victim of his or her own thought constructions:

> Like the legendary resurrected tiger which devoured the magician who restored it to life out of its skeletal bones, the concepts and linguistic conventions overwhelm the worldling who evolved them. At the final and crucial stage of sense perception, the concepts are, as it were, invested with an objective character.[29]

It is this mental moment that the anti-war Buddhists use, implicitly or explicitly, by calling those in favour of war to examine how their minds are working. To look at the process Nanananda outlines in more detail, the conventions of language enter the process of sense perception at the point where feeling gives rise to mental activity and concepts, as the consciousness attempts to place order on feeling through language.[30] This language immediately introduces the duality of subject and object. The 'I' enters, predetermined by the very nature of language. A feeling of aversion, therefore, becomes, 'I feel aversion'. What can happen after that, according to Nanananda, is that the structures of language take on a dynamism of their own. Concepts proliferate and leave the empirical behind, under the driving force of *tanha,* craving. Eventually, as the thought process develops further, what might appear to be reason in fact can cloak obsession, which can make the thinker, the victim. The very nature of language in the mind of one rooted in *avijja*, Nanananda argues, thus leads the perceiver further away from objectivity and discernment.

By way of illustration, a purely hypothetical progression from the observation, 'I feel aversion', one that I used in 1994, could be this:

> I am right to feel aversion. ... Therefore, the object is inherently worthy of aversion ... So, the object must threaten me and others ... Therefore the object must be annihilated ... I cannot survive unless the object is removed from my sphere of vision. ... It is my duty to annihilate this for my sake and the sake of others.[31]

27 B. Nanananda, *Concept and Reality in Early Buddhist Thought* (Kandy: Buddhist Publication Society, 1971).
28 *Majjhima Nikaya*, 18/1, 108-44.
29 Nanananda, op cit., p.6.
30 Harris, *Violence and Disruption in Society*, p.29.
31 Ibid., p.30.

In this progression, thought moves further and further away from what is empirically observed.

At one point in the *Madhupindika Sutta*, the fruit of *papanca* is linked with war.[32] The critique that Buddhists who oppose war in Sri Lanka direct to those who have supported it is that their thinking has become victim to the kind of process suggested by the term *papanca*. The clinging to an exclusive interpretation of nation, religion and language is one sign of this, they would say; the demonizing of the 'other' as terrorist or threat to identity, another. Both, they would say, are fuelled by the 'I' consciousness, personal or corporate, rather than objective analysis of cause. Both lead to patterns of response that can be none other than unwholesome.

In Conclusion

On the evidence of text and tradition, Buddhism does not condemn war in all circumstances. Buddhist ethics possesses a context-dependent element rooted in the importance it gives to the empirical. However, what it gives to a Just War theory with one hand, it takes away with another. For what Buddhism teaches about the nature of the mind and the arising of human dis-ease mounts a weighty critique of all justification of war. For, if a war is to be truly 'just' in Buddhism, those who take the decision to perpetrate war should be free of *avijja,* ignorance. They should have transcended the urge to relate all sense data to self, or by extension to their own group, ethnicity or nation. They should be able to discern quite clearly right view from wrong view and be able to stop any movement towards *papanca*, unwholesome proliferation of thought, before it begins. They should be utterly free of any tendency to construct a reality rooted in their greeds and hatreds. Only if these conditions are fulfilled can one be sure that a war is justified.

Buddhists who oppose war would argue that, in this round of birth and rebirth, these conditions cannot be met. Any decision to opt for war is a sign that *avijja* is present. It is a sign that the causes of conflict have not been adequately probed. Those who have opposed war in Sri Lanka, for instance, would argue that the causes of the conflict lie deep within the psyche of the Sinhala people and the errors of judgement they have made over the years. The solution, therefore, is not to meet militancy with militancy, violence with violence, but to analyze the causes of the conflict and to address them. And, as I write, there is hope that this is being done in the latest round of peace talks of December 2002.

The corollary of this is that only an enlightened person, a Buddha or an arahant, has the discernment to know if war can be just. And we are back to the question those who support war ask: Did the Buddha ever justify war or were his references

---

32 *Majjhima Nikaya,* 18/1, 113: where the clinging that leads to *papanca* is absent, 'this is itself an end of taking of the stick, of taking a weapon, of quarrelling, contending, disputing'.

to war in his recorded teaching simply part of his 'skilful means' to lead his listeners beyond the material towards spiritual truth?

Appendix to Chapter 6: Background to the Situation in Sri Lanka[33]

Sri Lanka is the home of four religions and three main ethnic groups. Buddhists form 69 percent of the population. Hindus rank second at about 15 percent. Then come Christians and Muslims, each about seven to eight percent of the population. The Buddhists are mainly Sinhala and the Hindus, Tamils. Christians stretch across both major ethnic groupings. The Muslims are best seen as a separate ethnic group, although many speak Tamil.

The Sinhala people are the majority in the south and central areas, although in the central hill country there is a sizeable number of 'Indian' Tamils, who travelled from India during the nineteenth century to work on the coffee and tea plantations. The Tamils are a majority in the north of the country and in some eastern parts, although the war has increased the number of Tamils in Colombo, the capital.

In the run up to independence in 1948, there were some who realized that a major issue in any independent Sri Lanka would be adequate representation for the minorities in the new centralized government. As early as 1938, the Tamil politician, G.G. Ponnambalam suggested that, in a proposed new legislature, 50 percent of the seats should be set aside for minorities and 50 percent for the Sinhala people. The Sinhala greeted this proposal with great derision. But ethnic politics did not go away. In the 1940s, several ethnically-based parties were formed, for example the All Ceylon Tamil Congress, the Sinhala Maha Sabha.

At independence in 1948, a cabinet containing both Sinhala and Tamil politicians was possible primarily because the Soulbury Constitution, which determined parliamentary structure, contained a section that protected minority communities from discrimination. But this did not satisfy all. In the 1950s, a Sinhala nationalism that demanded recognition of Sinhala culture, language and religion grew in the South. In some ways, it was an understandable protest against the post-colonial hegemony of English and western culture. After all, most parliamentarians, Sinhala and Tamil, were of the English-educated elite. But it had a disastrous effect on communal relations.

In 1956, there was a massive parliamentary victory for a Sinhala-dominated party that appealed to this Sinhala nationalism. One of its first acts was to make Sinhala the national language, linguistically crippling the 25 percent of the population that was Tamil-speaking and thus violating the Soulbury Constitution.

33 This is an updated version of an Appendix that first appeared in: Elizabeth Harris (ed.), 1999, *Sri Lanka: Making Peace Possible* (London: Churches Together in Britain and Ireland, 1998), pp.35-8. Much else has been written about Sri Lanka's ethnic conflict. Among the most useful works are: K.M. De Silva, *Reaping the Whirlwind: Ethnic Conflict, Ethnic Politics in Sri Lanka* (Delhi: Penguin, 1998); R. Gunaratne, *Sri Lanka's Ethnic Crisis and National Security* (Colombo: South Asian Network on Conflict Research, 1998); K. Rupasinghe (ed.), *Negotiating Peace in Sri Lanka: Efforts, Failures and Lessons* (London: International Alert, 1998); & S.J. Tambiah, *Buddhism Betrayed? Religion, Politics, and Violence in Sri Lanka* (Chicago: University of Chicago Press, 1992). A remarkable novel that charts Sri Lanka's twentieth century history through the eyes of the Tamil people is: A. Sivanandan, *When Memory Dies* (London: Arcadia Books, 1997).

Owing to the majoritarian nature of Sri Lanka's democracy, the Tamil voice in parliament had no power. Civil disobedience was tried but to no avail. Good lobbying of Sinhala leaders, however, led, in 1957 and 1966, to political pacts that would have granted limited devolution to the North and East. But neither saw the light of day. Pressure from opposition parties and the Buddhist monastic Sangha meant that both were torn up. Other pieces of legislation followed that the Tamil community saw as discriminatory.

Until 1970, the Tamil protest was constitutional, pressing eventually for devolution of power to the North and East along federal lines. This protest achieved little and it was this failure of peaceful methods that created Tamil youth militancy – the emergence of groups that aimed for a separate state in the North and East. This began in the early 1970s and soon conflict with the armed forces began. In 1979, a fairly draconian Prevention of Terrorism Act was passed. In July 1983, an ambush by Tamil militants killed thirteen soldiers in the North. This triggered a horrific wave of anti-Tamil violence in the South. Thousands of Tamils lost all they owned. Many left the island for the West, thus internationalizing the issue. In the years that followed the violence intensified with Sinhala, Tamil and Muslim civilian deaths. One Tamil group became dominant by weakening its rivals – the Liberation Tigers of Tamil Eelam (LTTE).

Since 1983, there have been three waves of war, each more devastating than the last. The first was from 1983 to 1990. The peace talks that ended it broke down. The second lasted from 1990 to 1994. During this time the LTTE ran a de facto state in the North. When, in 1994, there was a new government in the South, talks recommenced. But again they broke down. The third wave lasted until 2001. With another change of government in 2001, a unilateral ceasefire announced by the LTTE was reciprocated by the government. This lead to An Agreement on a Ceasefire, signed on 22 February 2002 by the Government of the Socialist Democratic Republic of Sri Lanka and the Liberation Tigers of Tamil Eelam, facilitated by Norway. A Sri Lanka Monitoring Mission was established to monitor violations of the Agreement. The first round of formal peace talks were held in Thailand from 16-18 September, 2002. Two further rounds have been held, with considerable success. As I submit this chapter, there is cautious hope in Sri Lanka, at least amongst those who have opposed war, that over two decades of civil war can be ended through a Federal Constitution that will give regional autonomy to the North and East. There are some voices on both sides that are speaking of a sell-out, but the hope of the majority is that they will be marginalized.

Chapter 7

Pain but not Harm: Some Classical Resources Toward a Hindu Just War Theory[1]

Francis X. Clooney S.J.

My intention in these pages is to further our understanding of just war theory in the Hindu context by reviewing debates about killing in the sacrificial context, the requirement of kings to exercise force, and the quest for an interiorized, non-violent apprehension of reality. I will consider the justification of violence from the perspective of the brahmin as both sacrificial practitioner and sacrificial theorist, and in light of the duties of the king as interpreted by theorists who argue that the use of force, and so the causing of pain, can be obligatory. While reflection on the royal exercise of power is more directly relevant to the formulation of theories about just wars, reflection on sacrificial violence and the brahminical justification of it within a wider context of nonviolence most clearly elucidates the categories and calculations making sense of reflection on royal power. I will not be suggesting that there is an exact Hindu parallel to just war theory as developed in the Christian mediaeval period and modern West, but only that there has been serious and relevant reflection on violence and the choice to be violent or nonviolent – and thus the foundations for a just war theory.

It is necessary to distinguish two meanings of 'violence' (*himsa*), a word that will not appear frequently in the following pages. Violence can be an exertion of force which causes pain (with killing as an extreme but not uncommon outcome); this differs from violence as an exertion of force which aims at harming an other who is designated one's enemy, out of motives of cruelty, anger, hatred, etc. Pain (as physically and psychologically undesirable) is suffering, to be sure, but it need not be harmful (as spiritually detrimental), nor need harming another be the intention of a person exerting force and causing pain; such a person may be genuinely reluctant, and acting thus only in order to fulfill a duty or achieve a higher goal which includes even the longer term good of the person(s) hurt. In what follows I will use 'pain' and 'causing pain' to indicate 'physical action

---

1 Portions of this chapter were presented at the International Conference on Religion and Violence held at Boston College in June 2000, and published as 'Violence and Nonviolence in the Hindu Religious Tradition' in *Contagion*, vol.9, 2002. Here the focus has shifted to the calculation of when violence is warranted.

causing pain to some living being', whereas 'harm' and 'intending harm' indicate acts generated due to cruelty, anger, hatred, etc., and aimed at doing damage to a hated other.

Intending harm is always condemned, but causing pain can and indeed must occur in certain situations. Thus 'nonviolence' (*ahimsa*) is both 'not causing pain' and also 'not intending harm'. It is always commendable to refuse to exert force in order to harm, but a general prohibition against causing pain remains subject to exceptions. Thus, in the most general terms, one can predict that no war motivated by base motives and energized by malice toward the other, who is to be harmed, can be justified. But some wars may be justified and even required, since the exertion of force causes pain but does not intend harm, and is governed by just concerns. It will also appear in what follows that causing pain is not a universal option; it is a duty reserved to brahmins (in sacrificial) and kings (in governing).[2]

Causing Pain and Animal Sacrifice

The primary starting point and perhaps earliest documented context in which causing pain is debated is the Vedic sacrificial context. From before 1200 BCE killing animals had been both an expected practice and a problem, already subject to practical critique by opponents of the bloodiness of Vedic sacrifice. Fundamental Hindu attitudes toward the causing of pain were worked out in discussions of the fate of sacrificial animals. Even in older Vedic hymns, killing animals is treated as peripheral to the primary and proper event, the performance of sacrifices which (happen to) use animal parts as an offering. In the Vedic sacrifices the focus is not on the killing of the animal itself; what matters is that there are animal parts available for use in offerings. The offering of animal parts is common, but the actual killing takes place outside the sanctified sacrificial arena.[3]

By attention to primary sacrificial language and second-order argumentation about sacrifices, one can trace ambivalences and compromises in Hindu religious thinking and practical reflection: a shift from the 'ordinary' killing of animals to limited sacrificial killing, to a complete cessation of killing even in sacrificial contexts, and consequently, to a transformation of the performer into a 'non-sacrificing person'. Harm is rejected and causing pain restricted, until finally and ideally causing pain is eliminated. (This transformation is also manifest, socially, in the later emergence of temple rituals in which animal sacrifice is exceedingly rare.)

---

2   On pain in the Indian context, see A. Glucklich, *Sacred Pain: Hurting the Body for the Sake of the Soul* (New York: Oxford University Press, 2001). For a comprehensive introduction to *ahimsa*, see C. Chapple, *Nonviolence to Animals, Earth, and Self in Asian Thought* (Albany: State University of New York Press, 1993).

3   On the changing attitudes toward sacrificial killing, see H. Schmidt, 'The Origin of Ahimsa', *Melanges d'Indianisme*, (Paris: Editions E. de Bocard, 1968), pp.625-55. On the related issue of beef-eating and the treatment of cows, see D.N. Jha, *The Myth of the Holy Cow* (New York: Verso, 2002).

Even when killing was still imperative, there was an acute awareness of the problems entailed. Thus we find instructions for sacrifice in the *Rg Veda* (before 1000 BCE) which conclude with an appeal to the horse to see the value of the pain inflicted on it:

> Let not your precious body grieve you, who are truly going (to the gods). Do not let the axe linger in your body. Do not let the greedy and unskillful immolator miss the members and mangle your limbs needlessly with his knife. Truly, at this moment you do not die, nor are you harmed. For you go by auspicious paths to the gods. The horses of lord Indra, steeds of the wind gods, shall be yoked (to their cars); a courser shall be placed in the shaft of the ass of the Twins (to bear you to heaven).[4]

There is uneasiness about causing pain, a recognition of its 'irreligious' nature, while at the same time room is left for causing pain as religiously obligatory.[5]

Implied by this sacrificial justification of certain acts of causing pain – but not harm, since heaven, and not death, is the outcome – is a broader prohibition of other acts causing pain and all acts intending harm (that is, 'death' without 'heaven'). The presumption seems to be that sacrificial pain was permitted while acts of harm were universally prohibited – at least, as will be clearer below, for brahmins. (The impulse of this wider prohibition as an internalization of conflict will be touched on toward the end of this chapter.) There is, however, no explicit indication that concerns about sacrificial pain and the exclusion of the intention to harm was imagined as more broadly applicable to debates about warfare or the legitimation of violence in ordinary life. Or rather, texts in which not only harm is rejected (such as the *Bhagavad Gita*, to which we will return below), but even too the causing of pain (such as the Buddhist *Kutandanta Sutta*), did not represent the mainstream of reflection on royal obligations. We shall return to this issue below.

It is not possible here to explore the religious and social transformations that occurred in subsequent centuries, after the primary Vedic period, but a pair of particular debates, in Mimamsa sacrificial theory and Vedanta theology, are worth noting. Centuries later theological exegesis and analysis in the Mimamsa and Vedanta schools aimed at a narrowly-argued rule-based analysis of intention in

---

4   *Rg Veda*, I.162.18-21. Slightly adapted from the old translation, *Rig-Veda Sanhita*, by H.H. Wilson (New Delhi: Cosmo Publications, 1977 (originally published in 1854)), vol.2, pp.119-20.

5   The same strategy is seen in the *Satapatha Brahmana* (before 900 BCE), where we find this indication of the desire to pacify the animal to be sacrificed: 'Next the Agnidh priest takes a (new) firebrand and walks in front. Thus he places Agni in front, thinking, "Agni shall repel the evil spirits in front!" and they lead the victim after him (to the slaughtering place) on a path free from danger and injury ... Regarding this some say, "That victim must not be held onto by the sacrificer, for they lead it unto death; therefore let him not hold on to it". But let him nevertheless hold on to it, since the victim which they lead to the sacrifice they do not lead to death'. (3.8.1.9-10) Slightly adapted from Julius Eggeling trans., *The Satapatha-Brahmana: According to the Text of the Madhyandina School* (New Delhi: Motilal Banarsidass, 1978 (originally published in 1885)), vol.2, pp.187-88.

assessing actions and results; the effect was to exclude acts intending to harm the other. Mimamsa theorists (from 200 BCE and thereafter) were renowned for their close exegesis of sacrificial texts and sacrificial activities. The key Mimamsa discussion of the justification of causing pain as long as one does not intend harm is found in the commentaries on the *Mimamsa Sutras* of Jaimini (c. 2nd century BCE). In commenting on the notion of *dharma* (moral, religious, social, cosmic rightness) as related to injunctive force mentioned at the beginning of the *Sutras* (in I.1.2), Sabara (c. 2nd century CE) asks whether sacrifices intending harm to enemies can be justified as in keeping with righteousness, simply because such sacrifices are mentioned in the Veda.

Sabara analyzed justifications for pain and harm, when he had occasion to exegete a problematic Vedic injunction, 'Let a person intending harm perform the Syena sacrifice', i.e. an 'eagle sacrifice' aimed at harming one's enemies. While this is not a required sacrifice and may be ignored by potential sacrificers without fault, it is mentioned and so seems appropriately counted among legitimate sacrifices. Because enjoined, the Syena should be counted in keeping with *dharma*; but its result is intentional harm, so it also seems wrong actually to perform the sacrifice. Sabara's decision is that the initial qualification of the agent – a person intending harm – excludes persons committed to righteousness, and so delegitimizes the Syena sacrifice by ruling out the possibility that any just person would actually opt to undertake it. The sacrifice is legitimate, but because it requires a person intending to harm others, there is never anyone available to perform the sacrifice legitimately.

Kumarila's comment in his *Slokavartika* (8th century) on the Sabara's passage extends for about 70 verses (*vartikas*).[6] Kumarila sorts out the complex issues raised by Sabara and, as this summary of his views shows, highlights points of great interest:

> Acts causing pain which have the sanction of scripture are not wrong, while it is always wrong for an agent of action to intend harm, since such an agent is misguided and spoiled by his evil motivations, and so the sanctioned action never has an authorized agent;

These distinctions require Kumarila to interpret the Syena sacrifice rather subtly, since one can confuse the Vedic authorization of the sacrifice with a further, unwarranted approval of becoming an agent who intends harm. Accordingly,

> the Syena sacrifice is evil because of its intention to harm. The core scriptural – 'Let a person intending harm perform the Syena sacrifice' – remains intact, so the Syena is indeed sanctioned; but insofar as the agent intends harm, he or she is always ruled unjustified in actually choosing to perform that sacrifice. It is an injunction of which there is no justifiable implementation.

6   *Slokavartika*, vartikas 201-76 under sutra I.1.2.   For a reliable translation, see Ganganatha Jha, *Slokavartika with (reference to) the Commentaries 'Kasika' and 'Nyayaratnakar'* (Delhi: Sri Satguru Publications, 1983).

By a peculiar but effective compromise, then, the Syena sacrifice was sanctioned as a legitimate sacrificial action, but also permanently prohibited, since normatively there is no performer who could justly operate with the requisite intention to harm others. The authority of the Veda is intact, but a 'real world' prohibition again harming others in facts vetoes the implementation of the optional Syena sacrifice.

Two subordinate discussions in Kumarila's comment are also relevant. First, he argues that a calculation of pain and pleasure is insufficient for determining right and wrong. That one wants to harm another, and might profit from that harm, does not justify acting in a harmful way. Likewise, of course, disgust toward the killing involved in sacrifice, such as would lead to its non-performance, is not allowed to become determinative, since causing pain is required when it is clearly enjoined. Factors such as pain, pleasure, and disgust vary, and one cannot depend on them in deciding what is right and wrong; right action must be decided in accord with the Veda alone, and to the exclusion of personal motivations. Second, a passing objection in Kumarila's text proposes that it is clear from the Veda itself – 'Do not enact himsa [pain, harm] toward any being'[7] – that killing is inherently wrong and always prohibited; if so, other Vedic passages cannot be used to justify sacrificial killing, since 'scripture neither adds to nor subtracts from the capacities of substances and actions'.[8] Kumarila rejects this line of reasoning, arguing that there is no natural, general validation or prohibition of actions. They are always to be explained and specified in terms of particular performers considering them under particular circumstances. The Veda provides the required specification which justifies sacrificial actions causing pain, while ruling out all actions intended to harm.

Vedanta theology is a subsequent (from 500 CE and thereafter) influential grouping of theological schools which inherit much from Mimamsa but widen the category of texts, acts, and objects of knowledge to be interpreted. Most particularly, in Vedanta emphasis was placed on an eternal self (*atman*) which could neither intend nor suffer either pain or harm. Most Vedanta thinkers had no problem with the legitimation of sacrificial pain as described above, while embracing the refusal to intend harm as a standard, requisite virtue in the life of the truth-seeker and renunciant. But because of their concern to maintain the authority of scripture, they extended the Mimamsa reflection on the problem of the sanctioned causing of pain. Sankara (8th century) puts the negative and positive positions this way, in his comment on *Uttara Mimamsa Sutra* 3.1.25.

It has been argued, 'Sacrificial actions are impure insofar as they are connected with animal-killing, etc. Therefore their results can be inferred to be evil'. But this is incorrect, since knowledge of what is religiously right (*dharma*) and religiously not-right (*adharma*) is derived from scripture, which alone is the source of knowing that one act is right, while another is religiously not-right.

7 A prohibition that seems to be a general, pervasive caution rather than an explicit command.
8 See vartikas 249-54.

Both the religiously right and the religiously not-right are beyond sense-knowledge, and they are not invariable for all places, times, and occasions. A deed that is performed as religiously right in relation to one place, time, and occasion, may become religiously not-right in relation to other times, places, and occasions.

Since no one can have knowledge about religiously right and religiously not-right unless it be from scripture, and since from scripture it is certain that the Jyotistoma sacrifice, which involves pain as well as favor, etc., is religiously right, how could it be declared impure? But scripture also says, 'Do not enact himsa toward any being', and thus shows that pain caused to any creature is impure. True, but that is only a general rule, and there is an exception, 'One should immolate an animal for Agni and Soma'. Both the general rule and the exceptions have a well-defined scope. Hence, the Vedic rites are quite pure. Moreover, they are practiced by good people and are not condemned by them.[9]

This complex analysis again affirms a distinction between killing in the sacrificial context, where it is required, and killing outside it, where it is forbidden. Sacrificial violence is justified simply because it is required by the Veda, whereas killing for mundane goals is *always* forbidden. As in Mimamsa, in Vedanta too there is no attempt to justify or rule out killing on universal ethical grounds; causing pain is simply assumed to be generally forbidden, whereas the possibility of a stricter and limited Vedic permission/obligation to cause pain is at issue. Whatever one's intent and whatever the effect might promise to be, if the causing of pain is enjoined, it is justified; if it is not enjoined, it is always prohibited. The presumption is that both intending harm and causing pain are ruled out, except when explicitly enjoined. But the calculus remains, as in Mimamsa, a matter of balancing competing rules which govern general principles and specific exceptions.

Kings and the Causing of Pain in the Life of the State

The situation and calculation are different when we turn to writings about the duties of rulers, who are not brahmins but of the second, ksatriya, caste (religious class). To kings is entrusted the obligation of the 'stick' (*danda*), to uphold righteousness by the use of force, and thus it is their duty on occasion to cause pain. It is assumed that kings must exercise force when it is necessary to maintain or restore order. Here the calculation has to do with necessary force and proportionate response. The ideal of a king who entirely forswears causing pain is

---

9   The basic Vedanta text, the *Uttara Mimamsa Sutras* (more commonly known as the Brahma or Vedanta Sutras) is a very laconic set of about 450 short verses, sutras. It is necessarily read with commentaries. I have used the translation by Swami Gambhirananda: *Brahma-Sutra Bhashya of Sankaracarya* (Calcutta: Advaita Ashrama, 1983), pp. 85-586, slightly adapted.

rarely introduced, given the realistic obligations binding kings. Let us consider some standard portrayals of the duties of kings in this regard.

The *Laws of Manu* (first century CE) is a highly influential text which establishes norms for proper living, as seen and shaped from the brahminical viewpoint. Brahmins are urged to a life of purity and focus on learning and meditation. The lower castes were thought to have no right to cause pain, either in the sacrificial context where it is generally reserved for the upper classes (brahmin and ksatriya) or in ordinary life, where violent actions are punishable as criminal or as an unwarranted assumption by a citizen of royal power. *Manu* notes instances where the causing of pain may be necessary, even in a society where pain should be lessened, the number of agents authorized to cause pain severely minimalized, and the intention to harm excluded. Kings are reminded of their duty to protect the kingdom and the right order of society. They were admonished to cause pain when punishment is necessary, even while they should also be ruling in such a way that causing pain is not needed. In all cases, the intention to harm is ruled out. Thus,

> For the king's sake the Lord in ancient times emitted the Rod (*danda*) of Punishment, his own son, (the incarnation of) Justice, to be the protector of all living beings, made of the brilliant energy of ultimate reality. Through fear of him all living beings, stationary and moving, allow themselves to be used and do not swerve from their own duty. Upon men who persist in behaving unjustly he should inflict the punishment they deserve, taking into consideration realistically (the offender's) power and learning and the time and place ... Properly wielded, with due consideration, (the rod) makes all the subjects happy; but inflicted without due consideration, it destroys everything. If the king did not tirelessly inflict punishment on those who should be punished, the stronger would roast the weaker like fish on a spit ... A king who inflicts punishment correctly thrives on the triple path, but if he is lustful, partial, and mean, he is destroyed by that very punishment.[10]

Just as brahmins were actually obliged to cause pain in a sacrificial context even though in general actions causing pain are to be avoided, here too causing pain is conceded a due place in the exercise of royal power; indeed, exerting force and causing pain lessens the overall amount of pain in the long run, and also prevents those intending harm from acting out their evil intentions.

Kautilya's *Arthasastra* (150 CE) is a manual of guidance related to governance aimed at ksatriyas and kings. It emphasizes that the exercise of force/causing pain is a right and duty reserved to kings:

> The pursuit of (the people's) welfare as well as the maintenance of the philosophic tradition, the Vedas and the economic well-being (the society) are dependent on the scepter wielded by the king. The maintenance of law and order by the use of punishment is the science of government. By maintaining order, the king can preserve what he already has, acquire new possessions, augment his wealth and power, and share

---

10 VII.14-16, 19-20, 27, in W. Doniger and B. Smith trans, *The Laws of Manu* (New York: Penguin Books, 1991). Their introduction, notes, and indices, are particularly helpful in sorting out Manu's views on violence and nonviolence.

the benefits of improvement with those worthy of such gifts. The progress of this world depends on the maintenance of order and (proper functioning of) government.

Force is a last resort:

Some teachers say, 'Those who seek to maintain order shall always hold ready the threat of punishment. For there is no better instrument of control than coercion'. But Kautilya disagrees for (the following reasons). A severe king (meting out unjust punishment) is hated by the people he terrorizes while one who is too lenient is held in contempt by his own people. Whoever imposes just and deserved punishment is respected and honored. A well-considered and just punishment makes the people devoted to *dharma*, *artha* and *kama* (righteousness, wealth, and enjoyment).

Unjust punishment, whether awarded in greed, anger or ignorance, excites the fury of even (those who have renounced all worldly attachments like) forest recluses and ascetics, not to speak of householders.

When (conversely) no punishment is awarded (through misplaced leniency and no law prevails), then there is only the law of the fish. Unprotected, the small fish will be swallowed up by the big fish. In the presence of a king maintaining just law, the weak can resist the powerful.[11]

Kautilya expresses no hesitation about warfare; one of the duties of the king is to defend the kingdom even by pre-emptive conflict if this is needed, and so the latter part of the *Arthasastra* is a full-scale analysis of ways to deal with the external enemies of the state.

Early Tamil-language literature shows a similar concern to balance the eschewal of pain and harm while yet also respecting the role of the king who exercises authority and keeps the kingdom in order, even by heroism in battle. These two poems from the *Tirukkural* (c. 2nd century CE), even today perhaps the most widely popular classic in Tamil, illustrate the views common in ancient south India. The first warns against killing:

The sum of virtue is not to kill, all sin comes from killing.
The first of virtues in every creed is to share your food and cherish all life.
The unique virtue is non-killing; not lying comes next.
Right conduct may be defined as the creed of not killing.
Ascetics fear rebirth and renounce the world: how much better to fear murder and renounce killing!
Death that eats up all shall not prevail against the non-killer.
Even at the cost of one's own life one should avoid killing.
However great its gains, the wise despise the profits of slaughter.
Professional killers are vile to the discerning.
A diseased, poor and low life, they say, comes of killing in the past.

By contrast, the second reminds the king of his duty to use force when necessary:

11 1.43-15, in *The Arthasastra*, trans. L.N. Rangarajan (New York: Penguin Books, 1987).

Searching inquiry, an impartial eye, punishment as prescribed are the ways of justice.
The world looks up to heaven for rain and his subjects to their king for justice.
The king's scepter provides the base for scripture and right conduct.
The king who rules cherishing his people has the world at his feet.
The king who rules according to the law never lacks rain and corn.
Not his spear but a straight scepter is what gives a monarch his triumph.

This second poem ends by emphasizing the balance that must be maintained:

The king guards the land, and his own rule will guard him if he is straight.
A king inaccessible, unprobing and unjust will sink and be ruined.
For a king who would guard and cherish his people to punish crimes is a duty, not defect.
The king who punishes wicked men with death is a farmer weeding the tender crops. [12]

Further verses in the *Tirukkural* explore righteous rule, the damage that unjust kings can do, the importance of good defensive measures, the importance of valour and courtesy in war, etc. On the whole, it sees causing pain as necessary, though rare in the kingdom of a just and wise king.[13]

Both brahmins and ksatriyas are therefore justified in their exercise of force. Animals should not ordinarily be killed, but must be killed in certain sacrifices; people should not be subjected to pain, but in some cases causing such pain is a royal duty. Both brahmins and kings would, in fact, be criticized were they not willing to cause pain on such occasions. It is generally not stated but understood that no one else is eligible to cause pain: no woman, and no one in the lower religious classes, the vaisyas, sudras, and outcastes.

The preceding theory can be exemplified with reference to the *Mahabharata* and *Ramayana*, the warrior epics in which the values and dangers of the ksatriya ideal are explored in the course of narratives of wars and the events leading to them. It is here perhaps that we see the emerging 'Hindu just war theory' most clearly.

The twelfth book of the *Mahabharata* famously exemplifies the tension between the ideal commitment to not intending harm and a sober acknowledgment of the inescapability of causing pain in some circumstances. As James Fitzgerald has pointed out, it is a prolonged argument in favour of the just war.[14] Yudhisthira, the eldest and leading prince among the five brothers who have been wrongly deprived of their kingdom and are approaching the moment of fighting to get it back, expresses horror at causing pain in war and is hesitant right up to the time of

---

12 Tiruvalluvar, *The Kural*, trans. P.S. Sundaram (New York: Penguin Books, 1990).

13 See Clooney op cit., for my comments on violence and its complex resolution in another Tamil work of literature, the *Cilappatikaram*.

14 In the introduction to his translation of Book 12 of the *Mahabharata* (University of Chicago Press, forthcoming). I am grateful to Professor Fitzgerald for lending me the unpublished text and allowing me to quote from the translation below. See also Chapple, op cit., chapter 4, 'Otherness and Violence in the *Mahabharata*'.

battle as to whether he should go to war. Before the battle can begin, he must be persuaded that causing pain is justified in this situation. In 12.96, Yudhisthira asks how warfare, even waged by one warrior (ksatriya) against another, can be justified. He discusses the matter at length with his revered uncle and advisor Bhisma. The latter replies first of all that a peaceful settlement with one's enemies, even after invading their country, is preferable to causing pain. Nonetheless, when one encounters a worthy ksatriya opponent, fighting may ensue. This causing of pain is moderated by specific guidelines:

> One should not attack chariots with cavalry; chariot warriors should attack chariots. One should not assail someone in distress, neither to scare him nor to defeat him. There should be no arrows smeared with poison, nor any barbed arrows – these are weapons of evil people. War should be waged for the sake of conquest; one should not be enraged toward an enemy who is not trying to kill him. If, upon an outbreak of hostilities among strictly righteous people, a righteous man gets into trouble on the battlefield, then one who is wounded should not be attacked in any way, nor one who has no son, one whose sword is broken, one whose horse has been destroyed, one whose bow-string has been cut, nor one whose vehicle has been destroyed. One wounded should be given medical treatment in your realm; or he may even be sent to his own home. One not wounded should be released – this is the everlasting Law. ... Therefore Manu son of the Self-Existent said that war must be waged according to Law.

Not convinced, Yudhistra continues (in 12.98) to object, and Bhisma insists on the virtue of just warfare:

> By restraining the wicked and encouraging the virtuous, and by rites of sacrificial worship and giving gifts, kings become pure and free of taint. Kings trouble their people when they seek conquest, but after they have won the victory they make their subjects thrive once again. They drive their evil deeds away through the power of gifts, sacrifices, and asceticism. Their merit increases through their kindness to their subjects. Just as the reaper of a field kills the weeds and the grain at the time he mows the field, but does not get rid of the grain; so, kings slay those they want to kill at the time they shoot their sharp-bladed weapons, and the entire atonement for that is the king's making the inhabitants flourish once again. The king who guards his subjects from the plunder of their wealth, from slaughter, from affliction by barbarians, he, because he gives life, is truly a king bestowing wealth and happiness. Worshiping with all the rites of sacrifice, giving safety as the present to the priests, that king will experience blessings and reach the same heavenly world as Indra.

A righteous cause can be justly pursued to its conclusion, no matter how much pain is entailed. If Yudhisthira can connect the upcoming battle with the support of the traditional values articulated by the brahmins, then he can and must fight the battle.

If Yudhisthira exemplifies for us the wise king who finally undertakes a just war, then Ravana, the demon king and villain of the *Ramayana*, exemplifies the flawed decision-making and psychological blindness that lead to an unjust war. When the *Yuddha Kanda* (Book of War) of the *Ramayana* begins, good prince Rama is on the Indian mainland opposite Sri Lanka, where Ravana is holding

Rama's wife Sita in captivity. Rama, assured of the justice of his cause, is about to invade Sri Lanka in order to defeat Ravana and win her back. Ravana by contrast exemplifies perfectly the ruler contemplating a quintessentially unjust war. At the beginning of the book, Ravana, his ministers, and his brother Vibhisana argue the wisdom of going to war to defend the kingdom from Rama's attack.

Ravana turns out to be entirely deaf to good advice, but he begins by asking for it. Addressing his advisors, he first points to three kinds of rulers who make their decisions in three different ways:

> There are three kinds of men in the world, the good, the bad, and the middling ... He who in his deliberations consults experienced counselors, his friends with whom he shares common interests, his relatives and his superiors and then pursues his design with energy and the help of God, is considered the foremost of men. He who enters into deliberation and pursues his duty by himself single-handedly, accomplishing that which should be accomplished, is considered a middling man. He who fails to weigh the advantages and disadvantages of a matter and refuses God's aid, merely saying, 'I shall do it', disregards his duty and is considered the least of men.

Ravana then ranks three kinds of advice:

> That judgment which is given after a clear-sighted examination of the question, and to which, reinforced by scriptural authority, the counselors agree, is considered excellent. Those deliberations where unanimity is finally reached after innumerable discussions are considered middling. Those in which each person continues to stand by his own opinion and opposes those of others and where no conclusion can be reached, are considered pernicious. Therefore, an undertaking that follows on wise deliberation will succeed.[15]

Ravana is not open to the good advice he seems to be seeking, since he is flattered by his courtiers who indulge in their own arrogance and play to Ravana's pride; and so he is doomed to fight an unwise and unjust war.

Ravana receives both support and an admonition from Kumbhakarna, one of his key generals. He promises to fight and win for the king, but he also cannot refrain from adding his complaint that Ravana has been foolish to put himself in this situation where animosity and lust are inevitably leading to the unjustified causing of pain:

> On first seeing Sita, the consort of Rama, who is accompanied by Laksmana, she who was brought here by force, your mind was wholly possessed by her as the waters of the lake are filled by the Yamuna river. O Great King, this conduct is not worthy of you! You should have consulted us at the outset of this affair. The king who acquits himself of his obligations punctiliously, O ten-faced king, and whose mind is concentrated on what he is about, has not to repent later! Those undertakings that are carried out carelessly and against the scriptural law turn out badly, like unto impure offerings poured into the sacrificial fire by those who are heedless. To seek to end where one

---

15 *The Ramayana*, vol.3, trans. H.P. Shastri (London: Shanti Sadan, 1985), p.17, with slight modifications.

should begin or to begin where one should end is to ignore what is proper and what is not. If an adversary examines the defects of one who is unrestrained, he soon discovers his weak points, as birds the fissures in the Krauncha mountains. You made this assault without forethought and it is fortunate that Rama has not slain you [thus far], as poisoned food the eater thereof![16]

Ravana's brother Vibhisana argues vehemently that Ravana should avoid fighting Rama:

> My dear brother, the wise affirm that when the end which is sought cannot be attained by three means (conciliation, gifts, sowing dissension), the conditions when force should be employed are determined by the tacticians. O Friend, deeds of valor which have been tested according to prescribed injunctions succeed against those who are careless when attacked, or who are in opposition to the divine power. Now, Rama is on his guard, he is eager for victory, he is upheld by divine power, he has subdued his passions and is invincible, yet you seek to defeat him.[17]

Moreover, Rama and his allies are exceedingly strong, and by fighting them Ravana is imprudently planning to cause pain in a battle he cannot win. Better to make peace in advance. When it soon appears certain that Ravana will side with those urging war, Vibhisana rebukes them all:

> You friends of this monarch who is dominated by passion, violent by nature and whose acts are thoughtless, flatter him as though you were his foes, to the destruction of the titans. Rescue and deliver that king who is helped fast in the illimitable coils of a serpent possessed of a thousand hoods and who is formidable and of exceeding energy. It is for the sovereign's friends, whose desires have been gratified by him, to save him, even were it by dragging him by the hair of his head, like one who has fallen prey to fiends of immeasurable power.[18]

But it is clear that Vibhisana's advice and scolding will fail, and soon Ravana expels him from the city, and then begins the battle.[19]

In the *Mahabharata* warfare is undertaken with reluctance; wars can be avoided if kings are prudent and just, but it is also the just and prudent ruler who will fight the needed war without qualms. By contrast, in the *Ramayana* Ravana typifies the foolish king who is willing to cause pain and harm others, caricatured simply as his enemies, without regard for righteousness and without consideration of his own moral readiness for the large task of fighting and inflicting pain, if need be, without intending to harm others. When to fight is ultimately a judgment made by a good king who listens carefully to advisors worth listening to and is then able to exert force, punish, and cause pain, but only for the ultimate good of those involved on

16 Ibid., p.19.
17 Ibid., pp.21-2.
18 Ibid., pp.32-3.
19 On moral reasoning in the *Ramayana*, see R.M. Green, *Religion and Moral Reason: A New Method for Comparative Study* (New York: Oxford University Press, 1988), especially chapter 8.

both sides. The foolish king acts without listening to advice or by disregarding it, and as a result he only does harm. Both epics and the earlier texts we have considered seem to assume, though, that there are more foolish kings in this world than wise ones, more intentions to harm than reluctant inflictions of pain.

Ending all Warfare? The Internalization of Conflict

A third and final way in which the causing of pain was dealt with was to conceive of it as necessary, sacrificial combat which could, however, be internalized and removed from the exterior sphere altogether. Pain is ritualized and then internalized, and defeated within, so that the prospect of war no longer pertains as a real-life ethical possibility. For the sake of brevity, I will sketch this approach by reference to a single work of contemporary scholarship.

In *The Broken World of Sacrifice*, Jan Heesterman has plausibly hypothesized that there was a religious/political conflict contest at the core of the ancient royal Vedic sacrifices: real-life and unpredictable danger was regularized and controlled by relocating it in (an increasingly ritualized) sacrificial context where combat was regularized, rendered regular and predictable, and then diverted into planned acts of animal sacrifice. In the period of the great Upanisads (after the ninth century BCE) the entirety of the context was internalized by brahmins and ksatriyas who were learning to transpose external conflicts onto an interior sacrificial arena or battlefield.[20] A combative and conflictual configuration of reality (secular or religious) is transposed into a matter of inner oppositions and inner balances which at least stand as prominent alternatives alongside continuing sacrificial and military practices. As sacrifice and sacrificial combat are tamed and made ritually predictable, the religiously significant world is increasingly internal, and it is there that real battles are to be fought. Some Upanisads (such as the *Mundaka*) take vehement stances against ritual, and in such contexts we come very close to what might be labelled a 'Buddhist position', whereby the realm of religiously justified killing narrows to the point of disappearing and the entirety of sacrifice and warfare are reimagined as interior, spiritual combat. Sacrifices and wars are the mistakes of those lacking in introspection.

Rhetorically at least, this view became widespread and was influential. In much of the Hindu tradition the real alternative to intending harm but also causing

---

20 In Heesterman's terminology, sacrifice 'is the arena of conflict and alliance, the field in which honour and position are to be won, the market for the distribution of wealth ... Combining in itself all functions – social, economic, political, religious – sacrifice is the catastrophic center, the turning point of life and death, deciding each time anew, through endless rounds of winning, losing, and revanche, the state of human affairs here and in the hereafter. Broken at its very center, it is forever hovering on the brink of collapse'. Ritual 'is the opposite. It is called upon to control the passion and the fury of the sacrificial contest and to keep such forces within bounds'. J. Heesterman, *The Broken World of Sacrifice: An Essay in Ancient Indian Ritual* (Chicago: University of Chicago Press, 1993), pp.2-3.

pain, lay within individual persons. The only just war is the inner war. External combat was judged simply the way of the world – a world which is such that suffering happens; some kill, other are killed; some do their duty; others seek gain or ambition harm to others – or interpreted as a misplaced externalization of interior struggle. Morally assessed, violence is condemned if it is due to unresolved inner conflicts, which instead became externalized, in bloodshed or in attitudes of anger and hatred which portray one's opponent as an enemy. Such violence is harm, not merely pain.

As is the case with all the materials considered in this chapter, the intended audience for interiorization was brahmins and ksatriyas; those to whom the causing of pain was permitted or assigned as a duty are those who are expected, in this strand of Upanisadic thought, to internalize sacrifice, combat, pain. Both brahmins and ksatriyas were offered an awareness that in ideal circumstances interiorization would be the more productive response to evil. At the farthest limit of that process, there eventually could no longer be any person such as would be able to perform sacrifices and fight wars. The obligatory duties remain in place to sacrifice animals or to fight remain in place, but there is no longer anyone in a position to be obliged by such duties. While most Hindu intellectuals remained committed to the legitimate possibility of both priestly and royal uses of force and pain, within Upanisadic thought the very justifications of sacrificial and royal pain were problematized by the awareness that there was almost always some internal rectification by which the need to cause pain externally could be avoided.

We can read the famous *Bhagavad Gita* in this light, even if it is true that the dialogue between Lord Krishna and the warrior Arjuna occurs on a battlefield where a highly bloody war is about to begin, a war justified by the teaching of the *Gita* as read in the wider context of the *Gita*. Traditional commentators, while not denying the war context, have generally seen the *Gita* as a teaching about the internal transformation of Arjuna, in whom the discovery of self-identity is accompanied by the rooting out of anger, fear, greed, and hatred, and the cessation of the practice of dividing the world into enemies and friends. Harm is entirely ruled out, and pain reduced to the warrior's duty in a world where pain need not harm either the killer or the killed. It is possible to imagine a world where wars would no longer occur, once everyone has rooted out his or her violent propensities and conquered the enemy within. But the *Gita* still presumes that in the 'real-world' the causing of pain will continue, even if the intention to harm is ruled out.[21]

Furthermore, against this background we can reconsider the remarkable role played by Mohandas K. Gandhi and his followers. Gandhi tapped into deep impulses of Hinduism (and Jainism too) in favour of a nonviolent attitude toward the world, and brilliantly adapted these ideals to the emerging independence movement and the shifting momentum against British colonialism. His *satyagraha* – that grasping of truth which is also a powerful positive rendering of not intending

---

21 For further reflections on the *Bhagavad Gita* and violence, see S.J. Rosen (ed.), *Holy War: Violence and the Bhagavad Gita* (Hampton, Virginia: Deepak Heritage Books, 2002).

harm and also not causing pain – has had a pervasive influence throughout India and the much wider world. Gandhi was in a sense a very traditional figure who rightly and powerfully taps into ancient Indian traditions of not intending harm by attacking the root causes of hatred, revenge, pride, etc.

A double emphasis on not causing pain and not intending harm as the highest ideal of Hindu culture is represented in continued reverence for Gandhi's teaching – and continued disappointment with any wider array of attitudes in Indian culture. We tend to interpret Indian culture so as to locate not causing pain and not intending harm as its highest ideal. It seems clear, however, that the 'highest ideal' can never be taken to be 'the sole ideal' if one is discussing the tradition of Hindu reflection on the topic. The complete avoidance of causing pain and the internalization of warfare was and is always accompanied by claims about the necessity of pain in sacrifice and especially governmental administration; war should be internalized, but war should also be fought justly.[22]

But however comprehensively Gandhi may have made the case for the ideal of not causing pain – much less intending harm – nevertheless he still represented only one key strand of Hindu tradition. He spoke and led as a remarkable, singular person and personality, to be sure, but also as a Hindu of his religious class; neither brahmin nor ksatriya, by tradition he had no authority either to engage in sacrifices or to punish evil-doers by causing pain. His ideal, however brilliant and inspiring it may be, was in part facilitated by factors specific to the (waning) colonial period. Indeed, as soon as he canonized the refusal to inflict pain, much less intend harm, as the greatest of Hindu ideals, the emerging independent India, which had the potential (and only that at first) of reestablishing the Hindu exercise of authority, immediately distanced itself from his ideals by turning to the state exercise of power, e.g., wars with Pakistan and China, the explosion of nuclear weapons, etc. Today, more than 50 years after Indian Independence (and although in a situation which is by no means a restoration of an idealized, ancient Hindu sense of kingship), Indians are manifesting again a wider range of attitudes toward causing and not intending harm. It should be clear by now that there is nothing surprising about this, since the Hindu tradition of the allocation of force would inevitably entail its exercise again when the opportunity would present itself.

Some Initial Conclusions Toward 'a Hindu Just War Theory'

In the preceding pages I have proposed some resources to aid us in understanding how limitations were placed on causing pain yet without envisioning its complete exclusion. I have touched on an array of topics: the sacrificial problematic of killing animals; theological distinctions regarding the causing of pain and the measures in accordance with which one makes decisions about pain and the avoidance of harm; the duty of kings to maintain order even if force is required for

22 For a perceptive analysis of Gandhi's views of violence, see M. Juergensmeyer, *Fighting with Gandhi* (San Francisco: Harper & Row, 1984).

this; portrayals of wise and foolish, conscientious and negligent kings, who use force moderately and blindly.

It is clear that one cannot ask merely, 'Is using force to cause pain to others right or wrong?' Rather, one must always differentiate the question according to the related question, 'Under what circumstances, according to which warrants, ought some particular persons perform acts which cause pain?' Brahmins were exhorted to avoid force and the causing of pain – except for killing animals during sacrifices; kings were mandated to create kingdoms in which the causing of pain was not necessary, and to become pure of any instinct toward harm – but also to be ready to be violent for the sake of the common good. All others were enjoined to refrain from using force at all, since such was not their prerogative.

Most Hindus eventually decided that blood sacrifice was cruel and unnecessary, and that the wider prohibition against such cruelty should curtail brahminical practice, and so in practice sacrifice of animals has been rare, uncommon. But the brahmin theorists never, to my knowledge, actually conceded the point. As sanctioned, blood sacrifice remained just and even a duty; it was just that over time the body of agents authorized to cause pain to animals in the sacrificial context diminished almost to the point of disappearance. It is the duty of a king who has to assess the factors presented to him in any given situation to be able to use force or wage war, as last resorts. While the royal defence of right order should in the long run make the causing of pain unnecessary, pain nonetheless remains a possibility which kings cannot rule out. War can at times be more just than refraining from war.

I have also noted the tendency in the Upanisadic tradition toward interiorization and, in the long run, a *de facto* ruling out of causing pain by both brahmin and ksatriya. It is important to notice this strand of thought, which undercuts theorizing about when causing pain is to be allowed, and yet also to see that it is just one strand of thought, not necessarily the privileged position promoted by 'true Hindus'.

Moving from these resources to a complete statement of 'the' Hindu view of the just war is of course a task that Hindu theorists, and not I, will have to undertake and test in the realm of public discourse among Hindus. But that discussion should also involve a broader consideration of Hindu materials, including both more contemporary materials and also a broader perspective of Indian thinking on these topics, with attention to a wider range of brahminical and non-brahminical views, most particularly those of Hindus who were not brahmins or ksatriyas, of Hindu women, largely left out of the classical discussions, and of non-Sanskritic vernacular and very local traditions. There are still other views - Jaina and Buddhist, Dalit, Christian, Muslim, Sikh, secularist – which have interacted with and helped shape the Hindu perspective over time. In the wider context, too, seemingly unconnected religious views become relevant. For instance, how one assesses the justice of causing pain is influenced by views on what life in this world amounts to – does one live in this world only once? So too, causing pain in other human beings cannot be entirely separated from the wider context and the extent to which one tolerates or causes the pain of other living beings. One may refuse to sacrifice animals for religious reasons, while having no hesitation to kill them for food; one may ask whether a diet of this sort falls into the category of justifiable or unjustifiable pain.

Chapter 8

Sikhism and Just War

Gurharpal Singh

Introduction

In April 1999 Sikhism marked the tri-centenary of the formation of the *Khalsa* (the Sikh brotherhood), an occasion that was celebrated throughout the globe. To commemorate the event in Britain, Sikhs invited Prime Minister Tony Blair to a reception in Birmingham to deliver the opening address. The choice of Blair was an appropriate one for not only was he the leading representative of 'New' Labour but also because as head of government he symbolized an enduring relationship between the Sikhs as a community and the British state. Blair's message to the Sikh audience was well received for, amongst other things, he chose to dwell on theme of just war in Sikhism by highlighting the on-going NATO campaign in Kosovo. This campaign, asserted Blair, vindicated a key element of the Sikh faith: namely, that when all modes of redressing injustice had failed, it was right and just to take up the sword.

This episode, even allowing for the natural opportunism of a gifted politician, illustrates how for non-Sikhs, the use of force in pursuit of justice is seen as a distinguishing feature of Sikhism. Over the last two decades there has been growing interest in the West in Sikhism fuelled by events in Punjab, India and the activities of the Sikh diaspora.[1] Most of the 20 million Sikhs live in the Indian state of Punjab, with about three million dispersed in other states of the Indian Union and overseas in North America, Europe, Asia, the Middle East and Australia. Since the early 1980s the Sikh diaspora,[2] which now is over a million strong, has been at the forefront of projecting Sikh concerns globally while in India, until the early 1990s, a violent struggle ensued between Sikh militants engaged in the campaign for Khalistan (a separate Sikh state) and India's armed and paramilitary forces.[3] What makes Sikhs militant is a question that has been frequently asked and answered in a variety of ways. As far as I am aware,

---

1   See C. Shackle, G. Singh and A. Mandair, *Sikh Religion, Culture and Ethnicity* (London: Curzon, 2001).
2   See G. Singh, 'A Victim Diaspora?', *Diaspora*, vol.8, no.3, 1999, pp.293-307; D. Singh Tatla, *The Sikh Diaspora: The Search for Statehood* (Seattle: University of Washington Press, 1999).
3   See G. Singh, *Ethnic Conflict in India: A Case-Study of Punjab* (Basingstoke: Palgrave, 2000).

however, only a few scholars have seriously examined the subject from the perspective of the ideals and values of the community itself.[4] The theme of a just war therefore is a useful point of departure to probe these issues and to locate it within the Sikh theological and historical tradition.

The rest of this chapter will address three aspects of this issue. First, by drawing on Sikh tradition it will outline the main characteristics of the Sikh equivalent of the just war doctrine. Second, with reference to recent events, more specifically Operation Blue Star in 1984, when the Indian Army stormed the Golden Temple, it will examine the relevance of the doctrine in providing the bases of resistance. And third, in light of the demise of Sikh militancy since the early 1990s, it will reflect on the likely influence of the doctrine in determining the future course of Sikh militancy.

Sikhism and 'Just War'

We need to recognize that Sikhism as a tradition has been very much influenced by historical events and there is no single key text that provides elaborate exegeses of the doctrine of just war. Such a doctrine, nevertheless, continues to exercise a powerful hold on the Sikh imagination. If it is implicit in the core elements of Sikh teaching, it is explicit in the emergence of Sikhism as a militant faith from the seventeenth century onwards. The evolution of the Sikh community has defined the nature of the doctrine; and, according to Sikh tradition, this development is marked by continuity from the first Guru (Guru Nanak 1469-1539) to the tenth Guru (Guru Gobind 1666-1705).

The essence of Sikh theology is found in the opening hymn of the *Guru Granth Sahib*, the Sikhs' sacred text:

> There is one supreme eternal reality; the truth; immanent in all things; creator of all things; immanent in creation. Without fear and without hatred; not subject to time; beyond birth and death; self-revealing. Know by the Guru's grace.[5]

Sikhs believe that God, who created the universe and everything in it, is omnipresent, immanent as well as transcendent, and omnipotent. Because God is formless, inscrutable and beyond the reach of human intellect, a relationship with the Creator can be established only by recognizing divine expression and truth. This relationship is possible through meditation on God's Name (*nam*) and Word

---

4   Among these are J.J.M. Pettigrew, 'In Search of a New Kingdom of Lahore', *Pacific Affairs*, vol.60, no.1, Spring 1987, pp.1-25, and The *Sikhs of the Punjab: Unheard Voices of State and Guerrilla Violence* (London: Zed Books, 1995); M. Jurgensmeyer, *Terror in the Mind of God: The Global Rise of Religious Violence* (Berkeley: University of California Press, 2001).

5   For a short history of Sikhism see G. Singh, 'Sikhism', *Encarta* (Microsoft: 2002).

(shabad) which are the revelations of the divine instructor (the Guru). Without the Guru's grace an individual is doomed to the perpetual cycle of death and rebirth.[6]

After Guru Gobind Singh the Guruship was invested in the *Guru Granth Sahib* (holy scriptures). Since then for Sikhs the Guru is spiritually present in the *Guru Granth Sahib*, which is the divine word, and He is temporally present in the collective body of the Sikh people (*Panth*) or any local congregation of them (*Sangat*). Sovereignty for Sikhs resides in the *Guru Granth Sahib*, not the state. Clearly as a community Sikhs' primary loyalty is to God. The teaching of the Gurus, the *Guru Granth Sahib*, and the formal interpretation of theses by the apex Sikh institutions have prescribed the rules for the community's existence.

Another important element in Sikhism's idea of a just war is the doctrine of *Miri-Piri*, the union of spiritual and temporal power that defines the indivisibility of the religious and the political. This doctrine emerged in the seventeenth century following the martyrdom of the fifth Guru. His successor symbolically donned two swords and, in defiance of Mogul authority, constructed the *Akal Thakt* (the seat of temporal authority) facing the *Harminder Shaib* (the Golden Temple). *Miri-Piri* is best symbolized in the *Nishan*, the Sikh emblem, in which two protecting swords shield the double-edged sword representing the purity of the faith. It was further extended by the tenth Guru who created the *Khalsa*, the Sikh brotherhood of *Sant-Spahis* (soldier-saints), who were to undertake a fearless defence of the community at a time when it was under continuous persecution. Above all, it is the *Khalsa*, with its emblem of the five ks, which represents popular Sikhdom, a pacifist creed turned militant by persecution. In sum, as Juergensmeyer notes, 'warfare is not only part of Sikh history but a central feature of its iconography'.[7]

In what context these ideals are to be defended – by force if necessary – can be gauged from the commentaries of the Gurus. Guru Nanak, the founder of Sikhism, often viewed by many as a pacifist, is said to declared that 'It is the privilege of a true man to fight for, and die in the cause of righteousness'.[8] Guru Gobind, who was involved in many battles during his lifetime in struggle with the local Punjab rajas and the Mogul court, in one of his most famous verses states:

Strengthen me, O Lord,
That I do not shrink from righteous deeds,
That freed from the fear of my enemies I may fight with faith and win,
The wisdom which I crave is the grace to sing your praises,
When this life's allotted course has run may I meet my death in battle.[9]

---

6   Ibid.
7   Jurgensmeyer, op.cit., p.96.
8   Quoted in S. Kapur Singh, *Sikhism: An Oecumenical Religion* (Chandigarh: Institute of Sikh Studies, 1993), p.193.
9   W.H. McLeod (ed.), *Textual Sources for the Study of Sikhism* (Manchester: Manchester University Press, 1984), p.55.

Gobind's own life was an illustration of this principle. In his *Zafernama* (Epistle of Victory) to emperor Aurangzeb, he enunciated the idea of just war in the famous couplet:

> When all other means have failed,
> It is permissible to draw the sword.[10]

Within the Sikh tradition, therefore, justice is the bedrock of political rule. Conversely, in conditions of injustice, or where the moral order is threatened, the defence of *dharma* (moral order) should be undertaken at all costs. The use of force, however, is sanctioned in defence of *dharma,* and then only as a last resort, as a defensive act for the protection of the oppressed and in the cause of liberty. The Sikh, it is made clear, should never be the first to draw the sword. A particularly important and lengthy political struggle is sometimes called a *dharma yud* (a war fought in defence of *dharma*). A *dharma yud* is viewed as a defensive act. Within Sikh tradition there is no legitimation for a pre-emptive war.

Finally, it is appropriate to mention the place of martyrdom within Sikhism, even though, arguably, martyrdom is hardly a collective communal act.[11] Yet martyrdom occupies a central role because in the development of the Sikh community resistance to oppressors has often been offered at the individual level. Heroic deeds against insurmountable odds represent a key component of the Sikh tradition. It would not be unreasonable to say that within Sikhism martyrdom is the 'supreme honour on those who give their lives to the cause'.[12] From the martyrdom of Guru Arjan (1563-1606), the creation of the *Khalsa* and vicissitudes of the eighteenth century when Sikhs faced organized massacres, the idea of a 'heroic death' has been a constant source of inspiration, especially, though not exclusively, when Sikh institutions have been under attack. But the emphasis on martyrdom is not absolute: it is tied to defence of righteousness, of a threat to *dharma* (the moral order).[13]

'Just War' in Practice: 1980s and 1990s

Sikh history since the late seventeenth century is characterized by a fundamental tension that arises from the ideal of a bounded community as propounded by the

10 K. Singh, *A History of the* Sikhs, vol.1: 1469-1839 (Delhi: Oxford University Press, 1991), pp.77-8.
11 Martyrdom, not unlike modern day reading of terrorism, can perhaps be interpreted as low-level warfare/resistance. For religious communities like the Sikhs, without a strong state tradition, the general doctrine of a just war is very much shaped by all modes of opposition.
12 Jurgensmeyer, op.cit., p.96.
13 L.E. Fenech, 'Martyrdom and the Execution of Guru Arjan in Early Sikh Sources', *Journal of American Oriental Society*, vol.12, no.1, 2001, pp.20-31.

Miri-Piri doctrine and the situation of a people sharing the plains of Punjab with other religious and cultural communities, principally Muslims and Hindus. Given that the concept of the *Panth* (community of believers) was never articulated as a spatial entity, as a relationship of land and people, the ideal political arrangement for Sikhs was a decentralized polity without a clear religious or ethnic identity. In the eighteenth century a loose confederation of Sikh factions provided the basis for the assertion of political power that culminated in Ranjit Singh's Kingdom of Lahore in 1801. Symbolically, Ranjit Singh deferred to the *Akal Takht*, but for all practical purposes his state was secular.[14]

With the arrival of colonialism in 1849 this tension was deflected because colonial policies, in particular Sikh recruitment into the Indian Army, nurtured a Sikh identity at ease with itself and one that was well adapted to accommodation in a multi-communal province and a multi-ethnic empire. Conventional wisdom now has it that Sikhism was substantially 'reinvented' around the *Khalsa* ideals following the colonial encounter with many of the rituals and institutions dating from this period.[15] The most serious confrontation between colonial rule and Sikhs over the management of Sikh shrines in the early 1920s was eventually settled amicably with a creation of a 'Sikh parliament', and an institution to manage Sikh temples.[16] Remarkably, neither Indian nationalism nor the militant Sikh tradition was able to construct a viable ideology of resistance to colonial rule in Punjab.

However the partition of Punjab and the independence of India in 1947 heightened the contradiction between community ideals and the new political configuration in which the *Panth* resided. On the one hand Sikh identity was strengthened by the creation of a Muslim Pakistan and predominantly Hindu India where the cleavages of language and religion were reinforced; on the other, economic and political integration into India threatened to undermine communal boundaries in a secular state which promoted individualism and proclaimed itself the source of all legitimate sovereignty.[17] This conflict set the scene for one of the most bitter campaigns for autonomy in the 1950s and the 1960s when the newly independent Indian state appeared to be beset with escalating demands for regional autonomy. New Delhi, however, managed the 'Sikh question' during these years through 'hegemonic control' – that is, it made an 'overtly violent ethnic contest for state power either "unthinkable" or "unworkable" on the part of the subordinated community'.[18] Sikh compulsions towards statehood after 1947 were contained by

14 J.S. Grewal, *The Sikhs of Punjab*. The New Cambridge History of India, II.3 (Cambridge: Cambridge University Press, 1990), ch.6.

15 See H. Oberoi, *The Construction of Religious Boundaries: Culture, Identity and Diversity in the Sikh Tradition* (Delhi: Oxford University Press, 1994).

16 R.G. Fox, *Lions of the Punjab: Culture in the Making* (Berkeley: California University Press, 1985).

17 Singh, *Ethnic Conflict in India*, ch.6.

18 J. McGarry and B. O'Leary (eds.), *The Politics of Ethnic Conflict Regulation: Case Studies of Protracted Ethnic Conflicts* (London: Routledge, 1993), p.23.

the parameters of hegemonic control established by the Indian national leadership and its alliance with secular Sikhs who successfully divided the Sikh community.[19]

But by the early 1980s a campaign for mainly economic demands led by the Akali Dal, a moderate Sikh political party, turned violent. Mrs Indira Gandhi, who led the national Congress-I government in New Delhi, resisted concessions on the grounds that the movement was religiously inspired – an argument no too dissimilar from the one used by her father Nehru who opposed the calls for a Punjabi-speaking state. Interestingly this campaign was termed the *dharma yud morcha*. Whether by default or design this struggle reopened the Sikh national question, and in the process became a 'freedom movement', a 'Sikh revolution in the making'.[20] At this critical juncture the ideological framework for the agitation shifted from secular concerns to Sikh historical and religious tradition. A critical catalyst in the process was provided by Bhindranwale, a charismatic leader who did not share the political culture of traditional leaders. By counter-posing an alternative vision for Sikhism, Bhindranwale's leadership gradually undermined moderate Sikhs. And if this vision drew its inspiration from Sikh history and religious tradition, its objectives were essentially modern and in tune with the ideals and values of the community: to recreate a political unit in which the Sikh community would be the true repository of political power where its traditions and values would flourish without interference and control.

Bhindranwale claimed that

Sikhs would lose their identity in a flood of resurgent Hinduism, or worse, in a sea of secularism ... [He] support[ed] the Sikh concept of *miri-piri*, the notion that spiritual and temporal power are linked. He projected the image of a great war between good and evil waged in present day – 'a struggle ... for our faith, for the Sikh nation, for the oppressed'. He implored his young followers to rise up and marshal the force of righteousness.[21]

In speaking directly to his followers at the Golden Temple, Bhindranwale gave vent to the grievance of rural Sikhs, thereby skilfully combining tradition and history to evoke a sense of revolt. 'You can only have justice', he claimed,

If there is the rule of law, someone to enforce it, and the right of appeal. Where will you go [for justice] when no one cares for the judge or for the law and they [the police] are all powerful? With your hands then you will have to solve your problems. They [the police and the government] are perpetrating atrocities on us, exterminating our youth, burning our Holy Book, and insulting our turbans. When this is so you don't need to file a writ or a suit. There is no need to get licence for arms. Neither Guru Hargobind took a licence from Jehangir nor Guru Gobind Singh sought one from Aurungzeb ... When atrocities on peaceful people pass the limit, youth tend to adopt the path of Guru

19 See B.R. Nayer, *Minority Politics in Punjab* (New Jersey: Princeton University Press, 1966).
20 G.S. Dhillion, 'Towards a Sikh Revolution', *The Illustrated Weekly of India* (Bombay) (10 April 1983), p.11.
21 Jurgensmeyer, op.cit., pp.98.

Hargobind Sahib the True Lord. After all when there is no law, proof and appeal left, the GurSikh [a baptised] Sikh has to adopt that path.[22]

Between 1982 and 1984 Bhindranwale attracted much support among the Sikh youth and the peasantry. The Golden Temple became the site of Sikh militants' religious and political resistance to the Indian state, dramatically climaxing in the Indian Army's operation Blue Star in June 1984 in which 1,000 lives were lost.[23] Seen in this light, Blue Star was not merely a security operation but a clash of two nations. As Pettigrew has commented:

> The sacrifice of Bhindranwale's life and that of his followers drew attention to the fact that Sikhs live by a model of society opposed to that for which India stood. They were slaughtered in defence of their conception of what society should be.[24]

The storming of the Golden Temple complex, the assassination of Indira Gandhi in November 1984 and the subsequent pogroms against Sikhs in Delhi in which almost 4,000 died in the full glare of the international media created an image of a community under siege. Sikhs had been militarily defeated and their main institution, the *Akal Takht*, seat of temporal authority, demolished. Punjab was placed under virtual martial rule with combing operations in the countryside by the security forces. Against this background a militant movement emerged that began a guerrilla campaign for Khalistan, a separate Sikh state. The mainspring of this movement's resistance was provided by Sikh historical and religious tradition which justified the right 'to use force to restore justice in a society as well as to resist in high spirits, cheerfully, and to offer unyielding resistance'.[25] But this time the Sikh diaspora took an active lead in organizing and supporting the resistance. Throughout North America, Great Britain and Europe a sustained campaign was launched to provide material, diplomatic and moral assistance to the Sikh campaign in Punjab.[26] Khalistani militants – in Punjab and overseas – portrayed themselves as reluctant separatists who were forced to pursue the path of separate statehood by terror unleashed by the Indian state against the Sikh people. They provided moral symbols of revolt by restoring them to memory. Many adopted the popular names of forgotten Sikh heroes and generals who had been part of the Sikh folklore. Sikh institutions dating from the eighteenth century were resurrected with the objective of re-establishing the corporate identity of the community which, it was argued, had been undermined by the emergence of the modern secular state. Practically, the vision of a new kingdom of Lahore was articulated in an

---

22 J.J.M. Pettigrew, 'Take Not Arms Against Thy Sovereign: the Present Punjab Crisis and the Storming of the Golden Temple', *South Asia Research*, vol.4, no.2, November 1984, p.113.

23 R. Jeffrey, *What's Happening to India? Punjab, Ethnic Conflict, Mrs Gandhi's Death and the Test for Federalism* (Basingstoke: Macmillan, 1986); and M. Tully and S. Jacob, *Amritsar: Mrs Gandhi's Last Battle* (London: Jonathan Cape, 1985).

24 Pettigrew, 'In Search of a New Kingdom of Lahore', p.12.

25 Pettigrew, 'Take Not Arms', p.31.

26 See Tatla, op. cit.

ambiguous definition of Khalistan and a regular campaign against the security forces and civilians that included a prohibition on dowry, alcohol consumption, and corrupt practices. [27]

Sikh militants established a significant base among the Sikh peasantry, and between 1989 and 1992, there was a real fear in New Delhi that militants had succeeded in creating a parallel government. One comprehensive survey in July 1992 described Punjab as 'an area of darkness' where people lived in constant fear of violence by militants and the security forces. The government found its 'boundaries rolled back and its political will undermined into non-existence'. The survey described rural life in the state as

> Almost at a standstill. The nights ... are almost eerie where trigger-nervous security men man roads. As darkness deepens ... the last few buses, before they are run off the road after dusk, are full to the brim with human freight. In the witching hours no trains function on the branch lines, and by late evening even bigger junctions are deserted. [28]

In the event Sikh militancy was crushed by the use of overwhelming force in which the central government mobilized over 250,000 military and paramilitary personnel. According to official sources, from 1984 to 1993 there were almost 30,000 fatalities in Punjab arising from operations by militants and the security services.[29] The physical elimination of militancy in the mid-1990s created the space for the revival of moderate Sikh politics and in February 1997 the Akali Dal won an overwhelming landslide in the Punjab Legislative Assembly elections. For the first time since independence the Akali Dal administration was able to complete its five-year term. Yet the secular demands that gave rise to the movement in the 1980s remain unrealised. In managing the 'Sikh question' New Delhi has once more reverted to hegemonic control.

'Just War', Sikhs and the Future

The recent developments in Sikh history have been discussed in length because they illustrate most clearly the dilemmas and responses of Sikhs to conditions in which the faith and the community are under threat. Today these conditions, moreover, are set against the background of a globalized community with significant settlements in the major developed nations. The Sikh diaspora is a key component of the Sikh nation in defining its future goals as well as responding to the wider concerns of the community emanating from India and elsewhere. In these circumstances it is useful to reflect on the contemporary relevance of the just war doctrine within Sikhism and to what extent it might provide guidance to the

27 Singh, op.cit., ch.8.
28 *India Today,* (New Delhi), 15 July 1992.
29 For discussion of the figures and how militancy was contained see Singh, *Ethnic Conflict in India*, ch.9.

understanding of the future course of Sikh militancy. In particular five matters need to be kept in mind.

First, it is clear that the just war doctrine within Sikhism is still understood as a defensive act. Nothing that has taken place recently or in the last century has modified this view. The Sikh struggle of the early 1980s turned violent mostly after 1984. Even then it did so after a period in which the central government reneged on promises to implement a political accord which would have met the secular demands of the Sikh campaign. Organized resistance was offered after counter-insurgency operations unleashed wholesale terror in the Punjabi countryside.[30] To be sure, there were acts of random terrorism by Sikhs, including the infamous downing of the Air India jet off the coast of Ireland. But Sikhism provides no justification for terrorism. Explanations of terror associated with militancy have to be sought within the culture of the *Panth*'s followers for many of whom normative values of violence and revenge are ingrained attributes of the honour code.[31] Others have suggested that the operational tactics of counter-insurgency primarily determined the banalization of Sikh militancy through terror.[32]

Second, the ideological primacy of the historical and religious tradition within Sikhism, as recent events have confirmed, tends to come to the fore in a situation where the Sikh conception of *dharma* is threatened. As we have seen, Sikh militants were able to draw on a deep reservoir of symbols, history and theology to construct an ideology of resistance based on a competing conception of sovereignty. This tradition in a real sense is part of everyday Sikh litany.[33] But restoring it to communal memory as bases of action requires a significant counter-hegemonic project that would also need to be supported by conjectural factors. If in the 1980s and early 1990s Sikh militants and the Indian state collided, history also suggests that a conflict between Sikh ideals and values and the political systems within which they reside is not inevitable. A decentralized, multi-communal society in which there is considerable room for autonomy for Sikh religious and cultural values would appear to be the ideal mode of governance for Sikhs as a community. Conversely a centralized polity with limited religious and cultural autonomy poses real dangers for Sikhs and Sikhism.[34]

Third, Sikhs' failure to emerge as bounded community guided by the doctrine of *Miri-Piri* has meant that even in extremis mobilizing Sikhs for a just war is fraught with practical difficulties. Alongside the heroic tradition that is normally emphasized in mainstream Sikh narratives is the counter tradition of betrayal, disloyalty and treachery against the *Panth*, in short, a willing compliance with hegemonic control. Historically the boundaries of Sikhism have remained porous with sizeable marginal groupings that have contested the drive towards

---

30 See Pettigrew, *The Sikhs of the Punjab*, ch.1.
31 See J. Pettigrew, *Robber Noblemen: A Study of the Political System of Sikh Jats* (London: Routledge and Kegan Paul, 1975).
32 See Singh, *Ethnic Conflict in India*, ch.10.
33 McLeod, op. cit., pp.102-103.
34 See Singh, *Ethnic Conflict in India*, ch.2

homogeneity. *Jat* Sikhs, who comprise nearly 70 percent of the Sikh community, are renowned for their factional feuds and their ability to forge alliances against each other in the pursuit of power. Not unnaturally the police and armed forces in the 1980s and 1990s pitted *Jat* Sikhs against *Jat* Sikhs to undermine the militancy.[35] Because of this cultural heritage some anthropologists have suggested that Sikhism does not easily lend itself to state formation.[36] This may well be so given the contemporary diversity of the *Panth* and the complex modes of social, economic and political integration in India and overseas.

Fourth, the doctrine of just war has now to be understood against a background in which the Sikh diaspora is playing a major role in the affairs of the Sikh community. This development simultaneously makes the community in Punjab more vulnerable to the external adulation of heroic Sikh ideals through long-distance ('romantic') nationalism and also opens up the possibility of Sikhism once again being 'reconstructed' as a faith, as overseas Sikhs begin to reinterpret the core elements of the tradition. One of the interesting consequences of the promotion of multicultural policies in developed western societies such as Great Britain and Canada is that Sikh traditions and values are, in some ways, far better protected than in India. At the same time these values are under tremendous pressure because of the competing pulls of assimilation and tradition.[37]

Finally, reservations about the limited prospects of just war by Sikhs notwithstanding, I want to add a cautionary note in light of current developments in Kashmir. Operation Blue Star in 1984 was followed by some mutinies by Sikh soldiers who were eventually arrested and court marshalled. In the testimony before the court trying non-commissioned officers of the Sikh Regimental Centre for desertion when the Golden Temple was attacked, Lieutenant-General Harbaksh Singh, in their defence, drew attention to the fact that 'Sikh soldiers were nurtured on religious tenets and tradition'.[38] Since then some of the Sikh regiments have become mixed, though Sikhs continue to occupy a higher proportion of the officer corps in the Indian army than the ratio of their population would merit. The strains apparent among Sikhs serving in the Indian armed forces in 1984 have been apparent in other forms in India's previous wars – 1962 (China), 1965 and 1971 (Pakistan).[39] It is of course difficult to anticipate how developments might unfold in the event of a serious possibility of nuclear exchange between India and Pakistan,[40] but given the location of Sikh troops and the place of Punjab and Kashmir as the main theatres of a possible nuclear war, Sikh soldiers will once again be confronted with a severe test of loyalty. Faith, community and nation,

---

35 Ibid., ch.10.
36 Pettigrew, 'In Search of a New Kingdom of Lahore', op. cit.
37 D.S. Tatla, 'Sikhs in Mutlicultural Societies: Lessons for Public Policy', in J. Rex and G. Singh (eds.), *Governing Multicultural Societies* (London: Ashgate, forthcoming).
38 *The Tribune* (Chandigarh), 6 June 1986.
39 See A. Kundu, *Militarism in India: The Army and Civil Society Consensus* (New Delhi: Viva Books, 1998).
40 See G. Singh, 'On the Nuclear Precipice: India, Pakistan and the Kashmir Crisis', *Open Democracy*: www.opendemocracy.net/forum/strandhome.asp.

together with prospects of annihilation may yet pull Sikhs and Sikh soldiers in different directions where a choice has to be made between the Sikh conception of a moral order and a nation-building effort defended by nuclear weapons.[41]

Conclusion

Among the religious traditions of South Asia, Sikhism has one of the clearest – and probably the simplest – conception of a just war. This conception arises out of the historical circumstances of the Sikh community's evolution – its gradual development from the fifteenth century through institutionalization, persecution, the establishment of a Sikh state at the beginning of the eighteenth century, colonialism, partition, and today, an uncomfortable location in the Indian Union. Within Sikhism a major preoccupation has been with the preservation of a sound moral order in which the faith – and other faiths – can flourish without interference. As a community with a history of persecution and ambiguous boundaries, Sikhs have evolved the doctrine as a defensive mechanism, a means of survival in a hostile world. But it is also a doctrine that goes to the very heart of Sikhism as a faith based on political rule where justice has to be the guiding value of political rule and the moral order. Recent history suggests that these features of the Sikh tradition provide an enduring psychological need, a need that was clearly demonstrated in the events before and after 1984. Current developments indicate that Sikhism is perhaps in the process of introspection in which some of the core elements of the faith are being contested against the background of 1984, the emergence of the Sikh diaspora, and the continuing failure of Sikh institutions in India to align community ideals with political and social power. Given the high degree of uncertainty that surrounds the community's future, it is unlikely that the doctrine of just war will diminish in its significance. More than likely, as Tony Blair rightly noted, it will remain one of the defining credos of Sikhs and Sikhism.

---

41 At the height of the confrontation between India and Pakistan in May 2002, some Sikh leaders, such as Simranjeet Singh Mann, were at pains to stress the neutrality of the Sikh position.

PART III
PRE-MODERN PERSPECTIVES

Chapter 9

Inauspicious Tools: Chinese Thought on the Morality of Warfare

Thomas M. Kane

The owl of Minerva, Hegel tells us, flies at dusk. Nowhere has this saying been more apt than in ancient China. The 'hundred schools of thought' of classic Chinese philosophy emerged during a six-hundred year era of uninterrupted warfare (800-206 BCE). This was a period when everything that the Chinese held sacred seemed to be in jeopardy. New technology and new ideas had placed power in the hands of crass and violent men.

Some of the greatest thinkers in Chinese history lived during this period. Confucius, Menicus, Lao Tzu, Sun Tzu, Mo Tzu and Han Fei-Tzu are but six of the best-known Chinese intellectuals of this time. These thinkers sought ways for rulers and private citizens to act wisely and honourably in a world where both lives and principles were in constant peril. The collapse of China's old empire forced these intellectuals to look beyond commonplace assumptions about social relations and search for fundamental principles that could remain valid even when tradition failed.

In the process, these thinkers had to consider the moral status of warfare. China's philosophers took a broad range of views on this subject. This chapter summarizes the positions of China's better-known thinkers. Since these thinkers remain influential today, this survey provides some insight into Chinese political thought from ancient times to the present. Chinese thought also provides a counterpoint to other nations' writings on this subject.

The Confucians

'If one were to characterize in one word the Chinese way of life for the last two thousand years', one compiler of source material on classic Chinese literature tells us, 'the word would be Confucian'.[1] Kung Fu-tzu, known in the West as Confucius, sought to recover the harmony of earlier times by continuing the traditional rituals of Chinese society and by educating individuals to practise

---

1 W.T. de Bary, W. Chan, & B. Watson, *Sources of Chinese Tradition* (New York: Columbia University Press, 1960), p.15.

virtue.   Confucius did not forbid warfare.   Nevertheless, Confucius' teaching encouraged people to hold military people and military concerns in contempt.

'Good iron is not used for nails', Confucius said. 'And good men are not used for soldiers'.[2]   One notes that this quotation does not condemn the existence of soldiers or the practice of war.   Confucius opposes, not violence *per se*, but the waste of superior people in an ignoble and dangerous enterprise.

The saying about good iron and good men appealed to the scholarly elite who dominated China's bureaucracy for much of history.   Certainly, the typical member of this class had little desire to endure the hardships of military life.   Confucius' moral teaching further encouraged such people to abstain from warfare.   Although Confucius did not categorically forbid violence, he undermined the most common arguments in its favour.

If a man practised virtue, Confucius suggested, others would willingly follow his example.   If they did not, the virtuous man would still hold the moral high ground.   Without such virtue, no material gain was worth having.   Martyrdom was preferable to moral compromise.   A good man, Confucius taught, always puts his ideals before practical concerns.

Certainly, in Confucian teaching, virtue should come before wealth.   'The gentleman occupies himself with the Way and not with his livelihood'.[3]   If necessary, the virtuous man will extend this principle to the point of self-sacrifice. 'The resolute scholar and the humane person will under no circumstance seek life at the expense of humanity [humane conduct].   On occasion, they will sacrifice their lives to preserve their humanity'.[4]

What is this virtue that comes before all else?   When asked to sum up his concept of morality in a single word, Confucius replied 'reciprocity'.[5]   The sage went on to state a principle similar to the Christian Golden Rule.   'Do not do to others what you would not want done to you'.[6]   This idea seems to rule out most military action.

Confucius explicitly applied these principles to statecraft.   A good ruler, he said, would have no need to impose the death penalty.   'Just as you genuinely desire the good, the people will be good.   The virtue of the gentleman may be compared to the wind and that of the commoner to the weeds.   The weeds under the force of the wind cannot but bend'.[7]

This principle also applied to a ruler's dealings abroad.   When one nobleman consulted him about the best way to deal with foreign bandits, Confucius responded, 'if you, sir, were not covetous, neither would they steal, even if you were to bribe them to do so'.[8]   Confucius did not, however, condemn warfare as

---

2   T.M. Kane, *China* (Austin TX: Steve Jackson, 1989), p.8.
3   de Bary, op. cit., p.31.
4   Ibid., p.27.
5   Ibid., p.25.
6   Ibid., p.25.
7   Ibid., p.33.
8   W. Baskin, *Classics in Chinese Philosophy* (New York: Philosophical Library, 1972), p.12.

unequivocally as he condemned capital punishment. When a man named Tzu Kung asked Confucius what sort of things a state required, the sage responded, 'the essentials are sufficient food, sufficient troops and the confidence of the people'.[9]

When pressed on this issue, Confucius returned to his customary idealism.

> Tzu Kung said: 'Suppose you were forced to give up one of those three, which would you let go first?' Confucius said: 'The troops'. Tzu Kung asked again: 'If you are forced to give up one of the two remaining, which would you let go?' Confucius said: 'Food. For from of old, death has been the lot of all men, but a people without faith cannot survive'.[10]

Confucius does not consistently advocate pacifism. When asked whether one should requite injury with kindness, he responded 'how then will you requite kindness? Requite injury with justice, and kindness with kindness'.[11] When Confucius describes the features of a well-ordered empire, he casually mentions military expeditions going forth.[12] Nevertheless, he has little use for men of action, and he rejects the principles of pragmatism which people typically use to justify war.

The Taoists

Despite Confucius' great influence, China's rulers often honoured his teaching more in word than in deed.[13] War and conquest have played a critical role in every phase of Chinese history. Furthermore, other influential thinkers differed with Confucius' very principles. One of Confucius' most prominent critics was his elder contemporary, Lao Tzu, author of the *Tao te Ching* and founder of the school of thought known as Taoism.

According to legend, these two thinkers met in person. Confucius asked the older man about his opinions concerning propriety and the rituals of ancestor worship. Lao Tzu is said to have responded, 'the men whom you talk about and their bones have already rotted. Abandon your arrogance, affectations and excessive ambition. That is all the propriety you need'.[14] Taoists traditionally saw Confucians as fatuous meddlers, and were particularly concerned about the Confucian tendency to interfere in politics.

Lao Tzu's writings were less confrontational. Indeed, there are points at which Confucius and the *Tao te Ching* seem compatible. Both, for instance, envision the ideal ruler as someone who can manage state affairs successfully simply by

---

9   de Bary, op. cit., p.33.
10 Ibid.
11 Ibid., p.27.
12 Baskin, op. cit., p.23.
13 A.I. Johnston, *Cultural Realism: Strategic Culture and Grand Strategy in Chinese History* (Princeton NJ: Princeton University Press, 1995), pp.x-xi.
14 Kane, op. cit., p.64.

practicing *wu-wei* (non-action) and letting nature take its course.[15]　In any case, Lao Tzu writes in cryptic epigrams rather than structured arguments.　Lao Tzu leaves readers to speculate about the full meaning of his thoughts, and thus he leaves them to speculate about his position vis-à-vis Confucianism as well.

The *Tao te Ching* does not oppose Confucius directly, but it suggests a different way of looking at the world.　As the earlier anecdote suggests, Lao Tzu is an iconoclast.　Where Confucius urged people to strive toward abstract standards of virtue, Lao Tzu saw the standards as artificial and the effort as vain.

> A truly good man is not aware of his goodness,
> And is therefore good.
> A foolish man tries to be good,
> And is therefore not good. ...
>
> Therefore, when the Tao [way] is lost, there is goodness.
> When goodness is lost, there is kindness.
> When kindness is lost, there is justice.
> When justice is lost, there is ritual.
> Now ritual is the husk of faith and loyalty, the beginning of confusion.[16]

Lao Tzu is, in fact, sceptical about theories, analogies, models and precepts of any kind.　Despite his mystical streak, he is an empiricist.

> [L]ook at the body as body;
> Look at the family as family;
> Look at the village as village;
> Look at the nation as nation;
> Look at the universe as universe.
>
> How do I know the universe is like this?
> By looking![17]

When one sees things as they really are, one may use that knowledge.　One may turn the inherent potential of things to one's own advantage.　By making use of natural developments, one may achieve results without risk or effort.　Again, Lao Tzu's pragmatism contrasts with Confucius' idealism.　Where Confucius exhorts people to set their high principles against mere necessity, Lao Tzu suggests that

---

15　Confucius praises the legendary sage-king Shun for governing through non-action, although he does not necessarily imply that all good rulers must follow the same method. He does, however, say '[I]f a ruler himself is upright, all will go well without orders. But if he is not upright, even though he gives orders they will not be obeyed'. de Bary, op. cit., p.32. Lao Tzu, meanwhile, writes, 'Tao abides in non-action. Yet nothing is left undone. If kings and lords observed this. The ten thousand things would develop naturally'. Lao Tzu, *Tao Te Ching*, trans. G. Feng & J. English (New York: Random House, 1972), p.37.

16　Lao Tzu, op. cit., p.38.

17　Ibid., p.54.

readers become 'the stream of the universe', flowing with the contours of the land and subtly wearing it into the shape they desire.[18] Where Confucius urged rulers to rely on their exemplary virtue to blow lesser people like grass, Lao Tzu warns that 'high winds do not last all morning'.[19]

By replacing idealism with pragmatism, Lao Tzu provides a justification for war. A Confucian might take a stand on pure principle. A Taoist might objectively appraise a situation and conclude that fighting is a natural response to the circumstances. A Confucian ruler might take quixotic pride in setting an example of humane conduct. Lao Tzu noted that 'the wise are ruthless. They treat the people like dummies'.[20]

Lao Tzu explicitly discusses war, and he takes a balanced approach to the subject. Weapons, he says, are inauspicious tools. 'Weapons are instruments of fear, they are not a wise man's tools', the *Tao te Ching* warns.[21] 'He uses them only when he has no choice'.[22] In other words, although the wise man is reluctant to use weapons, there are occasions when he must use them. Lao Tzu urges compassion and prudence, but not dogmatic pacifism.

Having established that war may occasionally be unavoidable, Lao Tzu urges rulers to avoid it whenever possible.

> Peace and quiet are dear [to the wise man's] heart,
> And victory no cause for rejoicing.
> If you rejoice in victory, then you delight in killing;
> If you delight in killing, you cannot fulfil yourself. ...
>
> When many people are being killed,
> They should be mourned in heartfelt sorrow.
> That is why victory must be observed like a funeral.[23]

Not only does Lao Tzu lament the human cost of war, he cautions rulers against the practical dangers of military adventurism. One of Lao Tzu's key teachings is that one should minimize one's risk and maximize one's chances for success by avoiding all forms of conflict. Clearly, this applies to warfare.

> Whenever you advise a ruler in the way of Tao,
> Counsel him not to use force to conquer the universe.
> For this would only cause resistance.[24]

'A violent man will die a violent death', Lao Tzu exclaims in yet another section. 'This will be the essence of my teaching'.[25]

18 Ibid., p.28.
19 Ibid., p.23.
20 Ibid., p.5.
21 Ibid., p.31.
22 Ibid., p.31.
23 Ibid., p.31.
24 Ibid., p.30.

Even for the victor, the *Tao te Ching* warns, warfare is wasteful and destructive. 'Thorn bushes spring up wherever the army has passed'.[26] War distorts peoples' priorities and diverts resources from useful enterprises. When people follow the right way, they put their war horses to work hauling manure.[27]

As Lao Tzu considers the cost of war, he proposes more general ideas about the relationship between rulers and the states they rule. In the process, he suggests a way of distinguishing between just and unjust wars. The *Tao te Ching* praises rulers whose action – or, better yet, wisely timed restraint – allow people to enjoy the benefits of a simple, peaceful life.

> Though they have armour and weapons, no one displays them. ...
> Their food is plain and good, their clothes fine but simple, their homes secure;
> They are happy in their ways.
> Though they live within sight of their neighbours,
> And crowing cocks and barking dogs are heard across the way,
> Yet they leave each other in peace.[28]

Rulers must not act out of personal ambition. Lao Tzu suggests that conspicuous consumption and unnecessary opulence are to be frowned upon. Aggression is dangerous folly. 'A good soldier is not violent', 'a good fighter is not angry', and 'a good winner is not vengeful'.[29] 'Robber barons' who wear gorgeous clothes and carry sharp swords while the granaries are bare are certainly not following the way.[30]

Not only does Lao Tzu distinguish between good and bad reasons for fighting, he distinguishes between wise and unwise ways of making war. His philosophical ideas provide him with a theory of strategy. Despite his antipathy to violence, he does not seem to have any qualms about advising generals, nor does he mind explaining his more abstract concepts through military metaphors. These facts underscore the point that he accepted the occasional necessity of war.

Lao Tzu advocates tactics of surprise, opportunism and manoeuvre.[31] This corresponds to his more general ideas, which hold that those who act in harmony with the natural way of things can achieve results with minimum effort. One may also surmise that he hopes to minimize the wastefulness of war. He warns rulers against overreaching themselves, while urging them to exploit the excesses of the enemy.

There is a saying among soldiers:

> I dare not make the first move but would rather play the guest;
> I dare not advance an inch but would rather withdraw a foot. ...

25 Ibid., p.42.
26 Ibid., p.30.
27 Ibid., p.46.
28 Ibid., p.80.
29 Ibid., p.68.
30 Ibid., p.53.
31 Ibid., p.57.

There is no greater catastrophe than underestimating the enemy. ...
Therefore, when the battle is joined,
The underdog will win.[32]

Chuang Tzu, a Taoist thinker who lived several centuries after Lao Tzu and Confucius, actually was a military officer.[33] Warfare serves as a backdrop to some of his writings. Although Chuang Tzu is not noted for addressing the question of whether or not war is justified as an institution, he develops the idea that a good commander should overcome the enemy through innovation. Chuang Tzu uses a military parable to expound upon the more general importance of creativity in life.

There was a man of Sung who was skilful at making a salve which kept the hands from getting chapped; and (his family) for generations had made the bleaching of cocoon-silk their business. A stranger heard of it and proposed to buy the art of the preparation for a hundred ounces of silver. The kindred all came together and considered the proposal. 'We have', said they, 'been bleaching cocoon-silk for generations and have only gained a little money. Now in one morning we can sell to this man our art for a hundred ounces; – let him have it'. The stranger accordingly got it and went away to give counsel to the king of Wu, who was then engaged in hostilities with Yueh, on which he inflicted a great defeat.[34]

Chuang Tzu does not elaborate here, but his readers would have been familiar with the legend of how the salve allowed Wu's archers to keep their hands supple when fighting from ships in the winter, thus improving their ability to wield their bows.

[The stranger who bought the recipe for the salve] was invested with a portion of the territory taken from Yueh. The keeping of the hands from getting chapped was the same in both cases; but in the one case it led to the investiture [of the possessor of the salve], and in the other it had only enabled its owners to continue their bleaching. The difference of result was owing to the different use made of the art.[35]

Chuang Tzu makes no moral comment about the justice of fighting Yueh, but he presents the clever stranger as a paragon.

Students of warfare may fear that Taoist writings on strategy contain a dash of wishful thinking. Strategem is not always a substitute for brute force. Overall, however, the *Tao te Ching* provides a realistic response to the endless wars of the 'robber barons' who were destroying China. Lao Tzu appreciates the evil of war, but he holds that one must address moral problems through practical means.

32 Ibid., p.69.
33 Baskin, op. cit., p.149.
34 Ibid., p.158.
35 Ibid.

The Mo-ists

Mo Tzu is no longer as well-known as Confucius or Lao Tzu, but he was prominent in ancient China. Menicus, an influential successor to Confucius, identified Mo-ism as one of Confucianism's most dangerous rivals. Like Confucius, Mo Tzu preached an absolute standard of humanitarianism, but like the Taoists, he was a pragmatist. Mo Tzu eschewed the more esoteric doctrines of Taoism, however. He was not so much a philosopher as a social activist who preached for frugality, equal distribution of wealth and the principle of impartial 'universal love'.

Mo Tzu directly addressed the issue of war.

> Humane men are concerned about providing benefits for the world and eliminating its calamities. Now among all the current calamities, which are the worst? I say that the attacking of small states by large states, the making of inroads on small houses by large houses, the plundering of the weak by the strong, the oppression of the few by the many, the deception of the simple by the cunning, the disdain of the noble towards the humble – these are some of the calamities in the world ... added to these, the mutual injury and harm which the vulgar people do to one another with weapons, poison, water and fire is still another kind of calamity in the world.[36]

Nor, Mo Tzu says, can one argue that aggressive war serves the interests of the interest of the state.

> Take the case of an attack on a town with its inner wall one mile, its outer two miles, in circumference. To capture this without the thrust of a spear or the death of a man would be an empty achievement. As it is, however, the deaths must be reckoned by the ten thousand, at least by the thousand and all that can be obtained is one or two miles of township. And all the time the great states have empty [i.e. half-populated] townships to be reckoned by the thousand waiting to be occupied peacefully – and uncultivated lands to be reckoned by the ten thousand – waiting to be opened up peacefully. Thus then the amount of land waiting to be possessed is in excess, the population waiting to be ruled in true kingly fashion insufficient. Now then: to bring the people to death and to aggravate the troubles of high and low in order to quarrel over a half-populated township, this logically is to throw away that of which you have too little and to double that of which you have too much. To put the affairs of state right in this fashion is directly counter to the interest of the state.[37]

If people adopted universal love, Mo Tzu suggests, these calamities would disappear.

> One who obeys the will of Heaven will practise universal love; one who opposes the will of Heaven will practise partial love. According to the doctrine of universal love, the standard is righteousness; according to the doctrine of partiality, the standard is force. What is it like when righteousness is the standard of conduct? The great will not

36 de Bary, op. cit., p.40.
37 Baskin, op. cit., p.104.

attack the small, the strong will not plunder the weak, the many will not oppress the few, the cunning will not deceive the simple, the noble will not disdain the humble, the rich will not mock the poor, and the young will not encroach upon the old. And the states in the empire will not harm each other with water, fire, poison, and weapons.[38]

To those who found his approach excessively idealistic, Mo Tzu preached as follows:

> The knights and gentleman everywhere to-day, however, say that although in theory this kind of all-embracingness is very good, none the less it is very difficult for universal application. The word of our Master Mo is: the leaders in society simply do not understand what is to their profit, nor do they distinguish the facts. Take the case of besieging a city. To fight in the fields, to achieve fame at the cost of one's life: this is what all men everywhere find very difficult. Yet if their sovereign calls for it, then the whole body of knights are able to do it. How very different from this is mutual all-embracing love and the mutual exchange of profit. To love and benefit another is to have him follow and love and benefit you. To hate and injure another is to have him follow on and hate and injure you. What is there difficult in this? The fact is simply that no ruler has [yet] embodied it in his government and no knight has embodied it in his conduct.[39]

To Mo Tzu, aggression is simply irrational. For this reason, his followers preached avidly throughout China, attempting to show people the practical advantages of universal love. The Mo-ists did not condemn self-defence. Mo Tzu assumed, however, that once rulers understood the futility of offensive war, defensive war would become unnecessary. This sage's ideas are appealing, but they had no more success at ending war in ancient China than similar philosophies have had in the West.

The Strategists

Other Chinese thinkers addressed the problem of warfare from the perspective of a military commander. The most prominent of these thinkers is Sun Tzu, whose *Art of War* sells well throughout the world today. Sun Tzu takes the existence of war for granted. He gives his readers military advice, not ethical precepts. Still, his discussions of how to fight imply certain assumptions about what his readers are fighting for.

Despite the practical nature of his work, Sun Tzu writes from an ethical standpoint. He opens *The Art of War* by reminding readers of their responsibilities. 'War is a matter of vital importance to the state; a matter of life or death, the road either to survival or to ruin. Hence, it is imperative that it be studied thoroughly'.[40]

---

38 de Bary, op. cit., p.47.
39 Baskin, op. cit., pp.99-100.
40 Sun Tzu, trans. Yuan Shibing, commentary by Tao Hanzhang, *Sun Tzu's Art of War: The Modern Chinese Interpretation* (New York: Sterling Publishing Ltd.), p.94.

Not only must a responsible leader understand war, he must not enter into it lightly. Sun Tzu suggests that one should only fight in self-protection, and implies that rulers should declare war only for national, rather than personal considerations.

> If not in the interests of the state, do not act. If you cannot succeed, do not use troops. If you are not in danger, do not fight a war. A sovereign cannot launch a war because he is enraged, nor may a general fight a war because he is resentful. For while an angered man may again be happy, and a resentful man again be pleased, a state that has perished cannot be restored, nor can the dead be brought back to life. Therefore the enlightened ruler is prudent and the good general is warned against rash action.[41]

To wage war responsibly, Sun Tzu suggests, one must wage it effectively. This means that one must reject scruples and superstitions that inhibit rational strategy. Sun Tzu dismisses divination, sorcery and appeals to the gods.[42] Thus, he rejects the quasi-religious beliefs of his day. Many thinkers of Sun Tzu's era, notably Confucius and his followers, argued that rulers should model their decisions on the presumably wiser and more moral actions of ancient kings. Sun Tzu rejects analogies with past events as completely as he rejects fortune-telling.[43]

The Art of War has no place for chivalry either. Legends from earlier generations tell how, when one archer fired at the enemy, he would then courteously wait for his enemy to shoot back before launching a second arrow.[44] Sun Tzu coldly advises commanders '[w]hen the enemy presents an opportunity, speedily take advantage of it'.[45] Likewise, Sun Tzu advises rulers not to follow the ancient practice of choosing a pre-arranged battlefield by mutual agreement with the enemy commander.[46] Rather, one should seize the ground the enemy values most.

Later generations of Chinese strategists were even more frank about advocating dishonourable ruses:

> Whenever about to engage an enemy in battle, first dispatch some emissaries to discuss a peace treaty ... Then, relying on [the enemy's] indolence and laxity, select elite troops and suddenly strike them, for their army can be destroyed. A tactical principle from [Sun Tzu's] *Art of War* states: 'One who seeks peace without setting any prior conditions is executing a stratagem'. [47]

---

41 Ibid., p.125.
42 Ibid., p.126.
43 Ibid.
44 F.A. Kierman Jr., 'Phases and Modes of Combat in Early China', in F.A. Kierman Jr. & J.K. Fairbank (eds.), *Chinese Ways in Warfare* (Cambridge, Mass.: Harvard University Press, 1974), p.43.
45 Sun Tzu, op cit., p.122.
46 Ibid., pp.122-3.
47 R.D. Sawyer, trans., *One Hundred Unorthodox Strategies: Battles and Tactics of Chinese Warfare* (Boulder CO: Westview Press, 1996), p.218.

Sun Tzu advises commanders to be equally pragmatic in handling their own troops. According to *The Art of War*, one should bestow rewards purely according to merit, not customary practice.[48] One should put deliberately troops in desperate situations in order to force them to fight desperately.[49] Compassion, Sun Tzu notes, can be a weakness in a general.[50] Nevertheless, Sun Tzu not only holds that one must use soldiers' lives as sparingly as possible, he holds that one must minimize civilian suffering as well.

This theme runs throughout *The Art of War*. Sun Tzu expresses it in ringing terms near the end of his work. In his final chapter, Sun Tzu admonishes rulers concerning the importance of drawing upon all possible sources of intelligence in order to make strategy as efficiently as possible.

> Now when an army of one hundred thousand is raised and dispatched on a distant campaign. The expenses borne by the people together with disbursements of the treasury will amount to a thousand pieces of gold daily. In addition, there will be continuous commotion both at home and abroad, people will be exhausted by the corvee of transport, and the farm work of seven hundred thousand households will be disrupted.[51]

Under these circumstances, Sun Tzu concludes, if anyone fails to do everything within his power to defeat the enemy and end these sufferings '[s]uch a man is no general, no good assistant to his sovereign, and such a sovereign no master of victory'.[52]

Sun Tzu, in short, acknowledges the evils of war and seeks to limit them. Although he does not condemn the practice of war altogether, he follows the Taoists in advocating restraint. His admirers in later centuries amplified the point that the army is 'an inauspicious instrument,' and warfare is 'a contrary virtue'.[53] War, like fire, will burn those who use it too freely. 'Even though a state may be vast, those who love warfare will inevitably perish'.[54]

The Legalists

China's thinkers, however, were not all humanitarians. Other writers of the period phlegmatically accepted war as the natural business of the state. Shang Yang, a prominent early member of a school of thought known as Legalism, declared bluntly 'the means whereby a country is made prosperous are agriculture and

---

48 Sun Tzu, op. cit., p.122.
49 Ibid., p.122.
50 Ibid., p.112.
51 Ibid., p.126.
52 Ibid.
53 Sawyer, op. cit., p.264.
54 Ibid.

war'.[55] A ruler should systematically organize society, Shang Yang suggested, to discipline people for these activities.

Shang Yang cares nothing about the moral qualities of the rulers, and he has no scruples against aggression.

> A country of a thousand chariots is able to preserve itself by defence, and a country of ten thousand chariots is able to round itself off by fighting [i.e. wars of aggression] – even [a bad ruler like the legendary tyrant] Chieh ... would yet be able to subdue his enemies.[56]

With military advantage, Shang Yang implies, a state will succeed. Without it, moral and intellectual qualities are worthless.

> [I]f one is incapable of waging war [to conquer territory abroad] and at home one is incapable of defence, then even Yao [legendary for his wise rulership] could not pacify for any misbehaviour a country that [normally] would be no match for him. Looking at it from this point of view, that through which the country is important and that through which the ruler is honoured is force.[57]

Shang Yang advised rulers to ignore public opinion.[58] In the same vein, he suggested that the state should feel free to introduce innovative policies, rather than blindly following tradition.[59] Later generations of Legalists proceeded to reject most ancient Chinese concepts of morality as incompatible with sound rulership.[60] Charity, these writers suggested, merely encourages those who fail to provide for themselves, and patronage of arts merely encourages people to take up unproductive occupations.[61] If one pays homage to philosophers who 'esteem life', one will merely complicate the problem of motivating people to risk death in war.[62]

Mo Tzu suggested that it would be more rational to cultivate unused land than to seize territory from other countries. Shang Yang and his followers also advocated farming wastelands.[63] To the Legalists, however, one of the primary reasons of doing so was to provide grain for the army.[64] A state that followed such a policy would be able to go on to conquer yet more land, and to use its produce to support yet larger armies and yet greater conquests.

The Legalists recognized no higher purpose than that of building up state power. Some Legalists directly advised rulers to use state power to gratify their personal appetites. 'To possess the empire and yet not be able to indulge one's

55 Baskin, op. cit., p.138.
56 Ibid., p.145.
57 Ibid.
58 Ibid., p.136.
59 Ibid.
60 de Bary, op. cit., pp.126-7.
61 Ibid.
62 Ibid., p.126.
63 Baskin, op. cit., p.136.
64 de Bary, op. cit., p.129.

own desires is called making a shackles out of the empire'.[65]   Other Legalist writings placed less emphasis on the ruler himself and more on the laws and organizations that comprised the government. All, however, agreed that ordinary individuals mattered only insofar as they served the purposes of the state.

Of all the ancient Chinese schools of thought, Confucianism may have had the greatest long-term effect on Chinese culture.   Legalism, however, had the greatest immediate effect on the course of Chinese history. In 350 BCE, Shang Yang secured a position as a royal advisor in the Chinese state known as Ch'in. King Hsiao of Ch'in reformed his country's laws along Legalist lines, securing both military and economic advantages over the other realms of ancient China.

Over the following century, Ch'in gradually grew more powerful.   The influence of Legalist thought grew as well.   King Cheng of Ch'in, who consolidated his rule in 238 BCE, greatly admired Legalist writings. Cheng invited Han Fei-Tzu, one of the greatest Legalist thinkers of the time, to serve in his palace. Jealous courtiers arranged to have Han Fei-Tzu killed. Nevertheless, one of Han's school friends, a Legalist thinker known as Li Ssu, rose through the ranks of Cheng's court to become Grand Councillor, the highest position in the palace bureaucracy.

Li Ssu guided his country through a series of military campaigns in which Ch'in systematically destroyed its rivals and established its dominion over the entire Chinese world. King Cheng crowned himself as Shih-huang-ti, Emperor of China. As Shih-huang-ti's chief advisor, Li Ssu governed the empire according to Legalist principles. Li Ssu's regime joined the earthworks along the empire's northern borders into the first Great Wall, and Li Ssu's regime notoriously attempted to burn most of the books in China. In the process, the Legalist regime exploited its people with a ruthlessness that shocked the Chinese world.

Ch'in's empire survived only a few years after Shih-huang-ti's death. The rebels who overthrew it condemned Legalism as immoral. Traditional accounts of Chinese history describe the Legalists as villains. Nevertheless, the Chinese continued to study Legalist texts, and most of China's imperial dynasties have used Legalist methods.[66]   Mao Zedong admired the Legalists, and the communist reformers who dominate the current Beijing regime used Legalist arguments in their struggle against the lunatic fringe of the Cultural Revolutionaries.[67]

Conclusion

China produced both moralists and Machiavellians. If the moralists never persuaded rulers to follow their teachings, the Machiavellians never extinguished peoples' drive to place kindness or, at least, utilitarianism above the wild brutality

65 Ibid., p.142.
66 A. Waley, *Three Ways of Thought in Ancient China* (London: George Allen & Unwin, 1939), pp.199-252.
67 M. Goldman, 'China's Anti-Confucian Campaign 1973-1974', *China Quarterly*, no.63, September 1975, p.441.

of war. In these ways, Chinese thinkers have covered much of the same ground as their counterparts in the West and produced broadly comparable results. Although one may note that Chinese rulers paid great homage to Confucianism but failed to act like good Confucians in practice, one might say much the same of Christianity.

None of these schools of thought prescribe detailed laws to regulate war. The ancient Chinese do not seem to have put much effort into exploring the logical consequences of self-defence either. Despite the fact that ancient Chinese military thinkers were well aware of the concept of pre-emptive attack, Chinese philosophers often seem to assume that one can easily distinguish between offensive and defensive wars. Those who seek a painstaking analysis of such matters may conclude that Chinese thought on the subject is simplistic.

Despite the lack of such analysis, however, Chinese thought is often quite practical. If Mo Tzu failed to abolish war, he still deserves credit for his attempt to unite a philosophy of 'universal love' with rationality. The doctrines of Nazi Germany and Soviet Russia had little to add to Legalism. Sun Tzu remains widely read for his military ideas, and even his moral thought presents a useful blend of ethical responsibility and pragmatism. All these practical theories take some inspiration from Taoism.

Taoism emerges as the basis for some of ancient China's most useful ideas on the morality of war. This school of thought is also the one which differs most from Western writings on the subject. A philosopher of the Socratic tradition will not be satisfied with Lao Tzu's willingness to rely on intuition. Nevertheless, Western philosophers such as Aristotle have acknowledged the role of practical experience in politics. Until philosophers develop a perfect theory of human affairs, this form of intuition is likely to dominate statecraft. Given that fact, theories that embrace the concept of such wisdom and explore its consequences may have a great deal to teach us.

Chapter 10

The Arabs, the Byzantine State and the Islamic Law of War (*fiqh al-jihad*) (7th-10th Centuries CE)

Frank R. Trombley

One of the underlying ideological features of the Muslim penetration of mediaeval Asia Minor was the concept of *jihad* or 'fighting in the cause of God'. The behaviour of *ghazi* fighters is well known for the Saljuq and early Ottoman periods, but less is known for the earlier period because the sources are less explicit about religious motives. The Byzantine writers are prone to describe the Arab fighters as 'godless sons of Ishmael' or 'sons of Agar',[1] but show little interest in Muslims except successful generals or soldiers who converted to Christianity, whereas for Arab writers the emphasis is more on the tribal values of valour typically expressed in the pre-Islamic *'ayam* ('days') or battle narratives.[2]

The religious motive of 'fighting in the cause of God' was an unspoken assumption in the narratives about the Arab wars against Byzantine Anatolia.[3] This was partly because *jihad* was a complex legal matter, something better handled by Muslim jurists than historians.[4] Arab expeditions had a legal dimension covering every aspect of warfare. The *amir* or military commander was also usually an *imam* or prayer leader to whom all questions covering the legitimacy of particular acts of war had to be referred. With a large expedition, a *qadi* or judge qualified to interpret Islamic law might be present; very rarely a *qadi* might himself lead an

---

1   F. Halkin (ed.), 'Saint Antoine le jeune et Pétronas le vainquer des Arabes en 863 (d'après un texte inédit)', *Analecta Bollandiana*, no.62, 1944, p.218, line 9f.; p.219, line 21.

2   F. Rosenthal, *History of Muslim Historiography* (Leiden, 1969), pp.66-71.

3   On ideological issues, see A. Noth, *Heiliger Krieg und heiliger Kampf in Islam und Christentum* (Bonn, 1966), pp.13-92.

4   On the law of war, M. Khadduri, *The Islamic Law of Nations. Shaybani's Siyar* (Baltimore: John Hopkins Press, 1966); M. Bonner, *Aristocratic Violence and Holy War: Studies in the Jihad and the Arab-Byzantine Frontier* (New Haven: American Oriental Society, 1996), with bibliography; M. Kister, 'Land property and *jihad*', *Journal of the Economic and Social History of the Orient*, no.34, pp.270-311; J. Kraemer, 'Apostates, rebels and brigands', *Israel Oriental Studies*, no.10, 1980, pp.34-73.

expedition in the course of a planned pilgrimage.[5]   All acts of war raised legal questions under this system, as for example the terms and procedure for accepting the capitulation of a fortress, the proper disposition of captives and portable booty, and the acceptable limits of destroying enemy property.   An expedition was not properly terminated until a *qadi* at the home base of the force saw to the final division of the spoils.[6]

The Qur'anic provisions for fighting in the cause of God are well-known: not long after the Islamic community at Madina took shape, Muhammad announced the fight to overcome religious dissension with the Makkans.[7]   After the Muslim conquest of the Near East the concept was expanded to take in the geopolitical realities of the Islamic state.[8]   State systems whose monarchs had been invited to accept Islam but refused were counted as part of the *dar al-harb*, the 'region of war' where conflict might justly be imposed until those who dissented became Muslim, or they formally submitted and became *dhimmi*. An early statement of this position is found in Abu Yusuf's *Kitab al-Kharaj* from the caliphate of Harun al-Rashid (786-809 CE); here the merit of *jihad* is emphasized, as is the maintenance of the garrison towns on the frontiers of Islam, which are called 'the prop of Islam, the bane of the enemy and the gatherers of wealth'.[9]   By the eleventh century it was generally agreed that an important obligation of the imamate was the waging of *jihad*, whether offensively or in defence of the lands of Islam.[10]   The task fell in theory to the caliph as the chief *imam*, but in practice it devolved to the initiative of local governors and, at the level of policy, to the *wazir*s of the caliphate.   The defence of the Byzantine land and naval frontiers was invariably against them, as for example Mu'awiya, first as governor of Syria, then as caliph; Ibn Tulun in ninth-century Egypt, and Sayf ad-Dawla the *amir* of Aleppo in the 950s. On occasion there were important caliphal campaigns, like the one launched by Harun al-Rashid, the heir apparent, which crossed Anatolia to the Bosporus in 781/2, and the one that reached Ankyra in 806.

A substructure of the Islamic law and ideology of war is expressed in the Muslim narratives about these campaigns. For example, in a poem by Abu al-'Athaniya, the Byzantine emperor Nikephoros I is celebrated as a protected alien or

---

5   This applies to all expeditions led by the caliph himself and, for example, to the case of Ibrahim b. Ahmad b. al-Aghlab who led an expedition against Sicily in 874/5.

6   The above categories can be found in the chapter summaries of Ibn Abi Zayd al-Qayrawani's *Kitab al-jihad*, in M. von Bredow (ed.), *Der heilige Krieg (Gihad) aus der Sicht der malikitischen Rechtsschule* (Beirut: Franz Steiner, 1994), pp.63-132.

7   Qur'an 2, 186-9; 190-3. On the Qur'anic period, see R. Firestone, *Jihad: The Origin of Holy War in Islam* (New York and Oxford: Oxford University Press, 1999).

8   F.M. Donner, 'The Sources of Islamic Conceptions of War', in J. Kelsay and J.T. Turner (eds.), *Just War and Jihad* (Westport: Greenwood, 1991), pp.49-52.

9   B. Lewis, *Islam from the Prophet Muhammad to the Capture of Constantinople*, vol.1 (Oxford: Oxford University Press, 1974), pp.156 & 165. The fiscal dimension is treated in P. von Sievers, 'Taxes and Trade in the Abbasid Thughur, 750-962/133-351', *Journal of the Economic and Social History of the Orient*, no.25, 1982, pp.71-99.

10   al-Mawardi, *al-Ahkam al-Sultaniyya*, cited from Lewis, *Islam*, pp.7-9.

dhimmi after the raid of 806;[11] later, when the emperor violated the treaty by refusing to pay the capitation tax agreed in the treaty, another court poet broke the news to Harun al-Rashid in a tactful composition that salutes him as the conscientious *imam* who like a *malik* or secular king goes in person to 'Holy War'; as the bringer of bad news, the nervous poet also reminds the caliph that 'warning the *imam* is a religious duty, an expiation and a cleansing for those who do it'.[12] There are traces of a religious substrate in accounts of the raids of this period – for example al-Hasan's raid of 779 against Dorylaion. After his return, as al-Tabari states, 'Hafs b. 'Amir al-Sulaimi was in charge of the judicial business of his camp and the spoil that was collected'.[13] Hafs was an *imam* and perhaps *qadi*, who supervised the division of the booty after the raid according to the accepted principles.

The preoccupation of the Islamic sources with data about the numbers of captives, important prisoners taken (e.g. a bishop of Cyprus in 805/6),[14] conditions of surrender, places of encampment, the cutting down of trees, and the like, were all part of the tally required by the religious system. The most detailed assessment from the early period of the wars is found in al-Tabari's account of the great raid of 781/2 that reached the Bosporus.[15] The pervasive legal and religious requirements of living in the camp of an army on campaign is seen in a report about Mu'tadir's capture of the rebel Wasif on 14 November 900 CE.[16]

> [Mu'tadir] passed on to 'Ayn Zarba where he constructed a camp and where he left Khafif al-Samarqandi with the baggage. He left in company with his generals in the direction of the eunuch Wasif. After the prayer of 'Asr he received the good news of the eunuch's capture … He accorded *'aman* to the eunuch's troops and had it announced that the [booty] in the baggage of what had been found coming from the sack of the eunuch's camp and had not been distributed to the soldiers should be put outside the law [of soldier's plunder]. The soldiers of Mu'tadid handed over the greater part of the objects in their possession taken in the camp of Wasif.

It must be remembered that Muslims inherited the pre-Islamic idea of 'fate' or 'time' (*dahr*) that saw all events in a deterministic way and, in Islam, as absolutely determined by God.[17] The idea was first expressed regarding war after the battle of Uhud: Muhammad received a revelation (Qur'an 3.154) that God willed all the actions of the men who fought on that day, to such an extent that he might have

---

11 Lewis, op cit., p.28f.

12 Abu al-Faraj al-Isfahani, *Al-Aghani* 17, 44-6, cited in Lewis, op cit., p.29f.

13 E.W. Brooks, 'Byzantines and Arabs in the time of the early Abbasids', *English Historical Review*, no.15, 1900, p.736.

14 Ibid., p.745.

15 Ibid., p.738.

16 Al-Tabari, *Ta'rikh* III, 2198f. M. Canard, *Byzance et les Arabes II/2: La dynastie macédonienne (867-959)* (Brusssels, 1935), p.15.

17 W. Montgomery Watt, *Islamic Philosophy and Theology* (Edinburgh: Edinburgh University Press, 1985), p.25f.

transported unwilling participants to the fighting solely by his will. This form of determinism is implied many times in the wars of Harun al-Rashid, as for example in the raid of 781/2: 'the number of beasts trained to bear burdens *that God delivered into his hands* was 20,000'.[18] Or about the raid of 779/80 when al-Mahdi was caliph: 'And God made great conquests by their hands, and bestowed conspicuous favour upon them in that land [of the Romans]'.[19] Or more vividly in 805/6, when Harun al-Rashid made a pointed cap for himself on which was written 'raider and pilgrim', inasmuch as *jihad* was considered a lesser form of pilgrimage. The poet Abu al-Mu'ali al-Kilabi is reputed to have saluted the *khalifa* in terms that mimic the *dahr* controlled by God alone:[20]

> And who would seek or wish to contend with you, whether in the holy cities or on the farthest frontier, whether in the enemy's land or on a high-bred horse or in the land of ease upon a camel's saddle? And none beside you subdued the frontiers.

In the summer raid of 802/3, when Harun al-Rashid did not participate in armed pilgrimage against Anatolia, he sent his son al-Qasim instead, with a view to fulfilling a sense of religious obligation: 'And he gave him to God and made him an oblation for himself and a propitiation; and he appointed him *wali* of al-'Awasim [the defensive zone behind the *thughur*]'.[21] The hand of God was seen even in the operation of the war machines used to attack cities by both Arabs and Byzantines. At the thirty-eight day siege of the fortress of Samalu, Harun al-Rashid 'set up siege-engines against it *until God took it*'.[22]

A harder question to answer is what level of religious consciousness motivated the ordinary fighters. Some answers to this are evident in Michael Bonner's discussion of saints and scholars on the Arab-Byzantine frontier.[23] It was necessary to remind ordinary fighters of this dimension, and elaborate provision was made to reinforce this with liturgical acts. The institutional form of this practice was the foundation of mosques hard against the frontier, as for example the one at Tyana in Cappadocia, an advanced base from which the Muslims carried on the war inside Byzantine Asia Minor.[24] Thematically important passages were recited from the Qur'an before battle, particularly when the obligation of holy war and pilgrimage were combined in a particular expedition. The information on this is not very detailed for Anatolia, so one must look further afield. There is an example of it from the Maghrib and Sicily in 874/5. Ibn al-Athir reports:[25]

18 Brooks, 'Abbasids', p.738.
19 Ibid., p.736.
20 Ibid., p.745.
21 Ibid., p.742. On al-'Awasim, see Bonner, *Aristocratic Violence*, pp.87-92.
22 Brooks, 'Abbasids', p.737.
23 Bonner, *Aristocratic Violence*, pp.107-34.
24 Cf. J.F. Haldon and H. Kennedy, 'The Arab-Byzantine Frontier in the Eighth and Ninth Centuries: Military Organisation and Society in the Borderlands', *Zbornik Radova Vizantoloskog Instituta*, no.19 (Belgrade, 1980), pp.79-116.
25 Ibn al-Athīr VII, 196f, in Canard, *Byzance et les Arabes* II/2, p.133f.

[Ibrahim b. Ahmad b. al-Aghlab] resolved to go on pilgrimage ... As he knew that if he wished to go to Makka he would have to go by way of Egypt, and the ruler of that country Ahmad b. Tulun would prevent his passage ... he resolved to take the route to Sicily with the aim of simultaneously accomplishing the duty of holy war and that of pilgrimage, and to conquer the rest of the fortresses of Sicily. He therefore collected the arms and money he had accumulated; he went to Sousse [in Tunisia] where he put on a garment of sewn-together leather as the ascetics wear on the first day of the year 289 [16 December 901] and left for Sicily with a fleet. After landfall he marched on Taormina whose inhabitants had prepared for battle. When he arrived they sortied against him. For this reason, a Qur'an reader recited the *aya* 'We have given you a splendid victory' (48.1). The *amir* then recited, 'Say, there are two adversaries who are disputing on the subject of their Lord' (22.20). The *amir* recited this *aya* and said, 'My Lord, it is I today who have a difference of opinion with the infidels, and I carry it before you today!'

The Muslims are then said to have routed the Byzantines, killing many and chasing them straight into the town.[26]

When battles could not be avoided on holy days or in the holy month of Ramadan the Muslims perhaps fought much harder, but the Arab annalists seldom have any additional comment to make, as for example the serious battle at an undisclosed location in Sicily that fell on the Id of the Sacrifices (8 May 952).[27] The Muslim sources are in universal agreement that the *mujahidun* of Tarsos conducted raids during the holy month of Ramadan, whether for reasons of opportunism or operational deception.[28] Governor Thamal led a deep penetration into Anatolia with a large force of cavalry and slow-footed infantry in Rajab 319 (20 July – 18 August 931), evidently knowing it might be difficult to finish the operation before the start of Ramadan. He reached and occupied 'Ammuriya, which the forces of the Anatolikon theme had evacuated, and then pushed northward to Ankyra, plundering widely in the territories of the Byzantine fortresses, and re-entered Tarsos near the end of Ramadan (17 September – 16 October 931). Thamal's late return was governed by a spirit of opportunism: the Byzantine defences were weak and, consequently, it was possible to collect a large number of captives. The gross receipts of their sale were 136,000 *solidi*, a figure suggesting that the human booty came to more than 5,000 persons.[29] Muslim forces energetically resisted Byzantine raids that occurred in Ramadan and engaged in manoeuvre warfare against them.

---

26 More broadly, see W. Granara, *Political Legitimacy and Jihad in Muslim Sicily 217/827 – 445/1053* (Doctoral dissertation, University of Pennsylvania, 1986).

27 Ibn al-Athir VIII, 371, in Canard, *Byzance et les Arabes* II/2, p.160.

28 On the Muslim *jihad* establishment at Tarsos, see C.E. Bosworth, 'The City of Tarsus and the Arab-Byzantine Frontiers in Early and Middle Abbasid Times', *Oriens*, no.33, 1992, pp.268-86, and 'Abu 'Amr 'Uthman al-Tarsusi's *Siyar al-Thughur* and the Last Years of Arab Rule in Tarsus (Fourth/Tenth century)', *Graeco-Arabica*, no.5, 1993, pp.183-94.

29 Ibn al-Athir VIII, 172-174, in Canard, *Byzance et les Arabes* II/2, p.152f.

Assemblies at mosques usually preceded the Muslim army's ceremonial exit from Tarsos as it went against the Byzantine defences. The only record we have of this is, however, about an expedition sent to the frontier to collect Muslim prisoners being exchanged for Byzantine captives. The incident took place in 896/7 CE:[30]

> [Ahmad b. Tughan invited the population of Tarsos to assist in the prisoner exchange on 17 September 896.] He left for the Lamis [river] where the Muslim camp was on [18 September]. After inviting the people to leave with him, he made the Friday prayer; leaving the cathedral mosque, he mounted his horse accompanied by Rajib and his clients. The notables of the town, their clients and officers left with him, as also the volunteers in splendid array.

Expressions of enthusiasm were not confined to the immediate frontier zone:[31]

> This same year [959/60 CE] the preacher 'Abd al-Rahim b. Nubata gave the sermons for holy war with remarkable technique. It is said that, after he composed the sermon, he mounted the lectern to pronounce it and that the mosque was full of listeners. When the left the mosque, the greater number left for holy war. This holy war against the Byzantines continued until the death of Sayf al-Dawla and his son Abu al-Malili Sharif.

Ideological pronouncements permeated the diplomatic dealings of the caliphate with the Byzantines. There was, for example, the letter of a ninth-century caliph to emperor Michael III (842-67) bidding him to accept Islam; the document may well have contained dialectical argumentation based on the Greek philosophical studies then proliferating at the caliphal court in Baghdad, for the Byzantine reply written by Niketas of Byzantium uses a combination of dialectic salted with ridicule in its attack on the Qur'an.[32] Ideological pronouncements were a feature of less pointed exchanges, like the letter of caliph al-Radi asking for a treaty and exchange of prisoners in 937/8 CE. Its prescript has a predictable content:[33]

> In the name of God the merciful the compassionate. From the slave of God Abu al-'Abbas, the *imam* al-Radi in the name of God, *amir* of the believers to Romanos, Constantine and Stephen, leaders of the Byzantines. Safety to him who follows the straight road, who supports himself with a sure support (Qur'an 2, 257; 31, 21) and marches on the path of safety and to the nearness of God. The *amir* of the believers praises God, one, eternal who has neither wife nor offspring, nor a companion or partner.

The letter goes on to cite more *aya*s on peacemaking and holy war, and concludes with a benediction on Muhammad. The ideological cant was at times perhaps meant to bolster the self-confidence of the Muslim ruling elites. One

---

30 Al-Tabari III, 2152f, in Canard, *Byzance et les Arabes* II/2, p.11f.
31 Ibn al-Azraq al-Fariqi, in Canard, *Byzance et les Arabes* II/2, p.117.
32 A.Th. Khoury, *Les théologiens byzantins et l'Islam. Textes et auteurs (VIIIe – XIIIe s.)* (Louvain and Paris: Editions Nauwelaerts, 1969), pp.110-62.
33 Sibt ibn al-Jawzi, in Canard, *Byzance et les Arabes* II/2, p.173.

thinks, for example, of the poetry of al-Mutanabbi, whose praise of Sayf ad-Dawla repeats the literary commonplaces of *jihad* in works designed to put a good face on some desperate engagements the *amir* fought while manoeuvring the Byzantine defences in the trans-Taurus steppe: their concentric attacks and blocking positions caused him to lose his booty and let him escape with only a small party of his elite guard.[34]

The Christian Arab historian Yahya b. Sa'id al-Antaki was conversant with the legal realities of the tenth-century wars, as revealed by his account of the transfer of the *mandylion* of Edessa to the Byzantine state in 944.[35] A Byzantine army had entered Mesopotamia and raided the countryside round Diyar Bakr and the old Sasanid province of Arzanene, marching clockwise around Tur 'Abdin, passing Nisibis and reaching Edessa, probably in 943.[36] There the Byzantine commander offered to exchange some of his Muslim captives for the *mandylion*, a cloth image on which the image of Christ's face was thought to have been impressed. The authorities in Edessa thought the matter sufficiently important, correctly as it turned out, to refer it to the caliph al-Muttaqi who asked for a clarification from the *qadi*s and Muslim jurists (*al-qadat wa-al-fuqaha*). The Christian Yahya summarises the main points at issue under Islamic law:[37]

> There was a long discussion in which some of the assistants explained the significance of this *mandylion*, to find out how long it had been in this church; [it was found] that none of the Byzantine emperors had reclaimed it, that the handing over [of the image] marked the degradation of Islam, and that the Muslims had a prior right to the *mandylion* of Jesus – may peace be upon him – in view of where the image was [at present]. But then 'Ali b. 'Isa said that the ransoming of Muslims from captivity and their escape from a life of impiety and the misfortune and oppression that [the Byzantines] were attempting were more necessary and urgent. All the assistants agreed with his words, and he and the other Muslim *qadi*s advised that they accept the captives and hand over the mandylion because they did not have sufficient force to use against them and did not have the means to purchase the captives back from their hands. So the *wazir* drew up the protocol and had his assistants sign it.

The agreement guaranteed the exchange of two hundred Muslim captives; the authorities at Edessa (*'ahl al-Ruha*) specified one additional condition, that the Byzantines give them immunity against future raids, and a treaty of 'eternal peace' was concluded. The Muslims' deliberations and negotiations with the Byzantines were long protracted, for the *mandylion* was not delivered to Constantinople until

---

34 M. Canard, 'Mutanabbi et la guerre byzantino-arabe. Intérêt historique de ses poésies', in C. Cahen (ed.), *Byzance et les musulmans du Proche Orient* (London: Varorium Reprints, 1973).

35 The incident is described at Yahya b. Sa'id al-Antaki, *Histoire*, ed. and trans. I. Kratchkovsky and A. Vasiliev, in *Patrologia Orientalis*, no.18, 1924, pp.730-32 [32-34].

36 Yahya dates the raid to AH 331 = 15 September 942 to 3 September 943.

37 Yahya, *Histoire* 1, 731 [33].

the following year, on 15 August 944. The *fatwa*[38] of the Muslim jurists relied on the argument of military and financial necessity, combined with the risk that the Muslims might apostasize under the burdens of Christian captivity. This risk outweighed the argument of Muslim ownership and Islamic theological correctness. The Muslims' prior entitlement to the *mandylion* was certainly seen in light of Qur'anic theology where Jesus is seen as an entirely human prophet, and therefore not entitled to the *proskynesis* and the other trappings of divine worship that Byzantine and Syrian Christians were all too willing to grant his image.

The Byzantines are frequently mentioned in the legal treatises on *jihad* because of the importance of the wars against their territories. A case in point is the work of Ibn Abi Zayd al-Qayrawani, a tenth-century jurist of the Malikite school, who on occasion makes entirely original observations like one that mentions the important fortress and quasi-urban conglomerate of Amorion (Arabic *'Ammuriya*). Al-Qayrawani's interpretation relies on a text or oral tradition that predates caliph al-Mu'tasim's destruction of the site in 838 CE:[39]

> And in this way the *katib* of the imam exchanges letters with their emperor at a place like Constantinople or 'Ammuriya, when not one of the Muslims has personally entered [the city] after the imam has written a letter to their emperor concerning *sulh* and has required him to write back to him concerning what he might be willing to agree to in this regard: [if] the tyrant [*viz*. Byzantine emperor] wrote the reply and sealed it, but one of the Muslims did not personally witness [this] – neither the envoys nor others – that it is his actual letter, and they were not present at his act of sealing it and the letter has arrived, the imam should read it aloud along with the agreement in it about *sulh*. So that when the Muslims enter the city (*al-madina*), if the tyrant refuses to acknowledge the letter and what they say in it, but the patriarch agrees with us about the capitulation, it is permissible for the [Muslims] to take possession of booty and there is *sulh* with regard to [the Byzantines'] *'aman*.

The recommended practice is at first sight hypothetical, since the Byzantine emperor was not present in 'Ammuriya when it received *'aman* in return for capitulation twice during the seventh-century wintering raids,[40] as for example in 663/4 when the town surrendered to Ibn Khalid with a pact (*sulh*) and housed a Muslim garrison that apparently evacuated the place in the spring of 664.[41] The town had refused to submit to a previous raid led by Mu'awiya b. Abi Sufyan that reached its environs in 643, and so the Muslims exercised their legal right to plunder its *territorium*.[42] They could easily have confused the site's metropolitan status with that of the patriarchate of Constantinople, so this poses no problem for

---

38 Ibn al-Athir VIII, 302f, in Canard, *Byzance et les Arabes* II/ 2, p.156.

39 al-Qayrawani, *Kitab al-jihad*, in Bredow, *Der heilige Krieg*, p.126, lines 3-9.

40 In general, see D. R. Hill, *The Termination of Hostilities in the Early Arab Conquests A.D. 634-656* (London: Luzac, 1971).

41 *Maronite Chronicle* in A. Palmer (ed. and trans.), *The Seventh Century in the West Syrian Chronicles* (Liverpool: Liverpool University Press, 1993), p.34.

42 For the less detailed Arabic sources, see W. Kaegi, 'The First Arab Expedition against Amorium', *Byzantine and Modern Greek Studies*, no.3, 1977, pp.19-22.

understanding al-Qayrawani's text. It is quite possible that his summary goes back to an early legal critique of the Arabic-speaking emperor Leo III's disingenuous dealings with the *amir* Maslama at 'Ammuriya and Constantinople in 716-18 CE, as reported in the *Kitab al-'Uyun* and other sources.[43] Al-Qayrawani's views are consistent with laws concerning *dhimmi*s giving evidence against each other where no Muslim witness was present; hence one could disregard the emperor's disavowal of a written capitulation by resorting to the testimony of a Christian bishop, but only in the absence of Muslim witnesses to the act of sealing.[44]

One side effect of endemic warfare between the Byzantine state and Muslim caliphate was the taking of large numbers of captives and their disposition.[45] The price of a healthy adult male slave remained in the vicinity of 25 *solidi/dinars*, approximately one-third of a pound of gold, making captive-taking a highly profitable activity, particularly when it came to artisans and skilled agricultural workers. Exchanges of prisoners were periodically negotiated between the Byzantine state and the 'Abbasid caliphate during the period when the latter still claimed to exercise some centralized control of the *dar al-islam*. The Muslim writer al-Mas'udi (d. 956/7 CE) reports ten official exchanges of prisoners between 830-946 CE in his geographical work *Kitab al-tanbih wa-al-israf*.[46] The details of prisoner exchange in 830 CE come from Ibn al-Athir:[47] the figures indicate the repatriation of 35,982 Muslim captives over a period of 117 years, or an average of some 307.5 per annum. This can hardly represent more than a small percentage of the Muslims forcibly detained in Byzantine Anatolia between 845-946. Mas'udi mentions the existence of reports about other prisoner exchanges in the years 797, 810, 816, 862 and 872 CE, but gives no figures and expresses doubt as to the certainty of this information.[48] The Muslims had specific legal and religious procedures for the prisoner exchanges. These are evident in Ibn al-Athir's account of the exchange that took place in 830 CE, where he is summarizing the more detailed but less coherent account of al-Tabari.[49]

43 E.W. Brooks, 'The Campaign of 716-718, from Arabic Sources', *Journal of Hellenic Studies*, no.19, 1899, pp.19-33. Text in M.J. de Goeje and P. de Jong (eds.), *Fragmenta Historicorum Arabicorum* I (Leiden: Brill, 1869), pp.16-37. Cf. M. Canard, 'Les expéditions des Arabes contre Constantinople dans l'histoire et dans la légende', *Journal Asiatique*, no.208, 1926, pp.80-102, esp. p.99ff.

44 The Greek *sigillon/sigillion* ('seal, document') became a frequent loan word in Arabic, *sijill/sigill*. G. Graf, *Verzeichnis arabischer kirchlicher Termini* (Louvain: L. Durbecq, 1954), p.58.

45 See the discussion of S. Patoura, *Oi aichmalotai os paragontes epikoinonias kai plerophoreses (4os-10os ai)* (Athens, 1994), p.83ff.

46 M. de Goeje (ed.), *Bibliotheca Geographorum Arabicorum* 8 (Leiden: Brill, 1894; repr. 1967), pp.190-95. H. Grégoire, *Byzance et les Arabes I: La dynastie d'Amorium* (Brussels, 1935), p.336f.; Canard, *Byzance et les Arabes* II/2, pp.405-8.

47 Grégoire, *Byzance et les Arabes* 1, p.353f.

48 Canard, *Byzance et les Arabes* 2, p.408.

49 Ibn al-Athir VII, 16f, in Grégoire, *Byzance et les Arabes* 1, p.353f.

The Lamis river was the recognized frontier between the Byzantine state and the *khalifa* on the Tarsos-Tyana axis.[50] The Muslim authority handling the exchanges of prisoners varied, depending on who controlled northern Syria, the status quo of which was subject to periodic change. The governors of the Thughur and ʿAwasim regularly appointed by the *khalifa* normally supervized the exchanges. This was the case between 830-860, but in 895/6 it was directed by Ibn Tughan, who represented Abu al-Jays Khumarawayh, son of Ahmad b. Tulun, who at that time controlled Egypt, the Syrian provinces, Diyar Mudar and other regions. The regularly appointed governors conducted the exchanges again between 905-938, but in 946 it was handled by a governor of the Syrian frontiers acting in the name of Sayf al-Dawla of Aleppo, who is styled 'ruler of the provinces of Hims, Qinnasrin, Diyar Mudar, Diyar Bakr, and the provinces of the frontiers of Syria and Mesopotamia'. On this occasion there were 230 more Muslim captives than Greek, so Sayf al-Dawla paid for their release out of funds.[51]

The inquiry by a *qadi* into the theological opinions of Muslim captives being released was a regular feature of prisoner exchanges. There was always the risk that they had apostasized while in Byzantine captivity, as the three following examples reveal. A Muslim prisoner who became Christian in captivity and then a Byzantine soldier was *khalifa* al-Muʿtasim's key informant at the siege of ʿAmmuriya in 838 CE; the man gave the location of a stretch of masonry in the curtain wall that had been undermined by a torrent and thereafter shoddily rebuilt; the Muslims entered the city at this spot after directing their siege artillery against it, thanks to this intelligence.[52] The informant had evidently intended to return to Islam when he defected. Apostates were sometimes not given this opportunity. In 927 the summer raid that Thamal led out from Tarsos surprised a Kurdish chieftain named Ibn al-Dahhak who had taken service with the Byzantine emperor after apostasizing from Islam. In return, the Kurd had received a fortress and extensive lands. He was executed with his entire family; it is unknown whether this was because he refused repentance or was given no chance.[53] There were many other ex-Muslim commanders in Byzantine service; even so, the status of apostate made close encounters with Muslim forces risky, as we learn from an incident early in the career of Saʿid b. Hamdan (autumn 931 CE):[54]

> Byzantine troops marched against Samosata and besieged it. The inhabitants appealed to Saʿid b. Hamdan, to whom [the caliph] Muqtadir had entrusted the government of Mawsil and Diyar Rabiʿa, stipulating that he should conduct raids against the Byzantines and attempt to take Malatya-Melitene back from them. The inhabitants of this city, feeling weak, had made peace with the Byzantines and handed over the keys of their city ... [Saʿid b. Hamdan] departed [from Samosata] in the direction of Malatya where he found a Byzantine force and the soldiers of Malih al-Armani, with Bunayy b.

50 E.g. Masʿudi, *Muruj*, in Grégoire, *Byzance et les Arabes* 1, p.329.
51 Ibn al-Athir, VIII, 352, in Canard, *Byzance et les Arabes* II/2, p.157.
52 Al-Tabari, *Taʾrikh* 1245, in Grégoire, *Byzance et les Arabes* 1, p.302.
53 Ibn al-Athir VIII, 129f, in Canard, *Byzance et les Arabes* II/2, p.151.
54 Ibn al-Athir VIII, 172-74, in Canard, *Byzance et les Arabes* II/2, p.153.

Nafis, [a former] officer of [the caliph] Muqtadir who had converted to Christianity and gone over to the Byzantines. When these people learned of the arrival of Sa'id b. Hamdan, they left Malatya, fearing that Sa'id would arrive below the walls of the city and that the population would revolt against them and massacre them.

The former 'Abbasid officer who accepted Christianity seems to have exercised subordinate command in an independent force led by Malih the Armenian. A Byzantine army led by John Kourkouas returned three years later and accepted the surrender of Malatya-Melitene on 19 May 934. A sizeable part of the population seems to have accepted Christianity, to judge from the arrangements made to separate them from the Muslims after the city capitulated on the condition of *'aman*:[55]

> [The] *domestikos* Kourkouas ... besieged and blockaded Malatya for a long time, in the course of which the greater part of the population died of hunger. He had two tents erected, one of which was overtopped with a cross; he announced that those who wished to become Christians should congregate beside the tent with the cross where they were to register their moveable property and families. Those who preferred Islam were to assemble at the other tent, received a guarantee of safety for their lives and were taken away to a secure place. The greater number of Muslims went to the side of the tent overtopped with a cross because they wished to recover their families and moveable property.

Kinship and property became a species of blackmail to compel as many of the legally free Malatyans to accept Christianity. The city remained under Byzantine control until the eleventh century, so it is difficult to gauge how many of these folk would have reverted to Islam, had the opportunity presented itself.

Sayf al-Dawla's amirate at Aleppo provided a significant challenge to the Byzantine land frontier in south-eastern Anatolia during the mid-tenth century. The operations he undertook were characterised by swift, deep penetrations into Anatolia, and at other times by lateral marches along the frontier to cut off Byzantine forces making raids into Muslim territory.[56] The ideological focus of Sayf al-Dawla's campaigns during these years is found in the writings of al-Mutanabbi, a court poet in residence at Aleppo.[57]

A great Byzantine offensive against the Muslim-controlled maritime and military frontiers began in the second half of the tenth-century.[58] The most battleworthy formations were placed under commanders like Nikephoros Phokas, who became emperor not long after his successful siege of Khandaq in 962, the principal fortress of the Muslim *amirs* of Crete, thereby clearing the Aegean

55 Ibn al-Athir VIII, 221f, in Canard, *Byzance et les Arabes* II/2, 154.
56 M. Canard, *Histoire de la dynastie des H'amdanides de Jazira et de Syrie* (Paris, 1953), pp.715-862.
57 R. Blachère, *Un poète arabe du IVe siècle de Hégire (Xe siècle de J.-C.): Abou t-Tayyib al-Motanabbi* (Paris, 1935), pp.144-87.
58 On the Byzantine military infrastructure of this period, see J. Haldon, *Warfare, State and Society in the Byzantine World 565-1204* (London: UCL Press, 1999).

coastlands of the Muslim naval threat.[59]   After this, the main resources of the Byzantine state were directed at gaining control of the Muslim military frontier zones, the Thughur and 'Awasim.   The armoured equipment of key formations in the field army was upgraded and a new system of shock tactics was developed.[60] The emperors Nikephoros Phokas (963-69), John Tzimiskes (969-76) and Basil II (976-1025) oversaw this process, which continued with some interruptions for half a century.

John Tzimiskes' autumn campaign against Dayr Rabi'a in 972 that ended in the sack of Nisibis caused great panic throughout Muslim Mesopotamia, despite his subsequent abandonment of the siege of Mayyafariqin and the destruction of an army commanded by one of his subordinates outside Amida.[61]   The people of Mawsil panicked; only the intervention of the governor Abu Taghlib b. Hamdan prevented them from migrating en masse to Baghdad.   The upshot of the raid suggests that the *jihad* spirit was still alive among the lower classes of Baghdad who marched on the sultan's palace in response to the news, carrying copies of the Qur'an upraised (*al-masahif al-manshura*), in an evident bid to reawaken a similar spirit in the caliphate.[62]   The arming of the populace on the advice of the *shaykh*s ended the public outcry.

Tzimiskes' subsequent operations were directed against Muslim Syria in 975.[63] He raided the territory of Ba'lbak in Ramadan (15 May – 13 June), a tactic designed in this instance to catch villagers outside the fortifications fasting during the long daylight hours of late spring.[64]   The Muslims launched raids against Anatolia during Ramadan in the ninth century, so Tzimiskes' action does not seem to have violated customary practice.

A well-known feature of the Muslim law of war was the immunity granted to Christian monks, as long as they did not take on the role of combatants. One such incident is reported to have occurred on 2 September 985, while Bardas Phokas was attacking Apamea. To distract the Byzantine army from the siege, and taking advantage of weak Byzantine security on its eastern flank, the Turkish chamberlain of the Hamdanid *amir* at Aleppo crossed into Byzantine territory and attacked the Greek and Syriac monastery of St. Symeon the Stylite the Elder at Jabal Sim'an:[65]

Qarghunya marched to Dayr Sim'an the Aleppine which is [located] in the farthest district (*amal*) of Antioch and at the beginning of the district of Aleppo. He besieged it

---

59 V. Christides, *The Conquest of Crete by the Arabs (ca. 824)* (Athens: Akademia Athenon, 1984), pp.172-91.

60 E. McGeer, *Sowing the Dragon's Teeth: Byzantine Warfare in the Tenth Century* (Washington, D.C.: Dumbarton Oaks Research Library, 1995).

61 Yahya b. Sa'id al-Antaki, *Histoire*, ed. and trans. I. Kratchkovsky and A. Vasiliev, in *Patrologia Orientalis*, no.23, 1932, p.353 [145].

62 Yahya, *Histoire* 2, p.354 [146].

63 P. Walker, 'The "Crusade" of John Tzimisces in Light of New Arabic Evidence', *Byzantion*, no.47, 1977, pp.301-27.

64 Yahya, *Histoire* 2, p.368f. [160f.].

65 Yahya, *Histoire* 2, p.416 [208].

for three days and fought a violent battle and conquered it by the sword ... He killed its community of monks – for it was a flourishing and populous monastery – and took captive people from the district who had taken refuge in it and entered Aleppo with them and they were sold at auction.

The monastery was fortified after the Byzantine reoccupation of Antioch and its surrounding territory in and after 969. It is possible that a small garrison of Greek soldiers was stationed there, and that the monks fought in defence of the site. If so, they would have been acting in accordance with Syriac canon law and at the same time would have forfeited non-combatant status under Islamic law.[66] The rural population that took refuge at Dayr Sim'an in 985 was mostly Christian Arabic- and Syriac-speaking, to judge from the early medieval epigraphy of the Limestone Massif.[67] Qarghunya's manoeuvre achieved its operational aim, for emperor Basil abandoned the siege of Apamea.

Muslim legal practice had to some extent become the customary law of war in Syria by the late tenth century.[68] The Byzantine emperor sometimes observed it in negotiating the surrender of towns and fortresses whilst personally leading the army. Basil II invaded Muslim Syria in the autumn of 999, marching up the Orontes river valley as far as Hims-Emesa. Upon reaching Shayzar-Larisa, his army cut the aqueduct (*sikkatu al-ma'i*) and besieged the town without result until 28 October, when Basil entered negotiations with the Fatimid governor to surrender the place:[69]

In [Shayzar] there was a governor loyal to al-Hakim [the Fatimid caliph] who was named al-Halman and known as Ibn Karadis. The emperor sent to him about surrendering the town and his desire for [to purchase?] it.[70] [The governor] did not reply. When the matter was protracted – the siege and the shortage of water for the people in the fortress – Ibn Karadis requested '*aman* from [the emperor], applying the stipulation to it that [the governor] should not have to step on the [emperor's] carpet during his departure from the town and that [the emperor] should not obstruct him or any of his companions who chose to depart with him. [The emperor] accepted these conditions and sent his cross (*salib*) to him; Ibn Karadis opened the gate and departed with all the people [of Shayzar] to Hama and from there to Aleppo.

66 The Rules of Ja'qob of Edessa § 7 (late 7th – early 8th c.) state: 'And monks who by force have been driven to cast stones by (war) machines shall not be blamed by the canons'. A. Vööbus (ed. and trans.), *Syriac and Arabic Documents Regarding Legislation Relative to Syrian Asceticism* (Stockholm, 1960), p.95f.

67 F. Trombley, 'Demographic and Cultural Transition in the *Territorium* of Antioch, 6th-10th c.', *Topoi*, no.12, 2002, forthcoming.

68 Cf. the use of '*aman*, *salam* and the Islamic tax categories in the tenth and eleventh century peace settlements negotiated between the Normans and Muslims of Sicily is provisionally suggestive of this. D.A. Agius, *Siculo Arabic* (London and New York: Kegan Paul, 1996), pp.68-71.

69 Yahya, *Histoire* 2, p.457 [249].

70 This is Cheiko's suggestion. I am unable to deduce this from Stem I of the root *waghaba*.

The agreement was in line with customary practice: *'aman* had probably by this time become a loanword in Byzantine Greek; and the handing over of the Greek monarch's cross lent force to the promise of safe conduct; the category of 'companions' (*'ashab*) was evidently applied to anyone who wished to depart with the *amir*, including elements of the Muslim civil population. So many departed that the emperor felt it necessary to repopulate Shayzar with Armenians.[71]   The Muslims' expectations were sometimes disappointed during the campaign of 999.

In conclusion, several points require emphasis. The first is that what is called *jihad* might more aptly be called the 'Islamic law of war', if not the Islamic form of international law.   Like other aspects of Islamic thought, the law of war embraces every aspect of human activity: 'fighting in the cause of God' implied a complex system of ethics and lawful procedure that was in the best of circumstances difficult to observe.   In contrast to the Arabs of the seventh-tenth centuries, the *ghazi*s of Saljuq and Turkmen Anatolia were observing an individualistic and simplified form of law inspired by the *darvish*es and Turkish folk custom. So, in speaking about *jihad*, it is important to recognize that it is as much about fighting as about the state of mind in which the fighter reached the battlefield and how he conducted himself afterward, about his religious motives as much as his actions.   And the 'his' is perhaps questionable, since women are known to have accompanied the armies as well. Al-Tabari reports such an instance in 756 CE.:

> [Salih b. 'Ali and 'Abbas b. Muhammad] made a raid against the Adata pass and invaded al-Rum. And Salih was accompanied on the raid by his sisters Umm 'Isa and Lubaba *banat* 'Ali who made a vow that, if the dominion of the Umayyads were ended, they would wage war in the cause of God.

71 See above, note 70.

Chapter 11

The Rules of War in Sub-Saharan Africa

Alexander Moseley

Introduction

Unsurprisingly, the tribes of Sub-Saharan Africa share similar rules and expectations of conduct in war with other societies around the world. War is a costly endeavour – increasingly so the longer it lasts – and belligerents tend to converge onto mutually beneficial rules of conduct that limit or narrow the extent, duration, and ferocity of war. Such conventions often emerge *spontaneously* through tacit agreements between belligerents, rather than because of any ante-bellum instruction booklet reasoned out in some form of Rawlsian Original Position[1] or Classical Liberal Social Contract.

Pre-colonial Sub-Saharan Africa offers an abundant area of research for just war studies. Anthropologists and other scientists were able to examine and report on tribes' beliefs before native groups were substantially affected by European colonization and commercial expansion, thus providing researchers with an excellent opportunity for examining a plethora of non-Western and non-industrial societies' rules of war.

This chapter reviews the state and development of the just war codes in Sub-Saharan Africa, and it analyzes the tendency towards and the reasons for a convergence or divergence in war's rules in indigenous wars. The history indicates why and how vastly different cultures were able to settle down to a peaceful *modus vivendi*, but it also highlights a significant obstacle to pacific intercourse in Sub-Saharan Africa, which was the lack of alienable land rights. The absence of a literary judicial tradition that could be referred to in explaining the nature and reason for the war codes means that other explanations must be sought, and the paper draws heavily on economics, especially the methods advanced by the 'Austrian school', which prove particularly useful in examining what can be classified as rule formation in pre-political societies.[2]

---

1   For relevant literature, see John Rawls, *A Theory of Justice* (Oxford: Oxford University Press, 1973); Thomas Hobbes, *Leviathan* (London: Penguin, 1968); John Locke, *Two Treatises* (Cambridge: Cambridge University Press, 1967); and Jean-Jacques Rousseau, *The Social Contract* (Harmondsworth: Penguin, 1968).
2   See the works of Ludwig von Mises, Friedrich Hayek, and Murray Rothbard.

The chapter begins with an explanation of the principles behind just war processes relating them to the tribes' rules and codes before reviewing the particular mores of individual tribes.

The Principles of Developing Just War Traditions

Africa presents a vast topic for any field of analysis – it is a land of hundreds of tribes and languages, and five races.[3] The pre-colonial economies ranged from hunter-gatherer communities and nomadic tribes to semi-settled and settled pastoralists. Clashes were frequent and, given the lack of proprietary institutions, inevitable. Aptly described as a 'scenic heaven of which man made a hell'[4] – Africa was conquered, and Africans enslaved, by other Africans and by Arabs, as well as later by Europeans. Except where geography acted to keep some tribes isolated from one another (as well as European expansion until well into the nineteenth century), wars were frequent. 'The whole history of Africa might be written with war as its keynote', writes Davie.[5]

Moreover, as with any vast area of human habitation, the codes of just conduct in Sub-Saharan Africa ranged across a broad spectrum of rules from the chivalrous to the absent. But why did such rules evolve or emerge in pre-political societies, and what explains their absence? Pre-colonial Sub-Saharan Africa offers a useful ground for witnessing the processes that generate and dissemble the codes of war.[6] What principles are learned here can also be applied elsewhere. Understanding the *process* of rule formation enables us to understand why disparate groups tend to converge onto similar regulatory patterns in fighting, as well as providing a basis for understanding why those codes can break down.

Regular convergence in war[7] can be examined from the methods of praxeology.[8] The study of human action provides a thorough basis for understanding the nature as well as the changes in African rules of conduct. That is, a review of the incentives and limitations to ethical conduct that the tribes faced helps to explain the rationale for mitigating warfare. However, contrary to 'positive economics' and Marxian interpretations of economic phenomena,

---

3   J. Diamond, *Guns, Germs and Steel: The Fates of Human Societies* (London: Jonathan Cape, 1997).

4   Employed as a chapter heading by V. Bellers in her 'What Mr Sanders Really Did – or A Speck in the Ocean of Time': http://www.britishempire.co.uk/article/sanders.

5   M.R. Davie, *The Evolution of War: A Study of its Role in Early Societies* (Port Washington, NY: Kennikat Press, 1968), p.56

6   Colonization presents an excellent field of research for how apparently disparate rules of war converge as the groups encounter each other and then settle down.

7   The model is derived from earlier work on the nature of war as a spontaneous institution. See A. Moseley, 'Is War a Spontaneous Hayekian Institution?', *Peace and Change*, February 2002; see also A. Moseley, *A Philosophy of War* (New York: Algora, 2002).

8   Praxeology is the study of human action. See L. von Mises, *Human Action: A Treatise on Economics* (Edinburgh: William Hodge and Company Limited, 1949).

incentives are not merely unvarying or objective entities that agents react to: all values are culturally and hence ideologically infused concepts that are *chosen and sustained* by individuals acting within a group. They are full of implicit and explicit *meaning* in the group's language and customs. They are the product of human action and design; nonetheless, intra-subjective values (and war codes are of this kind) are affected by the institutional rules and presiding arrangements that a tribe's people support and abide by.

If we begin with a principle of human interaction, we can assert that *a priori*, interaction can be either peaceful or violent. Generally speaking, when it is violent, pacific benefits diminish and their marginally increasing scarcity usually (but not necessarily) prompts warriors to admit and acknowledge spheres of peace within war. As a general rule, belligerent groups have a self-interested incentive to retain pacific elements to their violence, and this is especially so when they are militarily evenly matched. *Ceteris paribus*, recognizable rules cultivate beneficial arrangements for both parties that transcend myopic policies of aggression and total war.[9] For example, until their impressive rise under Shaka, the Zulu tribes followed a not untypical policy of settling disputes by pre-arranged combat in which the first side to buckle dropped its spears in surrender, so stopping further bloodshed.[10]

As with most forms and codes of moral behaviour, the rules of just war evolved through what can be described as the result (often unintended) of spontaneous interaction of societies at war and at peace. Historically, literary civilizations codified such rules and conventions,[11] but for the most part they reflected cultural mores that had developed over time with prolonged contact between warring groups. Hence groups adopting just war criteria were more likely to have traded with one another or at least had seen the benefits of restraining the outbreak and range of war, whereas those who lived in isolation or predated on other tribes rarely supported ethical codes of conduct in war.

But what happens to those rules and expectations of conduct when external pressures and internal changes alter the general intertribal dynamic? Human history in Africa is notably unstable: this offers an excellent opportunity for witnessing the clash of disparate rules between migrating groups or the stresses placed on existing arrangements resulting from extreme environmental or demographic changes.[12] *A priori*, after a short-term massive upheaval of previous rules, one should expect that new cultural modes of conduct in war would evolve. Thus far, the theory is simplistic and such processes would be expected; however,

---

9   I use 'total war' to mean the absence of all rules and 'totalitarian war' to mean the complete socialization of all property and production for war's purposes.

10 K.F. Otterbein, 'The Evolution of Zulu Warfare', in P. Bohannan, *Land and Warfare: Studies in the Anthropology of Conflict* (New York: Natural History Press, 1967), p.352.

11 That is, the just war codes predate the explication of the codes.

12 See R.B. Ferguson who writes, 'To the degree that warfare is shaped by kin structures, change in those structures [as a result of demographic changes] will produce changes in warfare'. R.B. Ferguson, 'Explaining War', in J. Haas (ed.), *The Anthropology of War* (Cambridge: Cambridge University Press, 1992), p.53.

when an important economic basis for rule formation – or the lack thereof – is added to African history, a deeper and sounder explanatory theory of comparative just war theory emerges.

What is evident in Africa is that *land* was the foremost driving value over which belligerents fought, and which was also the value that later European settlers sought to control. Second to land access and control were cattle, which effectively formed a store of value and currency in many parts of pre-colonial South West and South Africa.[13]

But the economic value of land, or cattle, is not a given, external quantity or invariable *objective* value that agents blindly react to – no economic value is.[14] Economic values derive meaning and hence exchange values precisely because they are useful to *traders*, who value the land for its exchange value,[15] or to chiefs, who usurp the produce of the land through violent, political control. Nonetheless, once it is deemed of use (or valued for whatever reason), then the economic value will adjust and alter as demand and supply conditions change, and only then can economic pressures make sense in explaining the rules and codes of war and how they in turn adapt to changing population pressures, famines, the development of property alienation, the monopolization of trade and the deployment of taxes and tariffs on commercial activity.

Times when the value of land increased were times when the population had grown beyond its ability to sustain itself. Before the rise of Shaka, the Zulus had cultivated maize and their population expanded on its product; but without intensifying the productivity of their own land through alienation, the Zulu nation turned to a savage *Lebensraum* war[16] to gain neighbouring lands and to steal their cattle. Similarly, prior to the infamous Zulu expansion in the region, the Nguni, who 'were far more crowded than they realised',[17] exploded onto neighbouring tribes massacring all the major Hlubi kraals to make room for themselves.

Under such circumstances, there are two general methods of adaptation: either find new lands or improve the lands on which the tribe resides. For such a huge continent with a relatively low population density, the former was the typical policy taken up. But that is not to dismiss land or resource improvement as being beyond the tribes' capabilities. Africa had produced several flourishing civilizations, but, as Bellers comments, 'it seems that steady progress and prosperity was elusive and all too often the powerful chiefs and their people

---

13 The geography of course affected which currencies gained local acceptance. In South West and Southern Africa cattle predominated for they were easily transportable relative to the denser forests of Nigeria and the Congo. On the evolution of monetary media, see C. Menger, *Principles of Economics* (New York: New York University Press, 1976), pp.257-85; and on African currencies in particular, see P. Einzig, *Primitive Money*, (London: Eyre & Spottiswoode, 1947), Part III.

14 von Mises, op cit.

15 The same, for example, could not be said, for instance, of the oil fields of Nigeria, which possessed no value to the pre-colonial era tribes.

16 *Lebensraum* was the defining economic policy of the Nazi Government in Germany. Its intellectual roots can, however, be found in Plato's *Republic* and *The Laws*.

17 D.R. Morris, *The Washing of the Spears* (London: Pimlico, 1994), p.55.

degenerated into depravity. The history of Africa, from what we can gather, was a rollercoaster of riches and famine, of peace and desperate tragedy'.[18] As with the empires of the ancient world, either the internal customs and institutions failed to adapt to increasingly complex social arrangements, or predatory and aggressive tribes[19] undermined the nascent civilizations' ability to evolve properly and independently.

Diniswayo of the Zulu, for example, adapted well to growing population pressures – he reorganized the army, defeated thirty local tribes with little slaughter, and solidified a powerful chiefdom that Shaka eventually took over.[20] Like many tribes who came to the fore of their region's history, the Zulus developed politically but not economically: their advance was still-born. In quickly reaching the limits with which they could provide for themselves, the Zulus turned to aggressive war as a solution, a solution that could only be short-lived and be destined to fail. Man is not a beast and therefore is not determined by Malthusian laws as lions and gazelles are; he is capable of progress in developing his productive talents and therefore capable, through co-operation and the market system, of supporting a higher population. As Ludwig von Mises describes:

> The natural scarcity of the means of sustenance forces every living being to look upon all other living beings as deadly foes in the struggle for survival, and generates pitiless biological competition. But with man these irreconcilable conflicts of interests disappear when, and as far as, the division of labour is substituted for economic autarky.[21]

In a sense, Shaka, and other chiefs who followed the customary policy to annex land and to aggress against neighbours, were rejecting the humanly possible and progressive policy of cooperation with others: they sought, in a manner of speaking, to act like the beasts and to wage war for their resources rather than to encourage increased productivity through peaceful trade and the rule of law.

Contrary to Richard Ardrey's powerful and influential treatment of territorialism, fighting over land use is not wholly reducible to an inherent disposition, as if all wars could be explained by reference to a biological drive to control land.[22] Despite the evidence that most African wars were about access to land and resources, Ardrey's thesis requests too little of humanity. Man is capable of continually forging new Malthusian limits to his existence through economic development, but where he refuses to permit development or his attempts are thwarted by others, then the destiny of his culture remains embedded in dismal Malthusian cycles.

---

18 Bellers, op cit.
19 Predatory tribes often inhabited the isolated mountains and were not crushed or subjugated until the arrival of European arms.
20 Otterbein, op cit., p.353.
21 von Mises, op cit., p.663.
22 R. Ardrey, *The Territorial Imperative* (London: Collins, 1967); see my critique in *A Philosophy of War*, chapter 6.

The lack of proper land alienation[23] meant that access and control of land was the vital component to African wars. The history of many of the tribes was one of perpetual migration and displacement. For example, one of the largest people, the Bantu, drifted around the continent for several thousand years. Its sub-tribes and clans settled on but never alienated tracts of land. Boundaries were formed by nature: rivers, hills, mountains.[24]   Accordingly, tribes remained in place until famine ('The food supply ... is a constant anxiety', wrote Leys in 1925)[25] or conflict pushed them on. Whilst a low-population density persisted, the openness of the Continent meant that the conflict within the group or with other groups was predominantly of a low intensity violence; but when migrant groups encountered a stable group who were reluctant to move on, total war was often the result until one tribe gave way or was annihilated.

The primary reason for continued war across the region was thus the inability of the indigenous peoples to break out of the Malthusian demographic cycle[26] by extending their division and specialization of labour through private property. The lack of economic progress constrained the tribes to a precarious existence,[27] which

23 E.g., in Kenya land control was politically controlled or entailed in common. Individuals were permitted conditional control but strangers were permitted no rights at all. And 'absolute ownership of land is an idea foreign to the thought of all the tribes in Kenya'. N. Leys, *Kenya* (London: Hogarth Press, 1925). The Kalahari Bushmen believed that all property is held in common, but they maintained strict internal divisions of property in which compatriotic trespassers could lawfully be killed. Henrich Vedder, *South West Africa in Early Times*, trans. C.G. Hall (London: Frank Cass & Co., 1966), p.81.

24 Accordingly, hostile relations developed over boundary and resource-use disputes. I. Schapere, 'Political Institutions', in *The Bantu-Speaking Tribes of South Africa* (London: George Routledge & Sons, 1937), pp.173-95.

25 Leys, op cit., p.40. In 2002, it remains so for those African nations pursuing anti-growth policies (e.g., Zimbabwe).

26 Whenever the population density increased it became vital for the land to be alienated to smaller groups and individuals who could better exploit its resources. As a praxeological principle, any failure to develop more intricate forms of land control is not expedient for peace – the lack of a thoroughly intricate division and specialization of labour means that any population growth either had to be subject to natural Malthusian checks of disease, and famine, or to migration and the displacement of neighbouring tribes. Those (temporarily) better placed for the exploitation of resources often used their power to subjugate neighbours rather than develop more complex forms of trade. Those who controlled the ports, for example, became the focal points of the Atlantic slave trade. T. Sowell, *Conquests and Culture: An International History* (New York: Basic Books, 1998), p.109.

27 Conflict often arises because of a lack of tradable property rights or their mutual recognition.   Politically, property promotes stability and constrains the power of government; morally, on Lockean grounds, the individual is entitled to the product of his labour; economically, the existence of property rights ensures a more equal distribution of resources than communal or common rights and one that continually ensures that resources flow to their most preferred ends; and psychologically, individuals may enhance their self-esteem and identity through property rights. Property rights are required for economic advancement. Richard Pipes, *Property and Freedom* (New York: Alfred A Knopf, 1999), pp.3-4.

in turn affected the manner in which they waged war. Where life was valuable across the tribes, clashes were bloodless; but when an increasing population relatively devalued the individual tribesman's life, clashes were more bloody.

Regardless of initial economic circumstances, whenever two tribes clashed and commerce or other ties became more frequent, differences between the groups regarding the *justum bellum* tended to dwindle. That is, local and prolonged interaction formed coherent and mutually beneficial conventions: unless there was an overriding ideology that curtailed such pacific expansion, or the stresses on the tribe were such that their very existence was at stake (e.g., a culture of parasitism on other tribes, or an irrational hatred towards them): at such times the value of intertribal commerce fell to zero.

Amongst the larger societies, the lack of free commercial initiative also meant that the group's productive and militant energies, and hence collective morale, was directed through political channels such as the institution and personage of the Chief or King.[28] In turn, the adulation of, or subjection to, a political elite retarded individuation and development of the division of labour and subsequent growth of trade that could enable a tribe to break away from war and poverty.[29] Conclusively, in Sub-Saharan Africa, land *control* dominated tribal claims; but because the lands were held collectively by the tribe and administered centrally by the tribal king,[30] the lack of any permanent alienation to more productive individual users precipitated the great upheavals that became inevitable whenever the local economic base could not support a growing and burgeoning population.[31]

What is of importance to any analysis of human interaction is who controls resource values and how they are recognized.[32] This, crucially, affects the development of intercultural rules and conventions not only in war but also in peace. The great tracts of land owned by the Zulu, the Ashanti, the Herero, etc.,

---

28 R. Furneaux writes: 'the Zulus were a noble race, refined and brave. But they were the victims of two dangerous national habits: superstition and militarism ... the Zulu army, created by Shaka to make his people great, had grown into a Frankenstein's monster ... not unnaturally the Zulu army clamoured for wars'. R. Furneaux, 'Boer and Zulu', in J.M. McEwan (ed.), *Nineteenth Century Africa* (Oxford: Oxford University Press, 1968), pp.418-19.

29 That is, a free market economy of independent traders and citizens has much more incentive to abide by common rules of war than a centrally commanded economy of dependent subjects. We can learn a lot about the emergence of war's conventions from the praxeology of cultural convergence from the peaceful integration that accompanies commerce and peaceful integration of communities.

30 The Zulus, for example, did not consider land to be alienable, except only for residence for a period of the King's life.

31 Typical of Sub-Saharan land policies is that of the Bantu: 'Absolute ownership of land is an idea foreign to the thought of all tribes in Kenya'. Leys, op cit., p.35; Schapera similarly reports on the communal ownership of Bantu land: 'All the land occupied by the tribe is invested in the Chief and administered by him as head of the tribe'. Schapera, op cit. p.156.

32 M. Rothbard, *Man, Economy, and State: A Treatise on Economic Principles* (Auburn, AL: Mises Institute, 2001), p.80.

were controlled by their leaders and entailed en masse to their descendants, which meant that land and its value were thus *politically controlled* rather than exchanged through markets. As an economic principle, property can never be abolished, it merely changes overlordship or control. In Sub-Saharan Africa, the boundaries changed and, in the absence of land alienation, they had to change through conflict, dynastic and internal fighting, and migration.

The Just War Codes

On the whole, and in common with the peoples of the earth, most African societies ensured that war was a policy of last resort and that its violence was contained in some manner or form. Unsurprisingly, where economic relations grew more complicated – and hence the roots of individuation and peaceful commerce began to germinate – the codes of war were stronger.

Preliminary research on the nature of Sub-Saharan African war discovers a wide range of war conventions amongst the hundreds of tribes across the continent. Some forged alliances and federations, while others tried to impose their will on neighbouring tribes, and some sought relative isolation, peace and independence.[33] Some groups refused to attack at night: others held to no such restriction. Most tribes promoted distinctions between legitimate and illegitimate targets – but not all. Those who possessed greater manpower and resources used their advantages to subjugate weaker tribes and often became centres of the slave trade to Arabia or to the Atlantic.[34] Some tribes, such as the Fida, turned their back on war as best as they could in favour of concentrating on agriculture; the Nilotic Kavirondo were peaceful but could fight well if the need arose; and the Bahina desired to live quietly and tend their cattle, but had to maintain a strict eye on neighbouring predatory groups. The Makalakas were excellent tillers of the soil, but were conquered by the Zulus. The Manansas were adept at balance of power politics: they were harried by both the Matabele and Bamangwato and to seek peace would tell the one group that they were subject to the other.[35] Most who enjoyed any prolonged mutually beneficial contact with other tribes converged onto a *modus vivendi* that could accommodate their economic and cultural activities, which only severe disruptions or disasters could overwhelm.

All tribes possessed rules of conduct governing the outbreak and ritual of war. Thus we read of the Zulu purification rite – that after killing an opponent, the warrior would leave the battlefield to purify his soul; we read of the highly regulated battles of the Herero, and many other tribes, whose warriors would line up in the Homeric style with bolder individuals casting insults and then spears before the group would run *en masse* against the enemy effecting a melee, in which injuries or fatalities would bring the battle to an end. Most of the pastoral tribes

---

33 For example, the small baPedi clan, whose Queen, the legendary Queen of the Locusts, possessed convenient supernatural powers of destruction that kept others away.
34 Sowell, op cit., p.109.
35 Davie, op cit., p.49-50.

had strict rules against the killing of women and children but a variety of rules is also evident: the Ba-Huana offered no quarter in battle but did spare women, whereas the Ama-Xhosa of South Africa murdered women and children without distinction. Groups in frequent contact usually saw prisoners as having a useful ransom or productive value, or the women and children were assimilated into the victorious tribe or sold on: the Masai, for example, had no use for slaves for themselves, and so would sell on enslaved prisoners.[36]

Generally, women did not fight. However, the West African Dahomey tribe proffers the exception. In 1792 it raised an 'Amazon' tribe that fought as ferociously as men, but who were subject to strict celibacy laws – on the point of death. The explorer Richard Burton noted that at one time 150 women had fallen to nature's temptation and were put to death.[37]

Most tribes employed warriors to defend and protect their interests, but some, such as the Masai and the Zulu, produced notable armies that were held in fearful awe for their capabilities and strength. The Masai conscripted children into the *moran* from an early age and trained them to uphold one of most militant, and predatory, societies in Eastern Africa.[38] The Zulus lived in their aged-based army cohorts until the Chief permitted them to stand down and marry. Pygmies, on the other hand, were gainfully employed as capable mercenaries by tribes in the Congo area: 'Owning no territory, they settled on the land of a Chief (usually of the Madobe tribe), a tacit bargain being usual that they shall remain there unmolested on condition that they give military assistance'. The Pygmies were renowned for their skill and prowess in fighting.[39]

In some wars, especially those between semi-pastoral or nomadic groups, the warriors usually converged onto similar patterns of expectations of insults cast and weapons thrown, of minimal injuries and fatalities;[40] attacks on each other centred on the collective pride of the tribes and were highly ritualized,[41] verging on what could be termed an aggressive sport. However, blood feuds between tribes applying *lex talionis* could be interminable, especially as some tribes, such as the Nuba, recognized no difference between intentional and accidental killing.[42] Yet even here, the draw of peace was operative: justice was satisfied once the injuries or deaths were equalized. In blood feuds, indiscriminate killing was usually prohibited and the public opinion of both groups could act to temper or even call a halt to the feud.[43]

---

36 Leys, op cit., p.89.
37 Davie, op cit., p.31.
38 Even today, the Masai hold themselves proudly independent from the encroaching civilization.
39 Davie, op cit., p.57.
40 Cowardice was not derided by all – the Bantu thought it appropriate to run from the field, but under British rule they became brave soldiers. Leys, op cit., p.61.
41 S.F. Nadel, *The Nuba: An Anthropological Study of the Hill Tribes in Kordofan* (London: Oxford University Press, 1947), p.147.
42 Ibid., p.349.
43 Davie, op cit., p.210.

But where neighbouring tribes maintained frequent connections, each group implicitly recognized the value of the other community (even if only as a source of women and hence genetic drift more than any potential for trade creation) and did not wish to see it exterminated.

Originally, given small population densities, the land held a relatively low marginal benefit compared to that of the cattle that the tribes controlled and used as media of exchange. The plundering of cattle was often a primary *casus belli*.[44] Cattle were portable and easily stolen by raiders, and they embodied great wealth and prestige. The Masai apparently raided only for the cattle and attacked people only if they attempted to defend their interests.[45] Enslavement also produced great profits for victorious tribes (although some tribes disdained slavery and others permitted the slave to divorce his master[46]), and to be used for purchasing more cattle. But a growing population cannot live by driving cattle alone – cattle require grazing lands. In the absence of secure proprietary rights that were subject to impartial justice, raids and counter-raids resulted, which often became increasingly costly on a tribe driving them to secure some form of peace. Vedder reports that, 'just as the Numa said, "Where by hunter's foot treads, is Numaland", so the Herero said, "Where my cattle have grazed is Hereroland"'.[47] In other words, seizure and wars over land access were inevitable as two or more parties would claim access and rights to the same resources. Accordingly, other causes of war evolved from the lack of proprietary rights over land and other resource uses, and it is in this context that various rules and conventions emerged to ameliorate the drive to war that could arise over boundary disputes or through sheer militancy.

The economics of land use played a fundamental role in forging just war codes, but it is important to recall that it is the *value* of land as perceived by the various groups that is relevant here. Value 'is not intrinsic, it is not in things. It is within us; it is the way in which man reacts to the conditions of his environment'.[48] What frames a tribe's reactions to its environment (or any person's) is the philosophy, mythology, or theology to which they subscribe. The economic analysis of just war codes deepens when the belief systems of the tribes is also employed to explain *why* the Masai were haughty warriors or the Bushmen universally despised or why the enemy could justifiably be eaten. The belief that the dead affected present affairs and had to be propitiated or counselled justified the practice of human sacrifice. In the Niger Delta of West Africa sixty or more people would be slain each year; in Benin murderers and undesirables were slaughtered, and if none could be found prisoners were taken in raids or slaves bought for the very purpose. The Batjwapong of South Africa grabbed a man and strangled him to secure rain. But war, and the potential calamities it could create even in victory, presented

---

44 Davie, op cit., p.84. The Masai were so adept at stealing cattle that they gained the respect of Lord Delamere, who, acknowledging their tenacity, refused to prosecute them. The Masai in turn adulated Delamere. See Bellars, op. cit., chapter 18.
45 Leys, op cit., p.88.
46 E.g., the Bantu of Kenya. Ibid., p.36.
47 Vedder, op cit., p.177.
48 von Mises, op cit., p.96.

common justifications for sacrificing. The Dahomey sacrificed four thousand Whydahs after conquering the state in 1727; the Ashanti sacrificed hundreds annually to obtain the deities' assistance. Such great waste of human life and productivity could only be afforded by the richer kingdoms – poorer and smaller tribes sacrificed rarely or on a more frugal basis. However, the trade-oriented and culturally complex Yoruba-speaking peoples rarely sacrificed, and then only with a bought slave.[49]

Similarly, many tribes ate the victims of war – and not always when they were dead.

> Probably the most inhuman practice of all is to be met with among the tribes who deliberately hawk the victim piecemeal whilst still alive. Incredible as it may appear, captives are led from place to place in order that individuals may have the opportunity of indicating, by external marks on the body, the portion they desire to acquire. The distinguishing marks are generally made by means of coloured clay or strips of grass tied in a peculiar fashion. The astounding stoicism of the victims, who thus witness the bargaining for their limbs piecemeal, is only equalled by the callousness with which they walk forward to meet their fate.[50]

Cannibalism was not always the result of desperation, although humanity often turns to it under stressful conditions. It followed from the beliefs and hence valuations the tribes made of human life, although one group, the Ba-Kwese seemed to have taken to it in a form of reprisal against a cannibalist tribe, the Ba-Pindi.[51]

Tribal ethics asserted a strict division between the internal ethical codes of the group and the values applying to outsiders. The internal codes also extended to family members living in opposing tribes, who, in some African tribes, were either exempted from fighting or were avoided in battle by their kin. All members of the Bantu of Kenya saw themselves as related and would not permit another Bantu to go without, but it was acceptable to let a stranger starve.[52] Others employed blood-brotherhoods to cement relations between tribes by artificially extending the concept of kin to those with whom one mixed blood by drinking and rubbing it into wounds.

Many writers on the just war tradition have noted that violent interaction *within* the group is not permitted, unlike the violence meted against foreigners.[53] 'In dealing with members of the in-group', Davie notes, 'right, fair play, and the like have been in vogue, for there were mores which guaranteed them, whereas in the relations of groups or nations to each other, mores – the international mores or law – have been only meagrely developed'.[54] The Tallensi possessed relatively strict

---

49 Examples from Davie, op cit., pp.130-35.
50 H. Ward, *A Voice from the Congo* (London: Heinemann, 1910).
51 Davie, op cit., p.73.
52 Leys, op cit., p.35.
53 See, for instance, Herbert Spencer, *Principles of Ethics*; and Robert Ardrey, *The Territorial Imperative*.
54 Davie, op cit., p.20.

rules of combat. Allegedly, they did not go to war for economic gain and were very superstitious of spilling blood (it brought a mystical retribution); their conflicts were mainly skirmishes, which after a few days would be superseded by diplomacy. The underlying reason was that their clashes were between clans of the same people; hence, ultimately, 'ties of ritual collaboration between clans demanded that different segments ... cooperate for the good of the community'.[55]

Nonetheless, imperviousness to human suffering within and without the community was widespread: Livingstone once remarked that, 'It is hard to make [the Makololo] feel that the shedding of human blood is a great crime; they must be conscious that it is wrong, but, having been accustomed to bloodshed from infancy, they are remarkably callous to the enormity of the crime of destroying human life'.[56]

Wherever outsiders were held in great suspicion, travellers and explorers in Sub-Saharan Africa had to approach a kraal or village with great care, otherwise a quiet entrance was likely to be met with a hostile response[57] – a fact the explorer and missionary David Livingstone soon adapted to. But not Stanley, who once met an aggressive response with overwhelming fire to punish the tribe as, so he described, a father would punish a stubborn and disobedient son.[58] What can be read from his encounter is that the general cultural expectation of unknown foreign contact in Sub-Saharan Africa was that it would often turn violent or prompt a plundering. Wanderers feared for their lives, Dundas writes: 'In those days a man is said never to have left his village to go far alone; no one could go a few miles without encountering others who were looking for someone to rob or slay'.[59] Tribes across the continent sought slaves to sell or victims to sacrifice.

Appropriately, modes of etiquette in approaching a neighbouring group evolved to dissemble possible aggressive responses. The Bangala beat a drum and sang to notify others of their visits to other groups.[60] Checks and balances on warriors were evident through the use of intertribal institutions, diplomats, or even clandestine social arrangements. For example, in commercially (and therefore politically) more developed West Africa,[61] 'secret societies' policed domestic issues but also acted to smooth intertribal relations; such organs acted as a form of judiciary and arm of government, even when no explicit governmental

---

55 M. Gluckman, *Order and Rebellion in Tribal Africa* (London: Cohen and West, 1963), p.68.
56 Quoted in Davie, op cit.
57 Ibid., p.4.
58 T. Packenham, *The Scramble for Africa* (London: Abacus, 2001), p.28.
59 Quoted in Davie, op cit., p.13.
60 Ibid., p.13.
61 The Ashanti had prospered through the slave trade: they traded slaves for guns and were thus able to strengthen their political might until 1874 when Sir Garnet Wolseley marched on Kumasi to take over. The Ashanti had developed complex proprietary arrangements in which land was owned by ancestors, who had to be appeased when land exchanged hands or was conquered. They considered it inconceivable that land could exist without an owner. R.S. Rattray, *Ashanti* (Oxford: Clarendon Press, 1923), p.216-22.

arrangements existed. Members of such organizations wore badges of distinction, which permitted their free movement – among the Bantu, the Ukuku secret society could end intertribal quarrels through their brotherhood, a power that often overarched that of the relevant Chiefs.[62] The existence and development of such institutions reflected a growing complexity in tribal and intertribal relations; arguably, these initially evolved out of fraternal connections but developed to include more than just the problems arising between kith and kin as commerce expanded. The use of ambassadors to maintain peace within and without thus evolved between groups that mutually benefited from commercial or from other forms of relations – e.g., among Nigerian head-hunters, women were held as sacred, as they often had relations on both sides of a dispute and could carry messages peacefully. Other groups, such as the Tira and Muro of the Nuba employed recognizable uniforms or modes of dress.[63] Many tribes, such as the Masai,[64] also revered their medicine men sufficiently to obey their commands not to fight – a trait they share with the ancient Druids of Celtic culture. The British official *Blue Book* reported that Lenana, a long-lived medicine man, kept his people in check while the British began to expand control over Kenya.[65]

But the alternative means of maintaining the peace, from ambassadors to secret societies, pale in comparison with the ability of a pluralistic, indeed, individualistic society to uphold peace and impartial arbitration as the rule. Without the advancement of the division of labour and the required alienation of property to smaller and smaller units, war remained economically attractive even amongst the advanced tribes precisely because, as Reisman notes, 'the non-division-of-labor society cannot assimilate the members of the division-of-labor society – it cannot even support all of its own members'.[66] That is, without land alienation, the division of labour and its peaceful commercial values could not expand and the population thus remained subject to dreadful limitations.

Accordingly, the Chiefs that maintained control over vast lands that yielded insufficient produce to support a burgeoning population had to maintain a strong *political* control over their subjects to secure their obedience. The Ashanti had a proverb that would be recognizable to a European feudal knight: *tumi nyina wo asase so*: all power is in land. However, increasing political control over a society often increases the propensity for the leaders to take their people into war,[67] and in turn wars promote increased centralization: monarchy, writes Leys, was certainly

---

62 Davie, op cit., pp.205-207.
63 Captured slaves who became fluent in both languages would become suitable ambassadors. Ibid., pp.184 & 187.
64 Leys, op cit., p.90.
65 Ibid., p.92.
66 G. Reisman, *Capitalism: A Treatise on Economics* (Ottawa, IL: Jameson Books, 1998), p.317.
67 '[T]he aggressiveness of the ruling power inside a society increases with its aggressiveness outside the society'. Herbert Spencer, *The Man Versus the State* (Indianapolis: Liberty Classics, 1982), p.72.

the outcome of warfare – especially of the slave wars in Eastern Africa.[68] It is also witnessed in the spectacular rise of the Zulu nation.

Conflict is a form of human interaction that is invasive; exchange (trade) and gift giving are forms that are non-invasive. Whereas the latter enables the expansion of the division and specialization of labour, the former destroys it. Peace and prosperity could hardly be forthcoming for the Bantu, who would surround a village at night, rush at it in the dawn, kill as many men as possible, and then beat a hasty retreat.[69] Robbery, war, enslavement, and fraud are all invasive forms of human interaction that limit a population's ability to support itself, and in turn they encourage further violence. The usually successful Masai raids for cattle suffered severe setbacks in the 1890s: their cattle were decimated by rinderpest, which in turn left the Masai weak and vulnerable to an alliance between their enemies, the Kikuyu and Kamba. Masai were slaughtered, enslaved, and sold – but the favours were returned once their strength had increased.[70] Across the continent, such reprisals would continue until a Chief sued for peace – but in time, that tribe could grow strong enough to withstand further predations and become itself the predator.[71]

However, the attraction of peaceful intercourse and the potential for vast economic improvement was systematically marred by the lack of alienable property and political-cultural systems that inhibit such individuation. The existence of neutral territory and legitimate and illegitimate targets in war reflected such immanent considerations – the Ba-Mbale, for instance, prudently established markets on neutral ground,[72] which suggests that they recognized the benefits of trade and wished to eliminate war's disruption of commerce; others made areas of natural deposits out of bounds for battle.

In economically shallow societies, the pride of a group was often at stake from the insults of other groups and formed a perennial source of conflict. Ironically, tribes that did not alienate their lands and provide individuals with the means to secure a more productive life on this earth were quick to assume the existence of a 'property right' in their reputation, which, if slighted, was to be defended against.[73] In turn, for powerful Chiefs, the reputation of the group became a means of uniting and hence controlling the people against an enemy – Shaka of the Zulu certainly was one to exploit any insinuations or defamations with swift and brutal repercussions. Tribes thus found just cause in insulting behaviour (i.e., insulting

---

68 Leys, op cit., p.37.

69 Schapera, op cit., p.193.

70 Bellers, op cit., chapter 1. Bellers also notes what is an ideological (or mythical-cum-theological) *casus belli*: 'The Kikuyu probably lacked protein because they had difficulty in keeping cattle. The hubristic Masai, believing that God had ordained that all cattle should be theirs, could not tolerate others keeping them'.

71 A history that repeats itself often in contemporary Africa.

72 Davie, op cit., p.186.

73 Vestiges of which we retain in the laws of slander and libel of course. But, 'a man has no such objective property as "reputation". His reputation is simply what others think of him, i.e., it is purely a function of the *subjective* thoughts of others. But a man cannot own the minds or thoughts of others'. Rothbard, op cit., p.157.

according to the King, who embodies the moral standing of the community), but also in claiming neighbours to be the cause of the tribe's bad luck, famines, etc.[74]

Yet we often see that such excuses for war were dropped as a *casus belli* when the protracted cost of defending a reputation outweighed the benefits that may have accrued. As a principle, this effectively arises when a society becomes more pluralistic – and ultimately individualistic. That is, when a society spreads its interests beyond those of the King's, some members of the group will find an insult against the King to be a rather weak reason for fighting a war. This usually occurs when market economies develop and hence more intricate forms of intertribal and international commerce and interaction evolve: individuals pursuing a broader or different set of values than their Chief will have much to lose and have little to gain from a costly war.[75] Consequently, in the more complex societies of West Africa, the diffusion of interests diluted the justice of a particular leader's personal cause, or that of his warrior class; instead the justification of war had to appeal to a more broadly utilitarian consideration – namely the interests of society as a whole, which become harder to identify as a group's interests broaden.[76]

The utilitarian element to the just war code implies that deontological exhortations to fight chivalrously (e.g., no ambushing or poisonous weapons) or with a due sense of justice (regardless of the consequences) are in effect *luxurious* ethical codes. Nonetheless, the utilitarian reason for their existence is more obvious than an appeal to the warrior's 'higher moral nature'. Such codes arose among the Sub-Sahara African tribes – codes that were analogous to European chivalric codes of the mediaeval ages – but they usually emerged where warriors were of a similar background (same tribal roots) and/or shared similar expectations of future interaction.[77] They disappeared once the assumption of future interaction and reciprocal arrangements was rejected, which explains the warrior codes of the parasitical, thuggish-like tribes, as well as those generally victorious in battle. The Masai, arrogant in the presumption of victory, were proud of the fact that they never attacked without giving notice.[78] But the belligerent Nuba only used such codes for their sports and games – for them, war meant victory at all costs.[79]

---

74 All sufferings in Africa were blamed on *someone* rather than something. Leys, op cit., p.45.
75 Of course, advanced civilizations do commit acts of aggressive war either by whipping up atavistic values of collective glory (e.g. Milosevic in Serbia [1989-1997]) or defraying the true costs of war through inflationism (a policy that practically all Western nations have employed).
76 The decline of the monarch's status in Europe was, however, replaced not with the pacifying individualism that the renaissance invited and celebrated, but with a shift towards the embodiment of morality in the nation: nationalism replaced monarchism, but in both the civilians were to identify their own moral standing with the moral standing with an overarching entity rather than their own personal interests.
77 Nonetheless, deontological rules cannot fully ignore utilitarian considerations: arguably, absolute prohibitions appeal to reason *because* their infringement is detrimental in its results.
78 Leys, op cit., p.89.
79 Nadel, op cit., p.147.

Moreover, what can be called 'predatory tribes', such as the Heiban of the Nuba,[80] conceived of no benefit in intertribal peace and saw no benefit in war conventions. Such groups were universally feared and could only be halted by their thorough defeat, subjugation, or annihilation.

Tribes that did not see each other as potentially being in a position to explore the mutual benefits of intertribal trade, but who rather saw each other as potential targets for plunder, for subjugation in some manner or form, or even purely for food,[81] had no reason to follow a *justum bellum*. Accordingly, when tribes looked upon one another as mutual competitors for land, cattle, or prestige – instead of potential co-operators in the fight against nature and poverty, then prisoners possessed no value except for the amusement, appetite, and ingenuity of torturers.

Until the upheavals following devastating plagues in the 1890s, the Masai fought according to strict *jus in bello* criteria, avoiding harm to women and not taking prisoners: their raids were almost bloodless. The decimated Masai population soon became prey to their neighbours who sought revenge upon them and this altered the face of war in the region – massacres and slavery ensued until the British imposed a peace on the warring factions.[82] In Uganda, the Hima aristocracy of the Banyoro waged internecine warfare that left a quarter of a million dead according to contemporary accounts;[83] the Masai almost exterminated the Awa-Wanga in 1904; the Laikipiak preyed on surrounding tribes until the Masai drove them out; 'the history of the Suk is simply one of migrations and a life-and-death struggle with all the neighbouring tribes', writes Davie; the Doigio were pushed to practical extinction by the Segallai, who in turn were exterminated by a combination of their foes. Some wars were so deadly that entire tribes were wiped out – the Basuto tribe, the Makololo, the Bakgalagadi, and the Bakalahari were all displaced into nothingness, while the Zulus quashed tribe after tribe, ten disappearing into forced integration and death between the Limpopo area and the Zambezi.[84]

However, although explicit codes of conduct prevailed amongst similar groups and were ditched once the apparent divisions between peoples became severe, often a prolonged or daily interaction between warring peoples recreated or

---

80 Ibid., p.147.
81 The Ba-Huana feasted on the bodies of slain enemies. The Monbutto cured human meat from the battle dead and drove the prisoners home to be later butchered. Cannibalism was prevalent in the Congo region, where human flesh was considered a delicacy. The practice was also wrapped up in the tribes' beliefs regarding witchcraft and the power of blood. Davie, op cit., pp.69-7; & 'Cannibalism', *Britannica 2001 Deluxe Edition*, CD-ROM. Interestingly, Shaka tried to stamp out cannibalism, although his predecessors had feasted on the fallen. Dr A. Coutts, 'The Cannibals of Kwa-Zulu-Natal: Fact or Fable', http://www.battlefields.co.za/history/cannibals/index.htm, accessed November 2002.
82 Leys, op cit., p.89.
83 Davie, op cit., p.258, quoting H.H. Johnston, *The Uganda Protectorate* (London, 1902), vol.2, p.592.
84 Davie, op cit., p.259-60.

initiated a unique *convergence* onto mutually benefiting rules;[85] they did so because it became mutually beneficial for the warring groups to abide by recognizable rules that delimited the breadth or voracity, and hence cost, of war.

The exception was cases where the enemy were considered to be beyond the human pale. Hunter-gatherers, for example, have been replaced through hunting and extermination by pastoral societies who have looked upon the hunters as too primitive to engage in commerce with them. Bantu and Herero hunted the San (Bushmen) as they would any predator or threat to their own survival: migrating tribes from the north pushed the Bushmen to increasingly marginal lands, while the Kaffirs would kill Bushmen without distinction of age or sex.[86] In turn, European colonizers saw the Herero and Bantu tribes to be displaced in favour of the more technologically advanced industrial society (or in the case of the Boers and Germans – the 'supreme race'), and in both cases more advanced division-of-labour societies ultimately vanquished less advanced:[87] the San's territory could not sustain the Bantu population and so they were increasingly marginalized; and under the reign of Shaka, the growing power and population of the Zulu kingdom led to the Mfecane (the Crushing) of neighbouring tribes and clans in the 1820s, which resulted in two million dead. In this case, prior population growth generated pressures that traditional land use and occupation could not sustain.

But most importantly for understanding the nature and extent of the rules of war beyond the rituals and intertribal alliances, the vulnerability of the relevant economies has to be emphasized. Much commerce and exchange between the tribes was subject to grave violations by marauding gangs – often underemployed regiments who would prey on passing merchants. 'This state of affairs is clearly seen in the case of the Tedas [in modern day Chad] and other African tribes among whom "exchange is made with weapons poised, the parties approaching and returning from each other's presence in crouching posture – ready to pounce or to flee – and in the most suspicious frame of mind"'.[88] Whilst trade was thus vulnerable to attack, the very nature of land control inhibited the extension of the division of labour and hence the basis for exchange and potential perpetual peace, as Kant foresaw.[89]

---

85 Such rules emerged rather spectacularly in the trenches of World War One, for instance, with tacit agreements to fire artillery at the same place and same time, and periodic exchanges – most famously the Christmas football matches of 1914/15.

86 Davie, op cit., p.261.

87 A theme taken up by F.J.P. Veale in *Advance to Barbarism: The Development of Total Warfare from Sarajevo to Hiroshima* (London: The Mitre Press, 1968).

88 Davie, op cit., p.199, quoting Gregory, Bishop and Keller, *Physical and Commercial Geography*, pp.195-6.

89 Immanuel Kant, 'Perpetual Peace', in *Political Writings* (Cambridge: Cambridge University Press). Kant argued that the expansion of trade will diminish prejudices and thereby bring peoples together.

Conclusion

Reviewing the just war codes of various African groups, we can see how important, in the absence of land alienation and ensuing pluralism, the ameliorating institutions of ambassadors, blood-brotherhood, secret policing societies, and religious taboos were in constraining the impetus to war. Just war rules and traditions are not exclusively Western or Islamic: all groups face similar praxeological rules that tend to produce a convergence onto mutually acceptable and beneficial rules of conduct in war and peace. Extreme conditions or ideologies can overturn such intertribal arrangements, but the cost and duration of war are likely to re-establish the *modus vivendi*.

Throughout the paper, I have emphasized the role of the economics and legality of land claims in the evolution and development of African war codes. The clash between cultures – whether intertribal or international – ultimately took on forms that related to the possibilities for the groups to deal with each other on a more individualistic and pluralistic basis. However, the collective ownership of land promoted and sustained bellicose assumptions and tribal prejudices of enemies, and it diminished or prohibited spontaneous trades and interaction that could, in the long run, have acted to produce a longer lasting peace. In the absence of such freedoms, especially in the free trade of goods *and land*, the initial cultural clashes between European colonizers and Africans followed a similar cycle to those between Africans. When population pressures pushed societies to the limits of their economic base, ethical conduct typically diminished; only complete victory, escalating military costs or military equality brought warring groups into peace. But so long as that peace was not substantiated by land alienation, the cycle of violence would recur.

PART IV
MODERN PERSPECTIVES

Chapter 12

Justifying Killing: US Army Chaplains of World War II

Jenel Virden

The priest goes to war as a man of peace. His armor is the Cross. His right hand is raised, not to take life but to give it. He blesses, he absolves, he breaks the Bread of Life to his men, he anoints them and closes their dying eyes, and over their graves he erects the Cross and chants the Requiem of a fallen hero.[1]

In the *Brief History of the United States Army Chaplain Corps* – an Army pamphlet produced in 1974 – the authors trace the history of Army chaplains from 1775 onwards. The chaplains who served in the military during the American Revolution were really serving 13 separate colonies with 13 separate policies and 13 different ways to organize chaplains' services. The Continental Congress had established the Army Chaplain, as a recognized position, on 29 July 1775 and a chaplain was supposed to be assigned to each regiment. George Washington, at the head of the Continental Army, directed that chaplains would hold Sunday services throughout the army and issued an order in 1776 that chaplains were to be paid 33 1/3rd dollars per month – and should be 'persons of good character and exemplary lives'.[2] As in subsequent wars, Washington, as commander in chief, recognized 'the blessing and protection of Heaven are at all times necessary, but especially is it in times of public distress and danger. ... The General hopes and trusts that every officer and man will endeavor so to live and act as becomes a Christian soldier, defending the dearest rights and liberties of the country'.[3] Indeed, some clergymen during the Revolution actually raised their own militia units.

So begins the ironic situation in United States military history, reflected in other histories of other nations, of the chaplain who is called not only to the service

---

1   The Society for the Propagation of Faith, *The Priest Goes to War: A Pictorial Outline of the Work of the Catholic Chaplains in the Second World War* (New York: Forward, 1946).

2   Department of Army Pamphlet, *A Brief History of the United States Army Chaplains Corps* (HQ, US Department of the Army, September 1974). J. Chambers (ed.), *The Oxford Companion to American Military History* (Oxford: Oxford University Press, 1999), p.602, puts the monthly salary at $20.

3   *A Brief History*, p.3.

of God but also to the service of the military. The office of Army Chaplain was modified over time. By the Civil War chaplains' duties were less about being soldiers and more about ministering to soldiers' spiritual needs. Yet some chaplains fought in the Civil War. More interestingly, they also began to cast their nets more widely in terms of their remit. The Army's official brief history notes that during the American Civil War chaplains ventured into issues of morality. The Headquarter report notes that one chaplain organized a Temperance Society in the Irish Brigade. This chaplain, Father Dillon, issued his own Temperance Medals to some of the 500 members who had given their temperance pledge.[4]

It was not until the First World War, however, that the US Army Chaplaincy, as an official organization, was created. Prior to this, military chaplains were individuals working for individual units, serving without 'universal denominational indorsement or supervision', and they did not have a clearly defined military status.[5] When two million American men went off to Europe after April 1917 the strains on this ad hoc system began to show. The General Headquarters of the American Expeditionary Force (AEF) discovered in 1918 that they had no idea of how many, what denomination, and which units the chaplains were serving. It was at this stage that training was established with the opening of the US Army Chaplain School at Fort Monroe Virginia in March 1918 (later moved to Camp Zachary Taylor near Louisville, Kentucky). In what appears to be a modern war curricula, courses for chaplains included 'international law, first aid, drill, rules of land warfare, and equitation'.[6] A second school was set up in France in July 1918 at Neuilly-sur-Suize, which offered a two week chaplain course.

Chaplains' duties, as outlined in regulations, stressed their primary role of preaching and offering pastoral care. Weekly reports of what each chaplain did record that they spent the bulk of their time giving sermons, writing letters for the men, visiting the sick, and conducting burial details. The latter job was taken over by the Quartermaster Corps in the Second World War. Clergy who participated in combat were by then the exception and not the rule. The Hague Convention of 1899 had prohibited chaplains from holding combat positions.

The National Defense Act of 1920 established the Office of the Chief of Chaplains. By 1925 there were only 1100 chaplains in the Army and the bulk of these held commissions in the reserves. Many, however, were called to duty in 1938 when the organizers of the Civilian Conservation Corps (CCC) decided to provide religious services and moral guidance to the young men participating in this New Deal project. By June 1940 there were only 383 active duty men in the US Army chaplaincy. However by the end of Second World War (against Japan), in September 1945, there were almost 10,000. Military chaplains were overseen by the Chief of Chaplains and throughout the Second World War this position was held by Chaplain (Major General) William R. Arnold. It was to Chaplain Arnold that the bulk of chaplain correspondence on problems was addressed. In the Second World War, for the first time, each chaplain on active duty was 'indorsed

---

4   Ibid., p.9.
5   Ibid., p.13.
6   Ibid.

by his denomination, ... regularly ordained, and ... adequately educated in basic military subjects'.[7] During the war there were chaplains from almost every conceivable denomination, ethnic background and race. The ratio of chaplains to servicemen was one to 975, depending upon the theatre of operations. The statistics suggest there were 28 percent Roman Catholic chaplains, 62 percent Protestant and just under three percent Jewish – roughly equivalent to the civilian population. Of those who served, a total of 124 were killed in action and 1,783 were decorated for their service.[8]

As noted earlier, the issue of soldiers' behaviour was introduced early on in the American chaplain corps. As with many aspects of the history of war, there are some interesting dichotomies in the story of clergy in war time. For instance, it seems that few clerics felt a particular need to justify the breaking of the sixth commandment (thou shalt not kill). As stated in the Bible this commandment was thought to refer to the act of murder whereas killing in war was the taking of life with legitimate authority.[9] As it turns out, 'An eye for an eye' was quoted more often than 'Thou shalt not kill'. The art of killing was seen as incidental to the goal, which was the defeat of evil, as long as one killed without hatred or malice. Yet the chaplains found the breaking of many of the other commandments, as part of human nature, very problematic. Of special concern, apparently, were commandments number three (blasphemy) and number seven (adultery).

Chaplains' duties during the war were subject to much debate. By 1944, official duties of chaplains were to:

- render moral counsel;
- propose suitable means to promote 'right thinking and right acting'; and
- promote character building and contentment.[10]

Also, 'under paragraph 5 of AR 60-5 the chaplain is the "logical consultant" of his commanding officer in matters involving the morale, morality and character building' of the soldiers.[11] The three areas of concern for chaplains, therefore, were men's morale, their moral well-being, and doling out forgiveness to those men who felt the need to justify their actions.[12] Interestingly, however, the latter point was not raised in the chaplains' correspondence. Instead, the majority of correspondence that chaplains sent back to the Chief of Chaplains revolved around problems the chaplains encountered while trying to fulfil moral obligations.

---

7   Ibid., p.17.
8   Ibid.
9   Joanna Bourke, *An Intimate History of Killing: Face-to-Face Killing in Twentieth Century Warfare* (London: Granta, 1999), p.273.
10   TM 16-205, Section II, Paragraph 12, 1944, in Memo to All Chaplains from Edward Trett, HQ, US Army Forces, China, Burma, India, 24 August 1944, National Archives, RG247, p.1. (All archival material comes from the National Archives Record Group 247 Chief of Chaplains).
11   Headquarters, United States Air Force, CBI, 24 August 1944, noted in Ibid., p.1.
12   Bourke, op cit., p.289.

The Chief of Chaplains regularly received correspondence on a wide range of concerns. These could be as pragmatic as requests for advice or help with difficulties encountered in conducting religious services without proper equipment or space. This type of complaint, however, was the least common. The bulk of correspondence was about vice and immoral behaviour, such as gambling, use of profanity, alcohol consumption, homosexuality, problems of discipline, suspect entertainment, indecent literature, and sex, of any kind. Clearly, many other problems occurred, but those listed above were the ones that generated most of the chaplains' correspondence back to the Chief of Chaplains office in Washington D.C. Most histories of the war or histories of the chaplaincy have overlooked the two areas of entertainment and indecent literature, which are explored here.

Most chaplains recognized the need to strike a balance between carrying out their duties as outlined officially and spiritually and not appearing to be too puritanical or prudish. Many, if not most, did not write to the Chief of Chaplains to complain, although they may have included comments on problems of morality in their monthly reports. The correspondence of the ones who wrote to the Chief of Chaplains, however, demonstrates very profoundly the huge impact the Chaplains Corps could have on a wide range of topics and policies affecting the American GI. A good example of this is in the area of entertainment and USO-Camp Shows.

A chaplain in the China, Burma, India (CBI) Theatre of war had views on the role of entertainment for the serviceman and the part chaplains could play in maintaining standards of decency. By entertainment chaplains mostly meant travelling USO-Camp Shows that played to GIs both at training camps and bases in the United States as well as at overseas locations throughout the world. Chaplain Trett laid out a clear indication of how he, as a chaplain, felt on the issue and his memo went out to all chaplains in the CBI, making its way eventually to the Chief of Chaplains himself. Chaplain Trett maintained that entertainment:

> is a great implement that can be used to bolster the fundamentals of the American Way of Life; the morale of the men in the services; the ideals of the American homes; can serve unobtrusively but none the less profoundly to convince, and to reinforce the conviction, that the traditions of the American Government and Nation are superior; the ideals of the American home sound; its manhood sturdy, capable, and dependable; its womanhood virtuous, true, capable; and that altogether America is well worth sacrifice, service and defense. Failure so to utilize this potent instrument in our hands [entertainment], is a failure to discharge, in this regard, our responsibility to the service men and women.[13]

With that Chaplain Trett made clear that entertainment was more than just telling a few jokes and taking the audience's minds off the current war situation. It had a function that was surely nearly impossible to fulfil. It was to be used to justify participation in war as well as substantiate the American dream. By inference, any entertainment that appeared to counteract these ideals would be considered unworthy.

13 Memo from Trett, p.2.

USO-Camp Shows, Inc. was an independent agency set up to employ entertainers to give performances to the troops. Despite its independent status, however, it was under constant scrutiny by, and in voluminous correspondence with, the Chief of Chaplains office. If a chaplain in the field wrote to the Chief of Chaplains office complaining of a particular act, play or entertainment event anywhere in the world, this information was passed on to the headquarters of USO-Camp Show Inc. for comment and action. In order to lodge a complaint the chaplain involved had to provide details, not only of the particular entertainment unit, where and when it performed, but also the exact nature of the offence. These reports are useful for considering what type of conduct some individual chaplains deemed problematic during the war.

For example, a complaint was lodged by Chaplain (Captain) Webb in February 1944 from an evacuation hospital. He wrote to the Chief of Chaplains office complaining about a visiting group known as USO Show #401. According to Webb the 'show contained several admirable specialities, but at times the good was made ineffective by the evil of the libidinous poison on the part of certain performers'. The examples he gave are enlightening on a variety of levels, not least of which is to demonstrate how times have changed. Chaplain Webb took exception to the Master of Ceremonies George Chatterton who had the bad taste to include in his act a 'burlesque routine'. He placed his arm around the waist of the girl with his hand upon her hip. He told her that he was trying to find her pulse. The girl became worried about this hand being where it was. Finally he said 'That is not the hand you have to worry about'. He also appears to have recited a poem entitled 'Son of a Beach'. A ventriloquist appeared on the same stage, Mr Wayne Fernilius, who also elicited complaints from Webb. Apparently, one 'remark he made was most ungentlemanly'.[14]

The usual reasoning behind the lodging of complaints by chaplains revolved around their firm convictions that, for the most part, and in the majority, servicemen were decent men. It became a fight for the chaplains to maintain a reasonable level of decency in the face of numerous countervailing forces. These forces were most often referred to as outsiders who seemed to think that 'when a soldier leaves home and loved ones he thereby lowers his ideals, his morals and his sense of decency'.[15] This, of course, was true. Increased rates of venereal disease and illegitimate births give some indication that this was exactly what did happen. However, the Chief of Chaplains office certainly took the opposite view, which was then projected to other agencies. For instance, in the example above of USO Show #401, the response of the Executive Vice-President of USO-Camp Shows Inc. to the news of the offensive performance outlined by Webb was to dismiss the entertainers for 'violation of script'.[16]

USO-Camp Show Inc. had very elaborate methods of what was, for all intents and purposes, censorship of the acts authorized for performance to GI audiences. A representative of the agency would view all acts prior to signing them, any act or

14 Letter, Chaplain Charlie Webb to Chief of Chaplains, 9 February 1945.
15 Ibid.
16 Letter, Lawrence Phillips to Chaplain Arnold, 26 February 1945.

play would then be carefully scripted, any objectionable material would be eliminated, and only then would the act be approved for assignment either in the US or overseas. All entertainers had to agree to perform only what had been authorized – no ad-libbing was allowed. Part of the contracts that entertainers signed included a section on this very thing. They were told that 'the attached script of your act is authorized for presentation by you on your overseas tour. By direction of the War Department, you may not add any material not contained in this script without written authority from the Special Service Officer, a copy of which must be mailed to me immediately'. The Executive Vice-President noted in this contract that this was for the protection of the entertainer should he or she be 'subject to criticism by Commanding Officers, *Chaplains* and enlisted men'.[17] The entertainers then had to sign an affidavit and have it duly notarized.

In the official contract which entertainers signed, clause 10 stipulated that the actor 'agree[d] that neither you nor any of your employees will give any indecent, immoral or offensive performance, nor conduct yourself or themselves in a manner offensive to public decency or morality and will not hold yourself or themselves to public ridicule, hatred, scorn or contempt'.[18] To clarify matters further, Executive Vice-President Lawrence Phillips provided all members of the production department with a memo listing 'material that is forbidden for use by any USO-Camp Shows unit either in the United States or overseas'. These included mention of: the President and his family, members of the cabinet or congress, political issues (either domestic or foreign), and Allied and neutral leaders. Certain words were to be eliminated completely from all acts including words of a religious nature such as: God, Jesus and Christ as well as hell and damn. No use was to be made of the words Catholic, Protestant, Jew, Mohammedan, Buddhist, or 'members of other sects, their prophets, [or] their church officials'.[19] It is difficult to see how one could construct any good entertainment while adhering to these restrictions. Ironically, there is very little mention here of sex – yet sex was the number one problem that Chaplains had with the USO Camp Shows.

It is not clear just how many acts were dismissed by Mr Phillips due to either their violation of standards of decency or conduct, and/or because of complaints filed by Chaplains in the field. It is clear, however, that dismissals did take place. Western Union Telegrams were sent to inform performers of their dismissal or back to headquarters to verify problems. For example, Mr Finn Olsen was performing in a revue entitled 'Hold Everything' and when he refused to eliminate objectionable 'gags', including 'the worn out woman gag, the brassiere gag, and the ladies powder room gag', he was promptly dismissed. He objected, of course, and proclaimed he was not 'doing risky stuff ... [and had] the greatest laughs of all the acts'. He also protested that it just was not fair.

Of course, from the point of view of USO-Camp Shows, Inc. there was another incentive beyond the attitudes of the Army chaplains. When objectionable

---

17 Standard Letter, USO-Camp Show Inc., 1945. Emphasis added.
18 USO-Camp Shows, Inc., Standard Contract, p.1 (paragraph 10).
19 Lawrence Phillips, Memorandum to All Members of Production Department, 21 December 1944.

entertainment occurred in shows it was not just the chaplains who complained. Reports of offensive acts often appeared in newspapers and, frequently, church or denominational magazines. In addition, parents or other civilians could write letters of complaint or protest. Mr Phillips noted the problems in numerous pieces of correspondence and recognized that 'entertainers who deviate from scripts' present a serious problem, not the least 'from the standpoint of public relations'. He noted that he 'cannot, of course, maintain discipline if we do not take action when an entertainer violates instructions', hence there was a need to dismiss. Although others might try to plead the case for dismissed acts Phillips noted that 'if we cannot run an entertainment program that is clean, we cannot run an entertainment program at all. The people of the United States who are putting up the money to maintain Camp Shows are not going to put it up for dirty entertainment. I can explain to these people why there is no entertainment, but I cannot explain to them why there is dirty entertainment'.[20]

The question becomes, what was it that caused offence or was considered to be 'dirty', at least to chaplains in the field? Importantly, the idea of individual taste was not meant to enter into the equation, hence the need for chaplains to give details of the offensive material in any report they filed. However, the reader of these complaints cannot help but wonder about the nature of the cleric making them. For example, in September 1944 a chaplain wrote to complain about Carole Landis who appeared with a touring show that included Jack Benny. While Benny had received some criticisms from other chaplains, Chaplain Moore was particularly upset about Ms Landis. It seems that 'so obscene and unladylike was this prominent movie actress that on every hand enlisted men and officers were severely critical'. He goes on to add that he had 'no personal grudge against Carole Landis – in spite of the fact that I was omitted from the large number that she promiscuously kissed'.[21]

Another famous personality to draw a broadside from a chaplain was Ray Bolger. Although the Executive Vice-President of USO – Camp Shows Inc. registered disbelief at the accusations, he still had to respond to the complaint lodged by Chaplain McMahon. Chaplain McMahon claimed that Ray Bolger, 'between steps, related filthy, disgusting stories each of which, without exception, had as its theme homosexuality, and on no less than three occasions shouted at the top of his voice the Holy Name of Jesus Christ'.[22] Yet most participants saw USO-Camp Shows, for the most part, as a great boon to the war effort and to the soldiers' morale. It is important to remember that the objections were coming from the clergy. While some servicemen also complained of indecent entertainment on occasion, the criticisms from this segment of the audience were most definitely in the minority.

Not surprisingly, relatively few complaints filtered back to the Chief of Chaplains about the big names in entertainment. Instead, most protests revolved around more obscure acts, which were the bulk of the shows. For example Jed and

20 Letter, Lawrence Phillips to Howard Hobbs, 12 March 1945, p.2.
21 Letter, Chaplain Moore to Chief of Chaplains Arnold, 26 September 1944, p.1.
22 Letter, Chaplain McMahon to Chief of Chaplains Arnold, 8 September 1944, p.1.

Audrey Dooley, the husband and wife unicycle and bicycle act in the Camp Show called 'Gee Eye Revue', apparently told dirty jokes which centered on the use of the French 'Oui, oui' meaning to use the toilet. Abe Sher, billed as a 'novelty whistling act' was the 'worst offender' in Camp Show Unit #50, according to the complaint. Once he had finished his ten minutes of whistling he spent the rest of his time 'telling dirty, smutty and suggestive stories'. Yet, the third member of this unit, Jerry Lawton 'the dressed up cowboy', was 'credible and entertaining'. Finally, some entertainers also came in for praise. Poogie-Poogie the magician was apparently 'so successful in the quality of his work that he has been requested to remain in the Pacific'.[23]

The sheer weight given to the views of the Chaplains Corps was amazing. Quite clearly there were those who took offence at the slightest provocation, e.g. the use of the word hell once elicited a very long letter. Yet regardless of the nature of their complaints their role as the arbiter of decency and morality was never called into question in the official record. Occasionally chaplains recorded that they took their complaints about indecent entertainment to the commanding officer in the first instance, which was the standard procedure in most cases. If, however, this approach did not evoke an appropriate response, they took the matter higher up to the Chief of Chaplains. Yet nowhere in the official record is there a suggestion that they did not know what was decent. Also, they could, and did, get some acts cancelled, recalled and/or re-written. The chaplains' opinions had weight.

This was also true in the case of GI literature. The question of indecent literature was taken very seriously by the Chief of Chaplains William Arnold. As early as 1938 he was including statements about indecent literature in his circular letters. He urged 'all chaplains to survey carefully the literature circulated in their posts, camps and stations; and further, to organize, wherever possible, groups, clubs and societies to combat indecent literature. Indecent literature and profanity are first cousins'.[24] More alarmingly, earlier in the year, the Chief of Chaplains had received a letter from a Corps Area Chaplain urging Arnold to institute a national campaign based on the First Corps crusade. This crusade included a chaplain visiting camps, giving a rousing speech against indecent literature, then holding a public bonfire of all indecent magazines, producing a series of news releases, and having volunteers sign pledge cards against indecent literature. The idea of US Army chaplains burning literature in 1938, in light of the grainy black and white images we have from Nazi Germany of something of a similar nature, is disconcerting.

Literature, in the sense used here, is very broadly defined and includes books, plays, newspapers, and magazines, but also cartoons and pin-ups. All of the areas listed, however, inspired chaplains to write to the Chief of Chaplains with objections. These complaints ranged from concerns about pin-ups in barracks and

---

23 Missive, no author, 'Illustrations and Examples of Indecent Matter', 27 December 1944. Letter, M.Sgt McFadden to National Catholic Welfare Conference, no date. Letter, Lawrence Phillips to James Norris, 21 December 1943, p.1.
24 Circular Letter #91, Chief of Chaplains, 22 September 1938.

mess halls, to the depiction of the female form in GI newspapers like *Stars and Stripes*. Equally problematic were novels that appeared on reading lists supplied by the army or brought to their attention by outraged readers, as well as distasteful cartoons with indecent or immoral themes. One aspect of this genre, however, attracted the most attention from the chaplains – commercially produced magazines.

By mid war the Chaplains Corps was helped along in its campaign against indecent literature by the United States Post Office Department. As early as July 1942 the US postal service began revoking the second class mailing privileges of certain magazines deemed to be indecent. Postmaster General Frank C. Walker issued a series of press releases. In these he outlined the rules and regulations governing postal privileges. From the Post Office point of view second class mailing privileges implied governmental approval of the material being posted, meaning it would be seen as 'a publication fitting and proper for unrestricted circulation by and in the United States mails. A second-class mailing permit is looked upon by dealers and distributors as a badge of merit, a certificate of good moral character of the publication'.[25]

In the United States, second class post was reserved for periodical publications and, as with all other classes, constituted a fixed rate for posting. The second class rate was the lowest of four classes and included the mailing of newspapers, magazines and periodicals. The government claimed, supported by the Supreme Court, that the second class rate meant that the government was operating this system at a loss, but it was worth it if it meant the wider dissemination of current information. This implied second class post was 'published for the dissemination of information of a public character, or devoted to literature, the sciences, arts, or some special industry'. Yet, second class material had to be what was known as 'mailable matter'. The government also believed that, closely linked to all of this, there was a need to understand that second class mailing rates were a privilege, which had to be earned, and not a right. As pointed out by the Postmaster General in July 1942, government regulation Title 18, Section 334 of the United States Code stated that 'every obscene, lewd or lascivious, ... book pamphlet, picture, paper, letter, writing, print, ... is hereby declared nonmailable matter'. The Supreme Court upheld this restriction, noting that its purpose was to oversee the mails to avoid 'the use of the mails to circulate or deliver matter to corrupt the morals of the people ... [especially] that form of immorality which has relation to sexual impurity'.[26]

The statutes, according to the Postmaster General, were not meant to stop all publications dealing with issues of sex or sexual instruction. On the contrary, serious information was allowed. What the Post Office hoped to stop was the circulation of material, which could be determined that, 'taken as a whole, has a libidinous effect'. As with entertainment, the issue quickly becomes one of whose version of libidinous is going to be used to calculate the decency level of a publication. The criterion for the decision was whether or not the publication was

---

25 Information Service, Post Office Department, Press Release, 16 July 1942, p.1.
26 Ibid., pp.3-4.

likely to 'arouse the salacity of the reader'.[27] The Postmaster General was quick to point out that these regulations/statutes did not contravene the rights of free speech or freedom of the press.

This particular press release related to the revoking of second class mailing privileges of the magazine titled *College Humor*. The Postmaster General issued an order (#18238), served upon the publisher, to revoke the privilege based on the evidence that, since the winter 1941 issue, the magazine had included articles entitled: Dream Majorette, Breezy Collegians Create Back-Draughts, Lady Be Good, You Can Have Anything You Wish, Outdoor Girls Initiated Indoors, Drum Major, and Collegiana: It Happened Here and There. All of these were 'accompanied by photographs and drawings of an obscene, lewd and lascivious character'.[28] A hearing was held, evidence taken, and a counter argument put forth but the Postmaster General concluded that *College Humor* was a publication that does '"no more than appeal to the salaciously disposed" and show[s] clearly that every issue was "plainly designed to catch the prurient"'.[29]

This and subsequent action on the part of the Postmaster General was quickly seized upon by the Chief of Chaplains. To his delight he had at his disposal, over the course of the next few years, documentary proof of the indecency of certain publications, which was provided by the United States government. Arnold was quick to realize, as well, that he could use this information to good effect in the Army post exchanges by getting the military to ban the sale of magazines which the government itself had determined to be immoral.

On 2 November 1942 the Chief of Chaplains issued a statement outlining his belief that 'any magazine that cannot use the second class postal permit ... should not be sold by any agency on a military reservation'.[30] Chaplain Arnold also noted that, when confronted with this information, the Chief of Administrative Services, SOS, stated 'it is not thought that any service or post commander would intentionally permit the sale of unmailable literature', and 'if and when chaplains, in their duties, observe any transgressions of decency or propriety on the part of the post exchanges they should bring that to the attention of the local post commander'.[31]

Feeling that Post Commanders would respond favourably if lists of banned magazines were brought to their attention, the Chief of Chaplains asked all chaplains, in a circular letter, to report the appearance of any magazine to the base commander. Some chaplains in the field needed little more encouragement to go off in pursuit of these immoral publications. Chaplain Dux at Fort Knox sent a memo to the Post Chaplain declaring that he had found for sale at the Main Post Exchange magazines which had been deemed to violate the National Organization for Decent Literature Code. This very long list included: Complete Detective, Crack Detective, Feature Detective, Gags, Gayety, Keep 'Em Laughing, National

27 Ibid., pp.5-6.
28 Ibid., p.8.
29 Ibid., p.10.
30 Information Bulletin #26, 21 June 1943.
31 Ibid., p.2.

Detective Cases, Pack 'o Fun, Ranch Romances, Scoop Detective and Secret Detective Cases. The problems concerned the articles within these publications as recorded in the press releases of the Postmaster General.

Not all complaints met with equal response. In January 1944 Chaplain Ott reported to the Chief of Chaplains office that he had noted copies of *Esquire* at the local PX. The non-commissioned officer in charge agreed not to display the issue and to send the unsold copies back to the distributor. Then the Lieutenant in charge discovered this and ordered the magazine to be sold. When Chaplain Ott approached him on the subject Ott was told to refer it up to the Major. He did this and reported to the Chief of Chaplains that 'the Major maintains that he can see nothing wrong with the magazine (he is a doctor in private life) and that in his opinion, the morales [sic] of the men are not thereby corrupted. He tells me I have fulfilled my obligation ... As a chaplain I happen to know that these kinds of magazines are at least a contributing cause in the deterioration of the morales [sic] of the men'.[32] He was advised by the Chief of Chaplains office to make no further protest until the status of the magazine was clarified.

In another case, the office of the Chief of Chaplains counselled a chaplain, complaining about a picture used in a camp paper, to avoid being too overzealous. Chaplain Elsam was informed that:

[Y]our attitude in this matter seems very judicious and intelligent. The understanding chaplain wishes to exert the maximum influence against whatever he believes to be pernicious or harmful to the contentment, morale, or morals of the men. He will see things of minor importance which he cannot approve fully but will not wish to gain the reputation of being a complainer about small matters in case something of a serious character should arise about which he should speak out positively. If we cry 'Wolf!' every time we see a rat, we will have nothing convincing to say if the wolf actually comes. The chaplains' judgment and sense of proportion must be his guide in this particular.[33]

Conclusions

The large issues one might expect a Chaplain to grapple with, such as death and war, are rarely ever mentioned in the files of the Chief of Chaplains. Postwar memoirs of chaplains and official histories of various branches of the chaplains corps discuss war in general, and fighting the Second World War in particular, in heroic terms. The chaplains, in this capacity, see it as their duty to prepare 'the boys' for possible death and to maintain their resolve in the face of fearful circumstances. Chaplains are cited as brave men themselves in these accounts of the battlefront, and as men who made useful and valuable contributions to the war effort.

The fact that the major concern of chaplains throughout the war was the moral behaviour of men rather than battlefield considerations is telling. This is true for a

---

32 Letter, Chaplain Ott to Chief of Chaplains Arnold, 13 January 1944.
33 Letter, Chief of Chaplains to Elsam, 1 August 1944.

couple of reasons. First, the majority of GIs were not engaged in combat. In any war it is only a minority of servicemen who are actually fighting and dying. The vast majority of men during wartime make up the service branches of the military that support those who are in harm's way. Hence, the vast majority of chaplains were dealing with men who were not engaged in killing. Second, one could argue that if there was any conflict of the twentieth century that allowed people to believe that the evil they did (i.e. killing) was justified, it was the Second World War. People were fighting, killing and dying for a just and worthy cause, even for sacred reasons.

Two other points are also clear. First, according to the official *Report on the Army Chaplain in the European Theater of Operations*, 'the degree to which the chaplain was utilized as a consultant in moral issues depended to a great extent upon local circumstances and upon the personalities of the chaplain and commanding officer'.[34] Some chaplains took a very active role in issues of morality, attempting to lead the way, as it were, in safeguarding the men in their care from corrupting influences. Equally, some chaplains felt more at ease in dealing with the spiritual and pastoral needs of their men than with bigger and broader behavioural issues. Yet, as self-selected men of the cloth they all, more or less, came to the job with firm convictions about what constituted morality and sin. The widespread protest of chaplains from all theatres against the establishment of brothels and the issuance of prophylactics gives a good illustration of the unanimity of purpose in the Chaplains Corps, although it is clear that commanding officers either followed up on complaints or did not as they, personally, saw fit. With the distribution of American servicemen around the globe, it would have been impossible to insure a uniformity of response to all complaints.

Finally, there can be no doubt that chaplains had a profound effect on the development of United States Army regulations and policies. For example, at the end of the war a report on the chaplains suggested that future instructions to chaplains include a recommendation that they work 'at every level of command in the production of entertainment for military personnel, with a view *to eliminating morally objectionable and offensive material*' from GI entertainment.[35] Their role as moral guardians in the Second World War was praised. Furthermore, in a post-war survey, 93 percent of chaplains surveyed said that they felt their service had been valued. Half stated that they found no conflict between military requirements and the performance of their religious duties. In a related study, one-third of GIs had some grievances with chaplains while fully two-thirds had found chaplains to be of comfort.[36] According to Joanne Bourke, the leaders of the chaplain study had assumed that chaplains, as educated 'philosophers' would spend more time debating the dilemma of wartime killing. Instead, I would argue, chaplains

---

34 The General Board, United States Forces, European Theater, *Report on the Army Chaplain in the European Theater*, Study Number 68, 15 May 1946, p.35.

35 Ibid., p.39. Emphasis added.

36 Richard Holmes, *Acts of War: The Behavior of Men in Battle* (New York: Free Press, 1985), p.288.

withdrew from that issue and focused on types of behaviour which would make good soldiers into good Christians.

Chapter 13

Conflicting Normative Dimensions of Justification: The Gulf War[1]

Brendan Howe

Introduction

While belief in the concept of a just war might approach universality, what actually constitutes such an action may well vary across nations, cultures and religions. This chapter focuses on the Gulf War as a case study in which both sides explicitly claimed justifications for their actions based on metaphysical rather than material criteria. Saddam Hussein described the conflict in terms of an Islamic Jihad, or divinely sanctioned just war against the infidel, whereas President George Bush Senior claimed in no uncertain terms, and on repeated occasions, that the Persian Gulf War was just. For him: 'We went halfway round the world to do what is moral, just, and right'. According to DeCasse, his moral claim before Congress capped months of unprecedented ethical talk by the President, the media, religious leaders, intellectuals, and working men and women.[2] Bush explicitly linked the concepts of violation of sovereignty, aggression and justice, in a classical Western and Christian just war approach to legitimacy. However, these claims have been challenged on both factual grounds and with regard to their degree of universality.

My research focus rejects the notion of immutability and contends that just war theory has moved on from the state-centric focus of *jus ad bellum* to a position where greater emphasis is placed on *jus in bello*. The ends no longer necessarily justify the means, and how the war is to be fought must now form an integral part of the analysis of the legitimacy of going to war. My research also rejects the concept of universality, but acknowledges an overlapping consensus in which different cultural traditions have independently or through collaboration and contagion thrown up agreement in certain normative domains. Thus the analysis of the justifiability of the Allied military intervention in the Gulf will be carried out with reference to the Christian tradition, anti-universalist/Islamic perceptions, an overlapping consensual approach to justification, and *jus ad bellum* versus *jus in*

1   This work was supported by the Intramural Research Grant of Ewha University.
2   D.E. DeCasse, editor's note, in J.B. Elshtain (et al), *But was it Just?: Reflections on the Morality of the Persian Gulf War* (New York: Doubleday, 1992), p.vii. It is interesting to note that at the time of writing a strikingly similar normative debate is underway with regard to the possibility of building a second coalition to wage war upon Iraq.

bello. Each of these interpretations provides a differently nuanced answer to the central question of whether what the Allies did was right, in stark contrast to Bush's claim that: 'It's black and white. The facts are clear. The choice is unambiguous. Right vs. wrong'.[3]

The Allied *Jus ad Bellum*

Statists and communitarians claim that the state is the only common value in international politics.[4] All such authors recognize the universal right of individual states to resist the crime of aggression, and for states friendly to the victim of aggression to come to its aid – i.e., to reverse the prior intervention. Other authors consider intervention to rise above aggression if sanctioned by the proper authorities. According to Hedley Bull we have a rule of non-intervention because unilateral intervention threatens the harmony and concord of the society of sovereign states, but if an intervention expresses the collective will of the society of states, it may be carried out without bringing that harmony and concord into jeopardy.[5] In other words, universality is achieved through the endorsement of universal international organizations or some other expression of the collective and universal will. These concepts form part of the just war, and more specifically, the *jus ad bellum* tradition concerning the decision to go to war. Thus, for Elshtain, although might never makes right, might may sometimes, in balance, serve right.[6] The essential canons of this tradition include:

(1) Just Cause – usually perceived as resistance to aggression, or the prevention of horrific practices. According to Elshtain, the 'annexation of Kuwait by Iraq, the subsequent brutalization of Kuwaitis, and the gutting of their country were clear and blatant injustices, violations of basic principles of international order which encode respect for the autonomy of states'.[7] For many, these actions were easily sufficient to justify coalition counter-intervention.

(2) Right Intention – wars for revenge, wars to satisfy bloodlust or imperial ambition, are not justifiable under the tradition's criterion of 'right intention', but the Gulf War was waged, at least superficially, to reverse great evil, repel an invader, to check offensive weapon development and to establish basic ground rules for the conduct of post-Cold War international political and

---

3 D. Campbell, *Politics Without Principle: Sovereignty, Ethics, and the Narratives of the Gulf War* (Boulder: Lynne Reinner, 1993), p.22.

4 C. Thomas, 'The Pragmatic Case Against Intervention', in I. Forbes and M. Hoffman (eds.), *Political Theory, International Relations, and the Ethics of Intervention* (New York: St. Martin's Press, 1993), p.91.

5 Quoted in N.J. Rengger, 'Contextuality, Independence and the Ethics of intervention', in Forbes and Hoffman (eds.), ibid. p.91.

6 J.B. Elshtain, 'Just War as Politics: What the Gulf War Told Us About Contemporary American Life', in Elshtain, op. cit., p.44.

7 Ibid., p.47.

economic affairs.[8] Any one of these would probably be enough to signify right intention.

(3) Competent Authority – each action of the Iraqis was condemned, and each counteraction of the coalition sanctioned, by unanimous or near unanimous resolutions of the United Nations Security Council – the highest competent authority on international security matters. Furthermore, the allied intervention was authorized by the democratically elected representatives of the major intervening states at the highest level. Where available, further legitimacy was provided through the assent of democratic balancing measures in these states (e.g. the Congress of the United States and the official parliamentary opposition in the United Kingdom.) Lest such bodies be seen as representative of only certain sectors inherently antagonistic to the Iraqi regime, and thus lacking in legitimacy or authority, backing was also sought from the major Arab states. This was forthcoming, not only in the Arab League condemnation of Iraq at the Cairo meeting (and throughout the action), but also in the form of Arab contingents sent to join the coalition forces. 'In short, the Gulf War was authorized, not just once, but in a continuing process of international agreement, by all the relevant "competent authorities"'.[9]

(4) Reasonable Chance of Success – despite playing up the difficulty of the task posed in defeating the world's fourth biggest army, allied planners must have been confident in their ability to deliver a short, victorious war, and to all intents and purposes, this criteria has been vindicated by subsequent events.

(5) Proportionality of ends – certainly 'war is hell', and a fair degree of suffering was to be anticipated, but in assessing the proportionality of ends the coalition leaders had to consider not just the likely effects of intervention, but also those of non-intervention. Saddam Hussein's actions had already caused a great deal of pain in many quarters, and considerably more was likely to follow if he was to be allowed to continue his activities unchecked.

(6) Last Resort – for Wiegel, this comes down to whether 'reasonable people can reasonably conclude that all reasonable efforts at a non-military solution have been tried, have failed, and in all probability will continue to fail', while bearing in mind the continued costs in terms of human suffering caused by any further delay.[10]

(7) The Goal of Peace – this condition is not universally ascribed to by just war theorists, but is popular among the more state-centric proponents of international order. As such, I feel that some consideration should be given to it in this section. Essentially, war is considered evil, except if waged in order to put an end to an existing conflict, or to ensure that war is less likely to take place in the future. Both of these justifications were claimed by the coalition.

8   G. Weigel, 'From Last Resort to Endgame: Morality, the Gulf War, and the Peace Process', in Elshtain, ibid., pp.21-5.
9   Ibid.
10 Ibid., p.125.

However, all of these points may be, and have been, challenged to a greater or lesser extent in the context of the Gulf War. Just cause has been challenged on grounds of cultural specificity regarding notions of justice and the state. According to Matthews, the contemporary concept of the state is a European phenomenon and the modern international system of nation-states is in essence a European construction. Thus, as moral principles are developed in human society within particular cultural contexts, different cultures will have developed different systems of ethics which may well dictate different moral principles to govern similar situations. 'So not only is some skepticism warranted when addressing the issue of the ethics of behavior within states there are particular difficulties when it comes to investigating the role of morality in relations between states'.[11]

Yet, far from being a uniquely Western concept and construct, Islamic scholars have traced some of the earliest state entities to the region in question. Iraq attracted condemnation for its actions from diverse sources not limited to the West, but rather including members of the 'second' or formerly communist world, the developing world, and even the Arabic world. Furthermore, Johnson and Weigel respond that every culture has a moral tradition that addresses the justification and limitation of war. 'Though the specific terms and structures of what has come to be called just war tradition are those that have taken shape in the West, their ideas represent a far broader concept of moral issues and limits of military force'.[12] Thus the specificity objection to just cause is probably not appropriate in the Gulf case.

The 'right intention' of the allies has been criticized on the grounds of double standards. Why was the West so keen to intervene in this case, yet barely voices criticism when it comes to similar misdeeds by its friends or those countries with whom it has an interest in maintaining friendly relations? The Soviet Union invaded a number of its neighbours with seeming impunity, China annexed Tibet, Indonesia swallowed East Timor, and most importantly and emotively, Israel was able to continue its illegal oppression of Palestine despite criticism from the United Nations Security Council (15 Resolutions since 1967).[13] It is also problematic for the nuclear-armed West to claim the manufacture of weapons of mass destruction to be in some way 'unjust' or illegitimate. Perhaps the 'intent' was the destruction of the economic and military structures of Iraq which constituted an Arab force, with the goal of establishing a strong Israel and mastery over Arab oil wealth.[14]

But if this were the case, such objectives would have been better served through total conquest of Iraq – something that was well within the power of coalition forces when the halt was called. The claim of double standards relying

---

11 K. Matthews, *The Gulf Conflict and International Relations* (London: Routledge, 1993), p.170.

12 J.T. Johnson & G. Weigel, *Just War and the Gulf War* (Washington D.C.: Ethics and Public Policy Center, 1991), p.5.

13 The Mundi Club Occasional Publication no.1, *The Gulf War had nothing to do with Kuwait: So you thought you knew what the Gulf War was all about*, p.7.

14 O. Ramsbotham, 'The Conflict in Comparative Perspective', in A. Dancher and D. Keohane, *International Perspectives on the Gulf Conflict, 1990-1991* (London: Macmillan, 1994), p.309.

on comparison with cases of non-intervention by the West may be countered in a number of ways. Firstly, Matthews claims that past breaches of any moral code should not preclude current conformity to that code.[15] This is a particularly important concept for those who see the Gulf intervention as setting new standards for adherence to an international normative rules regime. Secondly, in many of the cases commonly cited, neither did the acts of aggression supposedly justifying intervention amount to annexation of the entire territory of a state and its extinction as a viable political entity, nor was the status of the entity invaded itself essentially challenged. Thirdly, legitimations of intervention are essentially permissive rather than prescriptive – intervention will only happen when likely to succeed, when likely to reduce suffering rather than increase it, and, it must be admitted, often when such intervention will also serve the national interest of intervening states. 'No sane political leader would choose a war that brought millions or even hundreds of thousands of deaths, or that threatened the world with nuclear destruction, for the sake of Kuwait independence'.[16] Indeed, by any number of measures of morality, such a war would cease to be just.

Regarding competent authority, even were it true that the United Nations in general, and the United Nations Security Council in particular is in thrall to the United States, this is not sufficient to explain the backing the coalition received from non-aligned and even anti-Western states, and the criticism of the Iraqi leadership even by those states which would normally be the most sympathetic to them. The near unanimous voting in the Security Council meant an unprecedented degree of competent authority authorization for the coalition actions. Furthermore, the competent authorities within the major alliance states surely held greater claims to legitimacy through a democratic mandate than did Saddam Hussein's regime.

On the fourth point, with the benefit of hindsight, a number of critics have claimed that in fact Saddam Hussein won the Gulf War, as he is the only political leader from the time of the conflict to still be in power. He has maintained his resolve in the face of continuing sanctions and UN weapons inspectors, and at times it has looked as if the coalition fielded against him will crumble before he does. However, at the time of writing, Saddam Hussein has acquiesced to the return of UN weapons inspectors, the United States is working hard to build up a second coalition against him, and even though there are clear concerns among prospective coalition partners that for many reasons a future intervention against Iraq will not be as just as the previous one, it is also clear that even now, few, if any, other states would be willing to side with Saddam Hussein against an American-led military intervention. As recently stated by Ivo Daalder, former Advisor to President Clinton's National Security Council, 'nobody wants to be left behind in a sure victory'.[17] Thus any perceived triumph by the present regime in Baghdad may well be seen as short-lived. Furthermore, the main declared war aim of the allies in the Gulf War was to expel Iraq from Kuwait, and in this they succeeded remarkably well.

15 Matthews, op. cit., p.173.
16 M. Walzer, 'Justice and Injustice in the Gulf War', in Elshtain, op. cit., pp.7-8.
17 S. Sobieraj, 'Bush Slowly Builds Iraq Coalition', *Associated Press*, 13 October 2002.

The next two clauses are the most contentious. Firstly, with regard to proportionality, it is argued that war can never be legitimate under modern conditions because its costs will always be greater than its benefits. Such claims were particularly prevalent among religious communities during the conflict.[18] However, these positions equate fairly closely with pacifism – if it is deemed impossible for modern wars to be just, as costs in terms of human suffering will always outweigh benefits, the same could also be said of all wars throughout history. Far from the use of modern weapons automatically leading to a massive increase in the suffering borne by civilians and the innocent, it was hoped that new 'smart' munitions could limit so-called 'collateral damage' thereby making this and future conflicts more likely to meet just war criteria. Whether or not this was actually the case in practice is more precisely a subject of *jus in bello*, or justice concerning the way the war was fought, and will be dealt with later. In general, commentators have remarked that although some measures taken by the allies might be seen as excessive, it was the overall restraint of the allies in order to attempt to stay within the paradigm that is most noticeable upon a detailed evaluation of the evidence. At this point all that is necessary for legitimacy in terms of the proportionality maxim and *jus ad bellum* is the belief that the human costs involved in not intervening would outweigh those involved in taking action against Iraq. Walzer further questions pacific interpretations of the proportionality maxim in terms of figuring in the value of defeating an aggressive regime and deterring other, similar regimes. 'All values of this latter sort are likely to lose out to the body count, since it is only bodies that can be counted'.[19]

Coalition action may be more accurately challenged on the principle of last resort. According to Campbell, when Secretary Baker finally met Iraqi Foreign Minister Tariq Aziz in Geneva in 9 January 1991, he declared that his purpose had been 'not to negotiate... but... to communicate' and Chomsky has characterized US diplomacy during the conflict as being 'limited to delivery of an ultimatum: capitulate or die'.[20] Not only were diplomatic channels underused, sanctions were not given the time required to succeed.[21] Last resort shortcomings also feed back into other elements of the complex allied justification defence. The American

---

18 Thus on November 15, 1990, the National Council of Churches of Christ criticized the Bush administration for its 'reckless rhetoric and imprudent behaviour'. On the same date, Archbishop Daniel Pilarczyk, president of the National Conference of Catholic Bishops, wrote to Bush that he feared coalition actions could well violate just war criteria, 'especially the principles of proportionality and last resort'. (Elshtain (et al), op. cit., p.128). A Jesuit magazine in Rome with editorials reviewed by the Vatican Secretary of State expressed the opinion that 'just wars' cannot exist because even when just causes come into play, the harm wars do by their nature is so grave and horrendous that they can never be justified on the forum of conscience (P. Heinegg, translation of *Modern War and the Christian Conscience* from *La Civilta Cattolica*, ibid., p.117).
19 Walzer, op. cit., p.2.
20 Campbell, op. cit., p.58.
21 Sanctions might have worked – they were universally accepted; Iraq had no large friendly neighbours willing to help them break the embargo; and the allies were ready and able to blockade air and sea (Matthews, op. cit., p.145).

President was required to determine that 'the United States has used all appropriate and other peaceful means to obtain compliance by Iraq with the United Nations Security Council Resolutions' before being granted the legal competence to resort to the use of force, yet 'met that requirement on 16 January 1991 with a letter to the Speaker of the House and the president pro-tem of the Senate, in which he simply repeated, as fact rather than contention, the resolution's wording'.[22] Thus, without the legitimacy of 'last resort' it may be that at least in the American context, there was not competent authority.

However, even if there were other measures that could have been taken, this need not be a terminal failing for the legitimacy of the allied case. It may have been morally obligatory to canvass these possibilities and to weigh the likely consequences, it was not obligatory to adopt one of them, or a sequence of them, simply so that war would be a 'last resort'. As Walzer notes, 'last resort' would make war morally impossible. We can never reach lastness, or we can never know we have reached it, as there is always something else to do. 'Most competent observers, applying this or that version of rational decision theory, expected Iraq to yield before the January 15 deadline. When that did not happen, war was, though not a "last", surely a legitimate resort'.[23] Although sanctions are almost universally and perhaps unthinkingly regarded as morally superior to the use of force, they can conceivably cause *more* suffering to civilian populations – one of the prime measures of the morality of intervention. Furthermore, by most estimates, sanctions were likely to take at least a year.[24] Not only would great suffering on both sides be perpetuated perhaps longer than necessary during this time, the coalition might also have fragmented through internal tensions, leaving no end salvation to atone for the sufferings meted out by the means.

Finally we have the goal of peace. If this was the prime allied motivation, and they considered Saddam Hussein to be a serious threat to international peace and security, then coalition forces should have pushed on to Baghdad. Yet this would have resulted in the legitimacy of the allied effort being undermined by other just war considerations. This is a point to bear in mind concerning any future intervention to remove Saddam Hussein.

The Iraqi *Jus ad Bellum*

Iraq can be portrayed as a victim of Kuwaiti aggression. Some sources in the Middle East believed that in following a strategy of collapsing oil prices, the Gulf states were trying to bring down or contain Iraq in a manner similar to the way they had successfully weakened Iran during the Iran-Iraq war.[25] Indeed, Matti Shaba Matoka, the current Catholic Archbishop of Baghdad and leader of Iraq's Catholic community claimed that: 'Kuwait was stealing our petrol. I think Iraq was right to

---

22 Campbell, op. cit., p.57.
23 Walzer, op. cit., pp.5-7.
24 Matthews, op. cit., p.148.
25 Campbell, op. cit., p.45.

invade'.[26] Thus Walzer's concept of legitimate anticipation can be used to justify the actions of both sides, as it amounts to a claim that states may use military force in the face of threats of war, 'wherever the failure to do so would seriously risk their territorial integrity or political independence. Under such circumstances it can be fairly said that they have been forced to fight and that they are the victims of aggression'.[27]

Furthermore, if the occupation of Kuwait was wrong, so was the restoration of its undemocratic government and its unfairly privileged position. While the use of force to erase unnatural borders was wrong, more wrong was the forceful intervention of a non-Arab body to undo that erasure.[28] The inherent contradictions in the just war tradition complicate the task of assessing the justice of intervention based on the accepted criteria. Walzer attempts a clarification by prioritizing the criteria. For him, it is our abhorrence of aggression that is authoritative here, while the maxim of 'last resort' and proportionality play only marginal and uncertain roles.[29] However, Campbell points out that in Walzer's 'supreme emergency', a state that believes it is threatened, even if an act of aggression has not been committed, can take actions that might in other circumstances be considered unjust.

> As such, the identification of aggression and the ascription of 'justness' are not achieved by appealing to a neutral foundation or nonpartisan judge; they are achieved through a relation of power that constructs a hierarchy of superior/inferior, in which states associating themselves with the former can punish ones they represent in terms of the latter. Moreover, it means that just-war theory – rather than providing the critique of realism that many proponents claim it does – bears a striking affinity to the logic of raison d'etat.[30]

From a personal, and it must be admitted, Western standpoint, it seems fatuous to put the claimed motivations of the Iraqi regime on a par with those of the allies. However, that it is possible to make competing claims shows that more than one interpretation of justice is possible. Thus the universality and impartiality of *jus ad bellum* claimed by the allies to provide a clear distinction between the legitimate actions of the 'good guys' and the illegitimate actions of the 'bad guys' is in itself open to question, and we need to look elsewhere in our search for value-neutral justification. Increasingly, where right intention cannot conclusively be established, scholars are turning to the nature of actions carried out in the name of justice to assess the legitimacy of intervention.

26 D. Blair, 'Iraq's Catholics strike a bargain', *The Daily Telegraph*, 2 May 2002.
27 Quoted in Campbell, op. cit., p.49.
28 S. Nusseibeh, *Can Wars be Just? A Palestinian Viewpoint of the Gulf War*, in Elshtain (et al), op. cit., p.81.
29 Walzer, op. cit., p.2.
30 Campbell, op. cit., p.25.

Jus in Bello

Jus in bello consists of the proportionality of means doctrine, which dictates that no more military force is used than is necessary in order to achieve morally legitimate political and military objectives; discrimination – that every effort be made to preserve civilian life, even in the face of increased costs on behalf of the belligerents; and the concept of limited war – a more recent addition to the just war tradition that restricts the targets of belligerent states to those that will directly contribute to the reversal of the wrong that legitimized the intervention in the first place. In other words, targets that help perpetuate the wrong are legitimate up to the point where the wrong has been reversed. After that time, there are no legitimate targets, and during that period, it is unjust to develop alternative agendas and authorize military action to achieve goals other than those sanctioned by the original mandate.

Proportionality of Means

Lackey claims that there is a 'logical gulf between the demands of morality and the dictates of self-interest'.[31] The proportionality of means approach rejects this dichotomy – by virtue of our shared humanity, it accords with our self-interest to follow the demands of morality. In no form of politics is it possible to build a firewall between our wants and the consequences for others of our obtaining those wants. Hence Elshtain tells us that just war theory is not only about war, but rather it is a way of thinking that refuses to separate politics from ethics, public from private moralities, or to open up a sharp divide between 'domestic' and 'international' politics.[32] Therefore, we reject the realist notions of 'anything goes' in attempting to achieve political or military objectives – it is not just to push all of the costs onto our adversary or the operating environment in order to increase our payoffs and rational balance sheets.

The extraordinary lopsidedness of deaths and casualties in the Gulf War indicates that excessive firepower may have been used, and thus the proportionality maxim violated. In March 1991 the UN Undersecretary-General reported that the extent of Iraq's devastation was 'near apocalyptic'.[33] *The Guardian* newspaper reported around the same time that 'Iraq is doomed to being an economic cripple for years and, experts say, rebuilding the country could cost up to $200 billion and take a generation'.[34] Thus Brittain comments: 'No talk of a UN mandate, or a just war, can ever make the destruction of Iraq anything but a shameful stain on the conscience of the Allies rather than the victory of Operation Desert Storm hailed

---

31 R. Little, 'Recent Literature on Intervention and Non-Intervention', in Forbes & Hoffman (eds.), op. cit., p.27.

32 Elshtain, op. cit., p.43.

33 A. Cockburn, & A. Cohen, 'The Unnecessary War', in V. Brittain (ed.), *The Gulf Between Us: The Gulf War and Beyond* (London: Virago Press, 1991), p.1.

34 *The Guardian*, 26 February 1991, p.2.

by the Allied leadership and an overwhelmingly triumphalist Western media'.[35] Such a disqualification of legitimacy may be made not only in the event of actions being taken that consciously resulted in excessive harm to the opponent, but even should due care and attention to avoid unnecessary harm not be taken.

At the very least the allies were guilty of the latter. When asked in late March 1991 about the extent of Iraqi casualties, General Colin Powell replied, 'It's not really a number that I'm terribly interested in'.[36] For Schwarzenberger, the rules of warfare are the result of a continuous tug-of-war between two formative agencies: the standard of civilization and the necessities of war.[37] The coalition forces stand accused of violating the former without the justification of the latter – it was not necessary to the war effort or to secure discrete military objectives, to inflict the kind of devastation visited upon Iraq, nor was it necessary to continue to kill so many Iraqi troops even when they were in retreat. Attacking withdrawing Iraqi forces on Mutha Ridge did not violate international law. 'A retreating army is regarded as still within the bounds of war operations and as such is a legitimate target'.[38] Weigel points out that the retreating Iraqis could and should have surrendered, as did tens of thousands of their comrades, and a number of commentators have noted that an army in retreat is still an army, and thus poses a threat.[39] However, the doctrine of proportionate means demands that enough of a threat be posed for continued human cost to be inflicted, and it is doubtful whether this justification is available to the allied commanders.

Discrimination and the Protection of Civilian Life

Weigel notes that throughout the war there were strict rules of target recognition which were scrupulously obeyed, even to the extent of bringing back unexploded ordnance when targets were not directly identifiable.[40] Thus civilian casualties were unintentional and, while unfortunate, acceptable. However, these justifications are based on a false dichotomy between accidental 'collateral' civilian damage and deliberate targeting, or a straw man question of whether suffering outside the theatre of combat was directly intended or a result of legitimate military actions. Discrimination of action takes place, and thus legitimacy can only be claimed, if civilian life is actively and positively protected – i.e., all feasible precautions taken to avoid the loss of civilian life rather than just omitting to directly target civilians. Coalition supporters claim that although more non-precision guided munitions were used than guided ones, precision-guided weapons were used in situations where legitimate military targets were located in populated areas, and 'non-precision weapons were used to attack broad targets or

35 Brittain, op. cit., p.xii.
36 Campbell, op. cit., p.4.
37 Matthews, op. cit., p.157.
38 Ibid., p.166.
39 Weigel, op. cit., p.27.
40 Ibid., op. cit., p.28.

desert targets where precise locations were uncertain'.[41] However, as admitted by Walzer, strategic bombing of infrastructure, including attacks on power and water supplies (water most clearly), is very much like attacking food sources: 'they are necessary to the survival and everyday activity of soldiers, but they are equally necessary to everyone else. An attack here is an attack on civilian society. In this case, it is the military effects, if any, that are "collateral"'.[42] Yet much of the allied bombardment of Iraq focused on these very areas. Furthermore, according to the Pentagon Report on Persian Gulf War, the intelligence agencies were unable to assess bomb damage properly and to communicate targeting restrictions speedily to the air forces, so that far greater damage was inflicted upon Iraq's civilian infrastructure than originally intended.[43] Indeed, despite the massive allied 'Nintendowar' propaganda, only seven percent of explosives dropped were in fact 'smart', and 70 percent of the 88,500 tons of explosives dropped missed their targets.[44] This contributed to the 10,000 or more civilian deaths.

The former United States Attorney, Ramsay Clarke, who visited the southern Iraqi port city of Basra said that what he saw was 'a human and civilian tragedy', and he judged the allied actions to have exceeded the mandate given by the United Nations Security Council Resolution 678, with the destruction of residential areas, hospitals, night clubs, coffee shops, clinics and law offices.[45] Some observers have even gone so far as to accuse the coalition forces of deliberate targeting of civilians, making an even stronger case for the rejection of the legitimacy of allied actions on the grounds of discrimination (or rather, lack of it!). According to the Mundi Club, '[t]he timing of the air raids was also politically motivated to put the severest pressure on the population to rebel against the government. This deliberate bombing of civilian targets was plain mass murder, a war crime'.[46]

Limited War

Walzer acknowledges that attacks of the sort carried out by the allies and listed above, suggested a war aim beyond the legitimate one of 'restoration plus' – the liberation of Kuwait and the defeat and reduction of Iraqi military power. 'The added, though never acknowledged, aim was presumably the overthrow of the Ba'athist regime, which was to be proven incapable not only of defending its foreign conquest but also of protecting its own people'.[47] He notes that in this case both the ends and the means are unjust as except in extreme cases, like that of Nazi Germany, war aims do not legitimately reach to the transformation of the internal politics of the aggressor state or the replacement of its regime as such would require a prolonged occupation, massive coercion of civilians, and a usurpation of

41 Matthews, op. cit., p.162.
42 Walzer, op. cit., p.13.
43 Campbell, op. cit., p.11.
44 Brittain, op. cit., p.xvii.
45 *The Guardian*, 8 February 1991, p.5.
46 Ibid.
47 Walzer, op. cit., pp.9-13.

sovereignty – exactly what we condemn when we condemn aggression.[48] Likewise, for Hauerwas: 'Just warriors abjure the crusade because the "good cause" often overrides the limited moral purpose that originally justified the war as well as often shoulders aside the principle of noncombatant immunity'.[49] Yet the allies stand accused, not only of launching a crusade, but also of behaving in such a manner for causes other than a limited moral purpose. Brittain concurs that the war aims of the allies were 'not just Kuwait, with all its oil wealth, back under control of a pro-Western government, not only the ousting of Saddam Hussein, but also a new regime in Baghdad which would be destabilized neither by Shiites demanding an "Islamic republic", nor by a democratic movement looking for genuine participation and Kurdish autonomy'.[50] If the justification for the war was to get Iraq out of Kuwait, why did the coalition forces bomb Iraq and target the Iraqi nuclear capacity?

It is therefore doubtful whether even the allied commanders truly subscribed to all the tenets of *jus in bello*. Thus again any claims to impartial and universal measurements of right and wrong based on this tradition are flawed. In fact, only by consulting every individual in the world for their personal perceptions can we be certain of establishing universality. Naturally, this is impossible. We must search for the best approximation of this process. We cannot ask every individual, but we can go some way to assessing the views of individuals within those societies that openly consult with their internal constituencies. Likewise, assuming that the spokesmen of states acting in the global arena speak on behalf of their internal constituencies, endorsement within international organizations would also seem to indicate some degree of legitimacy. In pursuit of the universal legitimizing criteria to which they aspire, liberal internationalists look to the values attached to individual human rights and the judgment of the international community in order to assess the just war claims of states.

Internal and External Constituencies

Liberal internationalists essentially appeal to two sets of shared values in order to establish the legitimacy of action or inaction by any particular state entity, those belonging to the state's internal constituency, and those belonging to the external constituency of the international community. In the aftermath of the Gulf War the former Secretary General of the United Nations alluded to the first by proclaiming the end of absolute and exclusive sovereignty and the birth of a New World Order in which no state could consider itself immune to the demands and rights of its people, and to the second by holding states responsible to the standards set by the external constituency embodied by the United Nations, which would not tolerate the hindrance of its 'great objectives' of peace and security, justice and human

---

48 Ibid. p.9.
49 S. Hauerwas, 'Whose Just War? Which Peace?', in Elshtain (et al), op. cit., p.89.
50 Brittain, op. cit., p.xii.

rights, and 'social progress and better standards of life in larger freedom'.[51] Thus the rights of individuals and the constituent parts of internal communities as well as the demands of international communities constitute the final set of justifying criteria we will consider.

The Internal Constituencies

The Amnesty International report documenting abuses by the Ba'athist regime against civilians in occupied Kuwait was held up by some coalition leaders as the prime motivation for a humanitarian intervention. In a speech at the Lord Mayor's Banquet in London on 10 April 1991, Douglas Hurd the British Foreign Secretary claimed that 'there are occasions, as today, when the world calls out in anger and shared sorrow against cruelty and suffering within states and we, the diplomatic profession, have to work out what that response be'.[52] Thus for Ramsbotham in the end it was the moral justification that President Bush relied on most – 'the moral/legal principle of collective security, the hope of a morally just new world order, and, triggered by the Amnesty International press release of 2 October 1990, the Iraqi atrocities in Kuwait, which from then on became a *lietmotiv* in the President's own emotional engagement with the crisis'.[53] Yet Amnesty International has pointed out that similar reports on atrocities within the borders of Iraq had been disregarded by coalition leaders. As late as 7 March 1990, the UN Commission on Human Rights in which the major allied powers play active roles, had decided not to take action on a proposal for an inquiry into human rights violations in Iraq.[54] The citizens of Iraq had been suffering under the brutal regime for a long period before coalition forces took up arms to defend the rights of the Kuwaitis, and were to suffer even more as a consequence of the allied intervention. That close to two million citizens, from a population of 17 million, were in exile even before the turmoil of 1991 shows the extent of this suffering.[55] Furthermore, if we are to consider the rights of individuals as the prime justification for this case of intervention, we have also to look at the legitimacy of the Kuwaiti regime.

Reports in the western media and statements by western leaders frequently linked the brutal activities of the Iraqis with calls for the restoration of the legitimate government of Kuwait. Yet on an individual level, it is doubtful whether there ever had been a legitimate government of Kuwait. Any reference to restoring the legitimate government of Kuwait may be rejected on grounds of the

51 B. Boutros-Ghali, *An Agenda for Peace: Preventative Diplomacy, Peacemaking and Peace-keeping*, Report of the Secretary-General pursuant to the statement adopted by the Summit Meeting of the Security Council on 31 January 1992 (New York: United Nations, 17 June 1992), pp.2-5.
52 J. Mayall, 'Non-Intervention, Self-Determination and the New World Order', in Forbes & Hoffman (eds.), op. cit., p.171.
53 Ramsbotham, op. cit., p.307.
54 Cockburn & Cohen, op. cit., p.2.
55 Brittain, op. cit., p.xii.

link between legitimacy and representation or participation.[56]   Any form of political participation (and even then of only the most rudimentary nature) was and is limited to 'official' Kuwaitis, excluding the majority of the state's inhabitants. Particularly badly off were the Palestinian refugees, themselves victims of an illegal invasion that the international community seemed bent on overlooking despite UN Resolutions condemning Israeli actions.   Women also endure an underrepresented status, and Human Rights Watch has identified a system of institutionalized discrimination against the Bedoon community resident in Kuwait, the closure of all human rights organizations and a new round of human rights abuses at Kuwaiti hands since the restoration of the 'legitimate' government. Despite calls to defend human rights in rallying support for the war against Iraq, the reinstated Kuwaiti government has trampled on those rights at nearly every turn, often with the use of violence.   Murder, torture, arbitrary detention, and unlawful deportation have been the tools of this campaign of vengeance.[57]   Power only brings control not authority – authority is grounded in consent. A government that rules without consent is illegitimate.   Thus an action aimed at restoring or imposing such a regime is itself of dubious legitimacy, and if it involves military force must be considered unjust.

These then are the two main problems with the allies playing the internal community legitimizing card – they needed to show that what they were reinstating was legitimate in these terms, and they needed to show a consistent concern for the internal constituencies of states. They failed both tests. For Nusseibeh, the moral credibility of an intervention can only be established if there is at least a demonstrated resolve to address the underlying causes of injustice, regardless of the prevailing dictates of national interest.[58]   This was not the case in the Gulf intervention.   Rather, an awesome military force was mobilized to protect the independence of a state whose hereditary rulers had recently suspended the democratic rights of their own subjects.[59]   Furthermore, far from responding to their internal constituencies, the allies could also be accused of dictating to them and misrepresenting them. So the Gulf intervention can be seen as a war waged by one state's elite (after manufacturing the consent of its internal constituencies) on behalf of a second state's elite (with very little claim to represent its internal constituencies) against a third state's elite which systematically abused its internal constituencies.

Yet, as noted by Elshtain, no state 'escapes whipping when measured up against strong standards of justice'. But just war deplores creating false equivalencies: there is a big difference between being paid low wages for hard work; being denied the franchise; and being tortured or gassed because one's politics is 'incorrect' or because one is a member of an ethnic minority which cannot defend itself against a dominant and violent majority.[60]   Although it is a

---

56 Ramsbotham, op. cit., p.310.
57 http://www.hrw.org/pubweb/Webcat-59.htm.
58 Nusseibeh, op. cit., p.76.
59 Mayall, op. cit., p.168.
60 Elshtain, op. cit., p.47.

stretch to claim that allied actions were primarily motivated by concerns for the well-being of the people of Kuwait, it is still conceivable that the intervention was morally just on the balance of human rights violations. By any standards allied actions were less bad that those of the Iraqi regime, which accounts in part for the broad support enjoyed by the Allies, and comes close to providing a universal legitimation.

External Constituencies

The coalition made explicit appeals to the external constituency of a global community, and implicit appeals to the notion of shared humanity in an attempt to justify the intervention. Yet the rules of co-existence and interaction in the global community were drawn up by these same powers in order to reflect their world-view and preserve the status quo in their interest. While we have already seen that states were not uniquely a product of the Westphalian system, but may have emerged in other regions (including the Gulf) prior to European interaction, this does not mean that the same value is placed upon statism, or the prioritizing of the state as political forum. Saddam Hussein may have broken the rules of interstate interaction, but it is possible that he was appealing to a higher, or at least alternative, set of justifying criteria.

Matthews has identified how charismatic persons like Saddam Hussein can appeal to the peoples of the other Arab states over their leaders on the grounds of Islam, Islamic unity and orthodoxy; and secondly on grounds of pan-Arabism, Arab nationalism and Arab brotherhood.[61] Saddam Hussein told delegates at an Islamic conference in Baghdad that '[w]e are taking the right path for peace and jihad, not only for all Muslims but for all mankind ... the showdown is not for territory. It is not a limited showdown for temporary objectives'.[62] While the coalition attempted to play down the autocratic nature of the Al-Sabah regime in Kuwait, the Iraqis touched a Middle Eastern street nerve by arguing that the oil-rich Gulf Arabs were corrupt and decadent and that their wealth should be shared evenly throughout the region. The classical Muslim view is of a world divided into the dar-ul-Islam (the House of Islam or the House of Peace) and the dar-ul-harb (the House of War). Ideally, conflict should not occur in the house of Islam, but if it does it should be settled by Muslims themselves, rather than 'American women in shorts'. 'The polity of the Muslim world is seen as self-regulating and, by definition, non-Muslims from "the House of War" cannot bring peace to "the House of Peace"'.[63]

While to Western ears this sounds like sheer hypocrisy and unsubtle propaganda of the worst kind, the Iraqi portrayal of events met with some sympathy and success in the region. Matthews claims that the Iraqi invasion of Kuwait was seen by most Jordanians and other Arabs all over the region as the

---

61 Matthews, op. cit., p.21.
62 M. Woollacott, 'Saddam rallies faithful for war', *The Guardian*, 12 January 1991.
63 Right Rev. M. Nazir-Ali, 'Saddam rallies faithful for war', *The Guardian*, 12 January 1991.

beginning of the forced Arab unity that would bring the wealth of the profligate Gulf state Arabs to the service of the bankrupt and poverty stricken Arabs of the north.[64] Likewise Ramsbotham contends that the substantial demonstrations mounted in early 1991 in Algeria, Bangladesh, Egypt, Indonesia, Jordan, Morocco, Pakistan, Syria and Tunisia were not just a 'street' manifestation, but, according to most Arab or Muslim commentators, reflected widespread sentiment.[65]

However, even in Islamic terms Saddam Hussein's position is morally untenable as jihad is forbidden against fellow Muslims. Indeed Matthews points out that Iraq's invasion of Kuwait contravened explicit instructions to the faithful in the Qur'an, whereby Muslims are urged to 'fight for the sake of Allah those that fight against you, but do not attack them first. Allah does not love aggressors'.[66] Yet it does raise questions regarding the universalist claims of the West concerning the rules of global society. The values for which the coalition claimed to be fighting do form part of an external constituency beyond the state, but it may be that this community is just one of a number of such communities, none of which is universal in nature. If coalition values were limited to a smaller constituency than the global society then they may in fact have been merely an extension of the national interest of dominant states.

The implicit appeal to human rights is also open to question. If the coalition forces were truly motivated by concerns of a shared humanity they would have applied them more consistently and have shown more evidence of concern for the post-intervention order in both Kuwait and Iraq. Furthermore, they would have shown concern for the effect of their own actions upon the civilians of a defeated Iraq. In a meeting with Douglas Hurd, Farouq al-Shara the Syrian foreign minister, called on western countries to keep the promises they had made during the Gulf Conflict, unlike their behaviour after the First World War when many of their pledges were broken. '"These nice words about peace, security and the new international order should be honoured", he said in a clear reference to statements by US and British leaders that a solution to the Arab-Israeli conflict must be urgently tackled after the end of hostilities'.[67] That they reneged once again on agreements to get tough with Israeli abuses shows little more than lip service was being paid to humanitarian tenets, which would still lose out to national interest.

Likewise, the recent depleted uranium scandal is only the latest tragic human consequence of actions against Iraq. Having encouraged both the Kurds and Shias to rise up, after allied objectives had been achieved, the coalition abandoned these populations to the inevitable recriminations. The United Kingdom and United States have steadfastly refused to lift sanctions against Iraq despite the mounting humanitarian tragedy. They have even shown resistance to the concept of 'smart' sanctions, whereby a military embargo would be maintained, but humanitarian supplies would be allowed passage. It seems unlikely that they will agree to lift

---

64 Matthews, op. cit., p.56.
65 Ramsbotham, op. cit., p.309.
66 Matthews, op. cit., p.186.
67 R. Mauthner, 'The Gulf War: Enduring Middle East peace depends on Israel, says Syria', *Financial Times*, 8 February 1991.

sanctions as long as Saddam Hussein remains alive, and the American government has inbuilt a ten month delay into any process of lifting sanctions, which would lead to the death of an additional 5,000 Iraqi children.[68] Indeed, exiled Iraqi writer Faleh' Abd al Jabar pointed out that war would destroy the country but give Saddam Hussein another political lease of life as the military was the main force which could remove him and offer change. Phebe Marr of the National Defence University and specialists in the United States Defence Department belatedly came to the same conclusion *after* the war.[69] All permanent members of the Security Council have consistently opposed a general right of humanitarian intervention in General Assembly debates.[70] While China might well be concerned about adding an avenue of criticism over Tibet, and Russia over Chechnya, some of the doubts in Western minds might have concerned the creation of a duty rather than a right to intervene. Yet perhaps guilt over their previous association with and support of such an unpalatable regime is a more convincing motive for coalition posturing over human rights in the build up to the intervention.

However, even if allied actions cannot be universally justified, there is little doubt that those of Saddam Hussein are even less justifiable by any criteria. Most commentators accept that there are individual human rights, shared values within communities that constitute state rights, and a certain degree of global consensus or shared norms. What is needed is a way to reflect these three competing demands upon our evaluation of justice. Most contemporary societies (those not rejected by international society as pariah regimes) give a high priority to the freedom to choose. An international version of Rawls' overlapping consensus here comes into play. Rawls identifies his overlapping consensus as the only community shared value likely to endure without coercion – an institutionalized guarantee of tolerance of diversity *within* communities as opposed to mere toleration of diversity between communities.[71] He is also concerned with majoritarian popular support for regimes, but unlike communitarians, is convinced that in order to get a substantial majority of citizens to give their support freely, a political doctrine is needed 'that a diversity of comprehensive religions, philosophical, and moral doctrines can endorse, each from its own point of view'.[72]

Any state which does not practise this degree of toleration of diversity leaves itself open to universal condemnation. Any state which does not practise this degree of toleration *and* conducts itself in a manner towards its own citizens that any rational being would find abhorrent is illegitimate according to the shared norms of international society. Should the abuses be sufficient (according to the doctrine of proportionality) to outweigh the possible harm that would be done by

68 F. Halliday, Seminar on neutrality, Dun Laoghaire, 17 May 2000.
69 Brittain, op. cit., pp.xiv-xv.
70 A. Roberts, *The So-Called Right of Humanitarian Intervention*, lecture at Queens University Belfast, 9 December 1999.
71 J. Rawls, 'The domain of the political and overlapping consensus', in D. Copp (ed.), *The Idea of Democracy* (Cambridge: Cambridge University Press, 1993), p.198.
72 Ibid., p.250.

external intervention, then every state of superior moral standing not only has the right, but also the duty to intervene.

Conclusion

The Allied military intervention in the Gulf can be seen as essentially justifiable in traditional state-centric Western terms of *jus ad bellum*. Its justifiability is considerably more problematic when considered in terms of *jus in bello*. Internal and external constituency considerations raise further doubts about the just war credentials of allied actions, and despite the existence of a theoretical overlapping consensus that borders on universality with regard to the more illegitimate of state actions against their populations, the universality of the application of these principles by the West is certainly open to question. Yet although Allied claims of universality remain unsubstantiated, there is enough of an overlapping consensus universally to identify Iraqi actions as illegitimate and deserving of reversal – indeed, a universal declaration of human wrongs may better frame the global consensus than the Universal Declaration of Human Rights.

However, what commentators on the whole have failed to acknowledge is that for things to reach a stage where this debate is necessary and we have to resort to 'seat-of-the-pants judgment' represents a significant failure on the part of the international community. States do not fail on the basis of irreconcilable ethnic cleavages, they do not collapse through lack of indigenous moral fibre, extremists do not win the support of others by virtue of appealing to the extremist in all of us – rather, hatred is generated by individuals attempting to build a political power platform, and support for them comes from those groups suddenly disadvantaged by changing circumstances resulting in an expectancy gap. While we cannot escape the communitarian dilemma, we can get round the proportionality maxim by acting sooner to undercut support for inhumane ideologies by constructing palatable alternatives.

Chapter 14

Just War and the Perspective of Ethics of Care

Rob van den Toorn

Introduction

Just war theory is in principle a branch of ethical theory, since all justification of human actions can be viewed as a question of ethics. Throughout history, the classic ethical theories have mainly been formulated by men. Possibly not coincidentally, they are dominated by a Kantian code of rights and obligations which many perceive as particularly masculine. Since the 1980s, a group of philosophers has begun to explore whether there is an ethic of care which can be seen as characteristically feminine and opposed to the Kantian view. I propose to build on their work and investigate whether there can be said to be a separate feminine, or feminist, theory of just war.

Taking as their starting point feminist psychological empirical data, these philosophers have postulated, as Carol Gilligan put it in her book *In a Different Voice*, that women have a different ethical experience than men; that 'women speak in a different voice'. Gilligan asserts that women 'focus not on the primacy and universality of individual rights, but rather on a very strong sense of being responsible to the world'. It should be noted that Gilligan describes her empirical observations about the different voice as a distinction between two modes of thought, rather than as unvarying characteristics of male and female thought. She also argues that the two strands of ethics, Kantian and Care, are complementary aspects of a whole, neither of them complete in itself.[1]

Similarly, in her book *Postures of the Mind*,[2] Annette Baier suggests that there is a need 'to connect their [women's] ethics of love with what has been the men theorists' preoccupation, namely obligation'. Baier also sees this ethic of care as of equal value to the Kantian world-view. She has developed the concept into a theory of Ethics of Care, which she presents as an extension of Hume's account of sentiments, in opposition to traditional ethical theory. Her theory forms a good comparative basis for the beliefs of nations, peoples, religions and cultures outside

1   C. Gilligan, *In a Different Voice* (Cambridge, Mass.: Harvard University Press, 1982).
2   A.C. Baier, *Postures of Mind: Essays on Mind and Morals* (Minneapolis: University of Minnesota Press, 1985).

the Western world, but it remains restricted, as she, like Gilligan only advocates a complementary position for it.

As far as the justification of war is concerned, I would go further. If we accept these views, our acceptance implies that we must formulate a comprehensive alternate perspective on just war, breaking away from the previously standard line. This would take as its cornerstone Hume's thesis that morality depends on self-corrected sentiments. An ethic of Care demands that people support a non-individualist, non-egoistic version of human passions, and that they pay attention to the essentially interpersonal or social nature of those passions which are approved as virtues and to the fact that cooperation includes cooperation in unchosen schemes, with unchosen and unequal partners.

In her book *Moral Prejudices*, in a discussion of violent demonstration and terrorism, Baier explores the implications of the Care perspective for questions of armed conflict.[3] I propose to carry this line of inquiry further and apply it to a conventional military conflict, and specifically the justifications used to launch that conflict.

In recent history, the wars in Kosovo, Afghanistan, and Vietnam all offer, in my view striking examples for discussion. In this chapter I will take the Kosovo conflict as a case study and present an empirical study of the official justification by NATO of its move to action in the Federal Republic of Yugoslavia (FRY), as reported in NATO documents. As I will show, the ethical grounding for the NATO intervention in Kosovo and the FRY was morally mainly credited to humanitarian grounds. I will elaborate on the philosophical basis underpinning this humanitarian motivation and demonstrate how, in my view, an application of Ethics of Care could have influenced our judgment about the justification of the war.

Ethics of Care

Let us first examine the origins and general outline of the philosophy which has developed into the Ethics of Care code. The concept is a relatively recent one. In the 1980s a group of social and moral philosophers including Laurence Thomas and Annette C. Baier formed a kind of philosophical counter-culture influenced by the Harvard psychologist Carol Gilligan. Gilligan had conducted research with the central assumption that the way people talk about their lives and the language that they use reveal the world they experience. She interviewed hundreds of people, mainly women, about their conceptions of self and morality, and about their experiences of conflict and chaos. She found that woman mostly focus their ethical views not on the primacy and universality of individual rights but rather on a very strong sense of being responsible to the world. She then compared her results with the morality scheme of Kohlberg, who sees the moral development of mankind as a development from a pre-conventional level (where what is seen to

3   A.C. Baier, *Moral Prejudices: Essays on Ethics* (Cambridge, Mass.: Harvard University Press, 1995).

matter is pleasing or not offending parental authority figures), through a conventional level (in which a child tries to fit in with a group and its standards) to a post-conventional level (in which the conventional rules are subjected to tests, these final tests being based on respect for each individual's Kantian autonomy). Gilligan applied Kohlberg's questionnaires to both female and male subjects and found that girls and women scored consistently lower on Kohlberg's scale.

Gilligan repeated some interviews a few years later to find out whether the positions taken by the interviewees had changed during the interval. As a result she changed her views about her empirical observations. She maintained her view that men and women naturally tend to two different perspectives on moral and social issues, but modified it to propose that both sexes can alternate between the two modes of thought, although individuals will more frequently follow the gender-dominant one. The first perspective, the normally male one, she called the Justice view, while the second, normally female perspective, was termed the Care view.

The possible causes of this dichotomy remain incompletely understood. In her writings Gilligan links the care perspective of women with their maternal role, although critics have attacked her failure to substantiate this. She bases her assumptions primarily on Chodorow, who in turn relies on Robert Stoller.[4] These two researchers have explored the development of identity from early childhood onwards. According to Stoller, gender identity 'with rare exception [is] firmly and irreversibly established for both sexes by the time a child is about three'. Chodorow believes that identity formation takes place in a context of ongoing relationship, since 'mothers tend to experience their daughters as more like themselves', while in contrast 'mothers experience their sons as a male opposite' and vice-versa.[5] Further empirical data comes from Mead and Piaget's work on children's games during the middle childhood years. Mead and Piaget claim that children in games learn respect for rules and come to understand the way rules function. Janet Lever built on their findings through a study demonstrating that boys play out of doors more often than girls do, that boys play more often in large and age-heterogeneous groups, that they play competitive games more often, and that their games last longer than girls' games.[6] Lever also noted that when disputes arose in the course of a game, boys were able to resolve the dispute more effectively than girls. Her research confirmed Piaget's observation that boys even in early childhood are more concerned with legalistic rules than girls, while girls are more tolerant. One can conclude that there is some empirical proof that as early as their middle childhood boys have already developed a bias towards a

4   R.J. Stoller, 'A Contribution to the Study of Gender Identity', *International Journal of Psycho-Analysis*, no. 45, 1964, pp.220-26.
5   N. Chodorow, 'Family Structure and Feminine Personality', in M.Z. Rosaldo and L. Lamphere (eds), *Woman, Culture and Society* (Stanford: Stanford University Press, 1974).
6   J. Lever, 'Sex Differences in the Games Children Play', *Social Problems*, no. 23, 1976, pp.478-87.

worldview based on rights (and obligations), whereas girls develop differently psychologically.

In fact, further psychological studies in the 1980s showed that most men do indeed have a different concept of achievement motivation from women. The men studied tended to approach success and avoid failure, while the women feared success and were averse to competitive achievement. Research showed that men's orientation is generally positional within a group and women's is generally towards individual personal relationships. Men see affirmation of their positional sense of self as not merely pleasurable, but morally *good*, and as this masculine viewpoint prevails in society, they receive social confirmation that it is indeed right for them to succeed.

In Gilligan's view, the contrasting deference of women towards their social position is not only rooted in social subordination but also in their moral concern that 'sensitivity to the needs of others and the assumption of responsibility of taking care lead women to attend to voices other than their own and to include in their judgment other points of view. Thus women not only define themselves in a context of human relationship but also judge themselves in terms of their ability to care'.[7] As a result, Gilligan claims that women analyze moral issues in terms of conflicting responsibilities rather than competing rights. They consider moral problems in a contextual and narrative manner rather than within a formal and abstract framework. As Gilligan puts it, 'this conception of morality as concerned with the activity of care centers moral development around the understanding of responsibility and relationships'.[8]

'Ethics of Care' is the description coined by Annette Baier. She extended the perspective described above to examine a model of a community different from a liberal one, one which voices Gilligan's version of morality. Baier points particularly to the long unnoticed moral proletariat, the mostly female, domestic workers. Their perspective had long been ignored, but due to progress in the conventional moral theories which saw the concept of an individual person's rights as central, more and more categories of persons were included as equal individuals, and this at last brought forward their new voice in the debate.

Baier suggests that women should go beyond achieving acknowledgement of equal status as persons, and press for equal recognition of their different perspectives. Traditional (Kantian) moral theories are concerned with relationships between equals, and give priority to the freedom of choice and the priority of the intellect, but 'relationships between those who are clearly unequal in power, such as parents and children, states and citizens, doctors and patients ... have had to be shunted to the bottom of the agenda and then dealt with some sort of promotion of the weaker'.[9]

In Baier's view true equality of power is rare and hard to recognize when it occurs. She proposes a new approach to the design of institutions structuring the relationships between unequals and advocates the study of the relationship between

7   Gilligan, op cit., pp.16-17.
8   Ibid., p.19.
9   Baier, *Moral Prejudices*, p.28.

the more and the less powerful. She puts it quite baldly when she states that 'the liberal morality, if unsupplemented, may unfit people to be anything other then what its justifying theories suppose them to be, ones who have no interests in each others' interests'.[10] Baier also raises the question of the priority of rationalism over emotion and passion, supporting Laurence Thomas in his defence of the equality of emotional and rational capacities.

The connecting thread in all of this is a focus on relationships between parties that are and cannot but be unequal, and a recognition that not all morally important relationships can be freely chosen. Baier, drawing attention to the historic inattention to relations of inequality and the inattention to unchosen relations, says, 'The emphasis on care goes with a recognition of the often unchosen nature of responsibilities of those who give care'.[11]

In sum, the perspective which emerges from the above philosophical and sociological studies is of an ethical theory which gives more weight to the nature of unequal and unchosen relations and to emotional considerations than the previously accepted Kantian view. This is in keeping with Hume's position that morality depends upon self-corrected sentiments. This provides a valuable new perspective for the world community in its deliberations of the justification of war. The application of Ethics of Care theory to international relations will highlight the essentially interpersonal or social nature of those passions which are approved as virtues and the fact that moral cooperation includes cooperation in unchosen schemes, with unchosen partners, with unequal partners in close intimate relations as well as distanced and more formal ones.

Just War Tradition

The historical discourse of just war started with St Augustine and received much of its terminology from Hugo Grotius. The main tenets of just war doctrine are:

- that a war be the last resort to be used only after all other means have been exhausted;
- that a war be clearly an act of redress of rights actually violated, or defence against unjust demands backed by the threat of force;
- that war be openly and legally declared by properly constituted governments;
- that there be a reasonable prospect for victory;
- that the means be proportionate to the ends;
- that a war be waged in such a way as to distinguish between combatants and non-combatants;
- that the victorious nation not require the utter humiliation of the vanquished.[12]

10 Ibid., p.29.
11 Ibid., p.30.
12 R.J. Niebanck, *Conscience, War and the Selective Objector* (Board of Social Ministry, Lutheran Church of America, 1972).

These notions are generally accepted as the basis of present-day theorizing about armed conflicts. Their general thrust is compatible with an Ethics of Care philosophy, but as I will point out below, specific situations arise with respect to humanitarian war where Care theorists would interpret them very differently.

For this dicussion, I propose the adoption of the definition put forward by George Meggle of the University of Leipzig. He suggests that a humanitarian intervention is an intended intervention from a state or state group A in a second state B in favour of C (some individuals or some groups of individuals) under condition that A undertakes the intervention to prevent, to stop, or to diminish grave actual violations of humanitarian law against C by B.[13] It is noteworthy that humanitarian interventions are in Meggle's definition justified by their intent, regardless of their success. As this paper focuses on the declared motives for initiating a conflict, rather than on possible hidden motives, it will be assumed that in all cases party A is indeed acting in good faith in believing there to be a factual humanitarian emergency situation and wishing to help party C.

Even given this assumption, I postulate that a humanitarian intervention can only be justified in the case of a grave violation or threatened grave violation of international law. A military intervention can morally only be acceptable as a last resort and not every threat can justify an intervention. Judging the degree of gravity will always be somewhat arbitrary and dependent on the arbitrator in question. In addition, the existence of a sufficiently grave situation to justify intervening does not justify any and all means of intervention. There remain moral limitations on military intervention as a means, a fact which will prove of relevance to the study of Kosovo below. It is difficult to talk about 'least harmful' means in the case of military interventions. The most accurate description is to talk of 'appropriate' means, where the intervention achieves its goal with the least possible damage to the violator.

This conclusion implies that one cannot accept humanitarian intervention without simultaneously accepting the risk and responsibility for collateral damage, and such damage must be minimized. By contrast, Meggle argues that a humanitarian intervention should from the start aim to limit the damage to the intervening party itself as much as possible.[14] As an example, he would endorse NATO's decision in the Kosovo war to resort to high altitude bombing, which was expected to, and did, lead to far more collateral damage but carried a much lower risk of NATO casualties.

It is at this point that these views and those of the Ethics of Care diverge. In accordance with the Ethics of Care, and with a recognition of the duties imposed by unequal relations (between the bomber and the bombed), there should be an appropriate correlation between the risk to the intervening party and the collateral damage. One could say that there is even a duty by the intervening party to accept a high proportion of risk.

---

13 G. Meggle, 'Ist dieser Krieg gut? Ein ethiser Kommentar', in R. Merkel (ed.), *Der Kosovokrieg und das Voelkerrecht* (Frankfurt: Suhrkamp Verlag, 2000), pp.138-59.
14 Ibid., p.151.

The true nature of this particular problem is eloquently addressed by Jean Bethke Elshtain in her book *Women and War*. Examining the problem of Truman's bombing of Hiroshima, she concludes that his justification must have followed one of two possible calculi:

- it is better to certainly kill 100,000 people than to possibly see 100,000+ die, or
- it is better to kill Asians in any number than to risk the deaths of Americans ('Our Boys') in any number.

Elshtain lays clear the thinking which suggests that the lives of the intervenors are more valuable than those of the party being intervened against, and declares that the second calculus is to her not acceptable. She states that 'it is lodged, not in respect for human life, in which case one wishes the deaths or injuries of as few as possible, but in ethnocentrism, if not racism, holding the lives of one type of human (white American) dearer than those of another type (brownskinned, non American). Is this calculus allowable from any ethical (as opposed to straight realpolitiker) vantage point? I think not. ... It is sad'.[15]

A further facet of the topic which has become particularly relevant in the last couple of years is the morality of counter-terrorist, as opposed to counter-military, intervention. Annette Baier distinguishes between the self-deceived and the genuine terrorist, and poses an important question about the licence to kill given to soldiers. She tackles the question of whether a terrorist can also be considered legitimately licensed to kill for his cause. In Baier's opinion, our moral attitudes towards killing are 'bearers of the vestiges of attitudes acquired during our long history as a species which has lived by our lethal skills ... The important moral question has always been whom or what may I assault and kill and when and how may I kill it and not may I assault and kill'.[16] According to Baier, boundaries between human and non-human, military and civilian, attacker and defender, have to be learned. This process of learning constitutes our education in the morality of violence.

Baier examines our history as members of fairly well recognized groups with recognized territories and authority structures, groups whose rights to defend their official values were taken for granted. She notes that just war theory puts great weight on the distinction between intended killing and collateral damage. 'The doctrine of double effect ... gets a supplement for use on the battlefields in the doctrine of just war. Only as long as we can draw clear lines round some fields, marked "fields for battles between duly licensed and uniformed intentional killers" and other areas marked "enemy cities, suitable for strategic but not saturation bombing, for foreseen but not intended killing of civilians" ... can we continue to polish and treasure the distinction between deliberate targeted killing and knowing but deplored killing'.[17]

---

15 J.B. Elshtain, *Women and War* (New York: The Harvester Press, 1987), p.39.
16 Baier, *Moral Prejudices*, p.209.
17 Ibid., p.212.

Baier proposes that a terrorist group is an outlaw group and that for outlaws all fields are battlefields, and she advocates that the doctrine of just war should be extended into a doctrine of just violence. 'We need a new Grotius, or a new Hobbes, or both, to work out the rights of violence and non-violence for all groups at odds with other groups'.[18] The response to terrorism, she believes, should be a theory that codifies the art of successful peacemaking, of forming workable plans for lasting peace. Essentially, her view is that the response to terrorist violence should not be counterviolence or moral condemnation but inclusion and removal of the grounds for resentment.

There is an obvious tension between George Meggle's view that it is the duty of an intervening party to minimize the risks to itself, and Bethke Elshtain and Annette Baier's position that the intervening party should see itself in *loco parentis* and attempt to seek the most favourable outcome for both the attacker and the attacked. Both women take an Ethics of Care approach and place the intervenor in an equal position of responsibility towards the terrorist and the non-guilty victim, the powerful and the oppressed terrorist.

The sense of a moral obligation to place the interests of the guilty party at a much higher priority seems to clearly differentiate the Ethics of Care view from the classic just war view. I will now turn to the Kosovo conflict to see how this would apply in practice.

The Kosovo War

In 1999, NATO, citing a pressing need for humanitarian intervention on behalf of the ethnic-Albanian population of Kosovo, attacked the Federal Republic of Yugoslavia and pursued a bombing campaign which lasted until the Yugoslav leader, Slododan Milosevic, capitulated. For the purpose of this study, I will consider just one aspect of the war, namely the formal justification of it by NATO, as put forward mainly in statements to the press. This is not a study of the influence of political groups, commentators, and academics on the causes and conduct of the intervention, nor of possible secret motives among decision-making bodies, but of the ethical nature of those views which were presented as NATO's official moral position for beginning the conflict.

The motivation is first laid out in the key UN Security Council Resolution 1199 of 23 September 1998. This resolution refers to a humanitarian problem:

> Gravely concerned at the recent intense fighting in Kosovo and in particular the excessive and indiscriminate use of force by Serbian security forces and the Yugoslav Army which have resulted in numerous civilian casualties and, according to the estimate of the Secretary General, the displacement of over 230,000 persons from their homes;

> Deeply concerned by the flow of refugees into northern Albania, Bosnia and Herzegovina and other European countries as a result of the use of force in Kosovo, as

---

18 Ibid., p.213.

well as by the increasing numbers of displaced persons within Kosovo, and other parts of the Federal Republic of Yugoslavia, up to 50,000 of whom the United Nations High Commissioner of Refugees has estimated are without shelter and other basic necessities;

Deeply concerned by the rapid deterioration in the humanitarian situation throughout Kosovo, alarmed at the impending humanitarian catastrophe as described in the report of the Secretary General, and emphasizing the need to prevent this from happening;

Deeply concerned also by reports of increasing violations of human rights and of international humanitarian law, and emphasizing the need to ensure that the rights of all inhabitants of Kosovo are respected;

Affirming that the deterioration of the situation in Kosovo, Federal Republic of Yugoslavia, constitutes a threat to peace and security in the region;

- Demands that all parties ... reduce the risks of a humanitarian catastrophe.
- Demands also that the authorities of the FRY and the Kosovo Albanian leadership take immediate steps to improve the humanitarian situation and to avert the impending humanitarian catastrophe ...
- Demands further that the FRY ... cease all action by the security forces affecting the civilian population and order the withdrawal of security units used for civilian repression.
- Notes ... the commitments of the President of the FRY ... not to carry out any repressive actions against the peaceful population.[19]

In the first press statement after the beginning of the air operations, the Secretary General of NATO, Dr Javier Solana, again justified the start of the war with reference to humanitarian concerns, saying, '[A]ll efforts to achieve a negotiated, political solution to the Kosovo crisis having failed, no alternative is open but to take military action. ... We are taking action following the FRY Government's refusal ... [to] end excessive and disproportionate use of force in Kosovo'. NATO should take 'whatever measures were necessary to avert a humanitarian catastrophe'.[20] Solana continued:

This military action is intended to support the political aims of the international community. It will be directed toward disrupting the violent attacks being committed by the Serb Army and Special Police Forces and weakening their ability to cause further humanitarian catastrophe. ... Let me be clear: NATO is not waging war against Yugoslavia. We have no quarrel with the people of Yugoslavia. ... Our objective is to prevent more human suffering and more repression and violence against the civilian population of Kosovo. ... We know the risks of action but we have all agreed that inaction brings even greater dangers. ... We must stop an authoritarian regime from repressing its people. ... We have a moral duty to do so. The responsibility is on our shoulders and we will fulfil it.

In summary, Solana is stating that:

19 United Nations Security Council Resolution 1199, 23 September 1998.
20 NATO Press Release, no. 040, 1999.

there is no solution left other than a military action and inaction is unacceptable (last resort);

- measures are necessary to avert a humanitarian catastrophe (clear redress of rights actually violated);
- the international community favours intervention;
- the excessive and disproportionate use of force is not acceptable (means proportionate to ends);
- it is not a war against the people of Yugoslavia, it is emergency help for civilian (Albanian) Kosovars (distinction between combatants and non-combatants);
- the measures will only aim to disrupt the army and special police forces, not cripple the Yugoslav nation (victorious nation not requiring utter humiliation of the vanquished).

It would appear that all the criteria for just war are present, but there is no mention of any duty of care towards the guilty parties, whether that be the individual soldiers and policemen or the state apparatus and leaders directing their actions.

In subsequent press releases [041, 042, 043, 044, & 045] NATO claimed that the responsibility for the air strikes lay solely and fully with the Yugoslav President Slobodan Milosevic. All of the points mentioned above were repeated. The one given the most emphasis was the rejection of excessive and disproportionate use of force. The fact that the campaign was not a war against the people of Yugoslavia was the one next most frequently mentioned. An unbreakable distinction continues to be made between 'innocent non-combatants' and 'guilty parties', to whom no consideration is due.

The statement about the situation in and around Kosovo issued at the extraordinary ministerial meeting of the North Atlantic Council on 12 April 1999 opened with a broader perspective:

> The crisis in Kosovo represents a fundamental challenge to the values of democracy, human rights and the rule of law. ... [The usual arguments followed] ... The unrestrained assault by Yugoslav military, police, and paramilitary forces, under the direction of President Milosevic, on Kosovar civilians has created a massive humanitarian catastrophe. ... NATO's action supports the political aims of the international community ... [Once again] Responsibility for the present crisis lies with President Milosevic, who sustains the policy of ethnic cleansing. Atrocities against the people of Kosovo by FRY military, police and paramilitary forces violate international law.[21]

Thus, in official statements the moral justification for emergency assistance to avoid a humanitarian catastrophe was now embedded in an appeal to the universal declaration of human rights and the framework of international law. This is yet

21 NATO Press Release M-NAC - 1(99)51.

again a very legalistic, Kantian perspective, one which relies on rules and the right of the stronger party not to be challenged by a weaker party.

Throughout, it was repeated that NATO felt it to be a duty to help the Albanian Kosovars. The public discourse accordingly focused on the powerful party, NATO, and its view of its duty. There was much less said about the Albanian Kosovars' entitlement to help or even their desire for help, and there was virtually nothing said about any entitlement to consideration by the non-Albanian Kosovars and the other citizens of the FRY. They are relegated to the same low importance as the Asians in Elshtain's Hiroshima example.

Exactly one year after the war started the Secretary General of NATO made a personal evaluation of what had transpired. As background he cited the rising of ethnic violence, the suppression of democracy, a breakdown of law and order, systematic human rights abuses by ruling authorities and a refusal by the Belgrade government to seek, or accept, a political solution. One of the chapters of his report calls the intervention 'A just and necessary action'. Lord Robertson states that:

> The abuse of human rights by FRY and the humanitarian disaster threatened to undermine the values on which the new Europe is being built. ... If Nato had failed to respond to the policy of ethnic cleansing, it would have betrayed its values. ... NATO nations confirmed that common values and respect for human rights are central to the Alliance and all the world's democracies.[22]

In his report, the Secretary General addresses controversial questions such as: 'Could it have been done better? Did the international community insist on conditions that made a failure of the Rambouillet talks inevitable? Did the Alliance do enough to avoid "collateral damage", and did NATO planes fly too high to be effective?' He also answered the questions: 'Was NATO's bombing campaign poorly conceived and executed?', and 'Did NATO's air campaign itself cause the ethnic cleansing it intended to stop?'

As can be expected, the answers are diplomatically formulated. Robertson tried to avoid casting these as moral questions, and instead looked at them as practical ones. His avoidance of the moral issues suggests that while there was a clear moral justification for initiating a war, he was on less sure ground with regard to the design of the war.

Conclusion

NATO's justification for initiating the Kosovo war was dual, both political and moral. It was politically unacceptable to the powerful international alliance that one state leader, Milosevic, should refuse the terms dictated to him at Rambouillet. This was clearly not felt to be a strong argument, however, as Milosevic's position

---

22 Lord Robertson of Port Ellen, *Kosovo One Year On: Achievement and Challenge* (Brussels: NATO Press Release, 21 March 2000).

was only mentioned in the very first NATO press release. The moral nature of the justification was stressed throughout.   The press releases and statements all mention the humanitarian catastrophe (specifically the displacement of a large number of civilians and reported massacres of ethnic Albanians) and the moral duty of NATO to bring an end to that catastrophe. As an aside, I note that this acute sensitivity to morality was in sharp contrast to the crisis some years before in Rwanda. All the conditions for a humanitarian intervention were matched there: a massacre with more than one million deaths, brutal oppression, and expulsion of people. There was no interest in or empathy with the oppressed of Rwanda. In that case, the political lack of reward from an intervention easily outweighed any moral duty of care.

Examining the moral aspects of the Kosovo war alone, one can conclude that there was justification for beginning a humanitarian intervention in Kosovo whether using a Kantian or an Ethics of Care philosophy. Where an Ethics of Care viewpoint would have led the NATO leadership to act differently would have been in planning the type of attacks it would carry out during its campaign.   The Secretary General gave as his personal opinion, as stated before, that the collateral damage was limited in keeping with the laws of armed conflict. That may have been so from a legalistic perspective, but in the last month of the war the total infrastructure of FRY was destroyed, with not only military targets but also economic targets bombed to absolute destruction. The motivation for this was explicitly given as being to make the helpless innocent civilian population become discontented with Milosevic by causing them to suffer. This clearly contradicts the requirement for respect for the party intervened against which was outlined above by Elshtain, as well as ignoring the requirements towards the Yugoslavs which Baier implies would have been placed on NATO by a recognition of their unequal power relationship.

In conclusion, the traditional just war norms would appear to have been useful, but insufficient in achieving the most moral result. In future interventions, it must be hoped that the Ethics of Care philosophy will receive equal prominence to the conventional views.

Index